The Touring Musician

A Small-Business Approach to Booking Your Band on the Road

HAL GALPER

Alfred Publishing Co., Inc.

Acknowledgments

I would like to thank the following people and organizations for their invaluable encouragement, advice, expertise, and assistance in helping me become independent:

Tim Ford; Harry Pickins; Ray Drummond; Jay Schornstein, the National Jazz Service Organization; Fred Hersch; Alberto Alberti; Hubertus von Fallios; Jordi Sunol; Warren Vache, the New York State Council on the Arts; Hollis Headrick; Carl Jefferson, Concord Jazz, Inc.; Jamey Aebersold; Marty Kahn, Outward Visions; Peter Straub; Martin Mueller, the jazz division within the Mannes College of Music at the New School University; Zella Jones, the Delaware Valley Arts Alliance; David Udolf; Dr. Robert Marvit; Dr. Tom Crogan; Dave Liebman; Caris Liebman, Caris Music Services; Todd Coolman; Jeff Johnson; Steve Ellington; Jon Poses; and Phil Woods.

Special thanks goes to: Lillyan Peditto for her patience and for being a book widow during the time it took me to write this book; Bret Primack for his invaluable help in getting this manuscript into acceptable shape; Senior Editor at Billboard Books, Bob Nirkind, for his extraordinary patience; and Alison Hagge for her editorial expertise and for making this book readable.

THE TOURING MUSICIAN
By HAL GALPER
© 2000 HAL GALPER
All Rights Reserved. Used by Permission.
Exclusively Distributed by ALFRED PUBLISHING CO., INC.

Library of Congress Cataloging-in-Publication Data
Galper, Hal.
    The touring musician : a small-business approach to booking your band on the road / by Hal Galper.
        p. cm.
    Includes index.
    ISBN 0-7390-4689-6
    1. Music—Vocational guidance. I. Title.
ML3795.G245 2000
780'.68—dc21   99-046522

Table of Contents

Part I: Preparing Yourself to Run a Small Business

Part II: Booking Your Tour

Foreword

I've known about Hal since his days in 1972 and 1973 with Cannonball Adderley, and from *Wild Bird,* a record he did on Mainstream in 1971 as a leader. I first heard him live, with Phil Woods, in the early 1980s at the Village Vanguard. His playing that night was both fluid and invigorating, and his solos were rife with harmonic adventurousness and sophistication. Little did I know at that time that in addition to being a musician and teacher, Hal is also an outspoken, highly opinionated fellow.

When the World Wide Web arrived full-force in the 1990s, Hal set up his own Web site. There's an area on his site (http://www.upbeat.com/galper) called "Rants and Raves" where he takes on everyone—from major record labels to jazz critics. Around the time that I discovered Hal's site, he discovered mine, Bird Lives (http://www.birdlives.com). My site also focuses on issues that are important to the jazz community. Hal started E-mailing responses to some of my diatribes. Soon thereafter we met in person, and he revealed that he was working on this book. He asked me to help out, explaining that he needed someone to clean up his prose. I accepted the challenge and for the past six months, we've been sending files back and forth over the Net.

Hal *lived* this book. A jazz professional for more than forty years, Hal has played and traveled with some of the best musicians of his time, including Chet Baker, Cannonball Adderley, Stan Getz, and Phil Woods, as well as led his own groups. How did Hal go from sideman to leader? By booking his own band. This has been a challenging responsibility that he continues to execute with remarkable finesse.

The sum total of Hal's experience as a road warrior, self-agent, manager, publicist, and booker appears on the pages of this book. Many musicians have lived the jazz life, but few are able to write about it as expertly and candidly as Hal. A perceptive and witty fellow who's been on the road for most of his life, Hal has learned his lessons the hard way—through experience. Now, as a jazz tribal elder, Hal offers fellow musicians a tool of empowerment. If you choose to embark upon a similar journey, this book will serve as a detailed and systematic road map. Accordingly, it's invaluable and—not surprisingly—highly entertaining.

Hal has written a survival manual for jazz musicians who seek to control their own destiny. In the jazz world, controlling your destiny means leading your own group. Because of the highly competitive nature of the jazz business, musicians can no longer rely only on record labels, agents, managers, or promoters to guide their careers. A successful musician must learn his or her craft *and* understand the business of jazz in order to function effectively. In this book, Hal shows how you can take hold of the reigns of your career.

It's been a fascinating journey, helping Hal to mine his knowledge and present it in a straightforward, unvarnished way. In addition to featuring chunks of invaluable information, this book includes a number of stories that Hal gathered during his remarkably colorful career. Believe me, parts of this book will have you laughing out loud! Playing jazz and booking a band is serious business, but thankfully Hal has retained his sense of humor.

Hopefully, *The Touring Musician* will not only inform you, but will inspire you to, like Hal, take an activist role in your career.

—Bret Primack
writer and jazz editor for GMN.com

Introduction

If you've picked up this book, you're one of the many musicians who are looking for an answer to the question "How do I survive in the music business?"

There is no *one* answer. There are as many answers as there are people asking the question. Ultimately, you have to assess the career choices that lie before you and find your own way. Booking a band and taking it on the road has been my answer, and could be yours as well.

I've written *The Touring Musician* to encourage you to dream, to give you the information you need to take control of your career, and to convince you that it *is* possible for you to make your dreams come true—because, ultimately, your career will be rewarding only if you pursue your dreams. If you have something valuable to offer the world and if you believe in it strongly, hard work and thoughtful dedication *will* make your dreams a reality.

Your ability to survive in the music business depends on a number of factors, including your talents and abilities, your music and life goals, and your willingness to apply yourself to whatever path you choose. The success of your career will be based both on how accurately it reflects the realities of the world in which you live and on the rewards that you expect to receive. Being well informed is an essential factor in determining whether or not you can achieve your goals and enjoy their rewards.

This book offers invaluable information for musicians at every level—young musicians still developing the necessary basics for a career in music as well as working professionals—and from every musical genre.

Understanding the complex processes involved in booking and leading a band will strengthen your professionalism and—even if you decide ultimately that leading a band isn't right for you—will help you to recognize and take advantage of the many career opportunities that working and touring with other bands can provide.

The Touring Musician is divided into two sections:

Preparing Yourself to Run a Small Business begins with an assessment of the mental and emotional essentials you should develop before you begin to book and tour your band. And then it presents the step-by-step basics of how to organize your business, including how to determine which kind of business venture is right for you; how to set up your office, including how to finance your start-up costs; how to select and package your band, including how to develop an educational component of the group's repertoire; and how to manage your time and information. This section also includes numerous sample worksheets and checklists to keep you organized, as well as sample legal documents that cover a wide range of situations.

Booking Your Tour introduces successful techniques that I've used to book my bands. You'll learn how to research your venue contacts, including how to scout and evaluate the many different kinds of venues that are available to you; how to successfully contact venues and negotiate gigs, including a list of the eight rules for booking a band; how to manage tour routing and budgets; how to manage your tour finances, including how to prepare your personal and band taxes; and how to manage your promotional activities. You'll learn how to identify and avoid the pitfalls of arranging transportation and accommodations for U.S. and foreign travel. This section also includes sample scripts to help you navigate a range of negotiation scenarios, solid advice about exchanging foreign currencies to your advantage, *plus* five sample tour calendars *and* five sample tour budgets. These last two items will help you see for yourself how to balance travel, performance, and free time while on the road *as well as* how the numbers work.

I'm certain that each reader will customize my advice to fit his or her own personal style. And soon you will discover that booking a band can be a challenging, creative, and educational experience. As you begin to assimilate and use the information in this book, you will realize that the process of booking and touring a band constantly changes. You will discover new ideas daily, as well as redefine old ones.

Throughout the book, I've included personal anecdotes from my forty plus years working as a jazz pianist. Some are hilarious, and others tragic. All serve to both entertain and educate.

During those forty plus years—and especially since 1990, when I began my career as a full-time bandleader—I perfected the techniques that I discuss in this book. There's an old saying that goes something like "It's a wise man who learns from his own mistakes; it's a genius who learns from others." My experiences in the music business give me a unique vantage point from which I can offer career advice to musicians who want to travel similar paths.

It's been my good fortune to have toured and performed with a Who's Who of the world's jazz greats. It's your good fortune that I've also made or observed nearly every possible mistake that can be made in this business.

In his books about the Mescal Indians of Mexico, author Carlos Castenada sums up my attitude about how musicians should approach the music business by comparing human beings to warriors in the Battle of Life. That attitude was reinforced by my early mentor, the great jazz pianist Jaki Byard. When I asked him for advice about whether or not I should leave Boston and move to New York City, he said, "Sure, man! Get your shield and spear and go to New York."

PART I:

Preparing Yourself to Run a Small Business

Chapter 1
Getting Your Attitude Together

"Attitude is everything!" (Jazz proverb)

The above proverb has been a recurring theme throughout my career. When I first heard it I said, "That's really hip!" although I had no idea what it meant. It wasn't until many years later that the real meaning of this proverb dawned on me—knowledge is useless unless you know how to apply it. This is true in life as well as in music.

Collecting information isn't hard. As musicians, we all know people who are connected to the industry—other musicians, teachers, music fans, perhaps even some club owners, critics, or promoters. We talk with these people, find out who's playing with whom and where, who's recording on what label, which bands are forming, which have broken up. That kind of thing. Many of us also read magazines like *Down Beat* or *JazzTimes*, or check out music-related Web sites. We all do these things—usually without even thinking about it as "work" or approaching it in any sort of systematic way. At some level, this comes naturally to all of us, just because we're involved with and interested in music. We collect all kinds of information every day—often without really thinking too consciously about it. However, as I mentioned above, *collecting* information is only part of the equation. After you have the information, you need to know what to do with it—how to make it work for you. Learning how to *apply* your knowledge is the artistic part of the process, and it is often more challenging than collecting the information. This is where attitude and the "art" of booking a band come into play.

The fact that you're reading this proves that you're willing to invest some time to learn about the creative process of booking and touring a band. This book will give you the information you need to take control of your musical career. As I mentioned in the introduction, if you have something valuable to offer the world and if you believe in it strongly, hard work and thoughtful dedication *will* help you to realize your professional dreams. Forming your own band and taking it on the road is one way to survive—and flourish—in the music industry. However, before you commit to this goal, it is important to make sure that you really *want* to become a bandleader. The next section will help you evaluate your professional and personal attributes—and help you to ensure that this venture is right for you.

ANSWERING FIVE TOUGH QUESTIONS

Every profession has its upsides and its downsides. Being a bandleader is no exception. This section will help to give you a general idea of the kinds of things that you will have to contend with as a bandleader. I've tried to dispel some of the common myths about the music industry—like that there aren't enough gigs out there to keep you working or that touring automatically creates a freewheeling lifestyle. It is a unique person who can thrive on the freedom of a life on the road and yet remain focused on the goal of the tour—to play and promote your music.

In this section I play devil's advocate at times, painting a portrait of what it takes to become a seasoned and effective "road rat." The idea is for you to think through these scenarios and see if you think that this lifestyle suits you. In this section, I pose the following five questions: Why would anyone choose a career as a bandleader? Can I handle life on the road? Is there enough work out there? Where do I fit into the scheme of things? and Why can't I get a gig?

Try on the answers to these five questions. See what resonates with you. The discussions that follow each question will help you clarify your thoughts about booking your own band and taking it on the road.

Why Would Anyone Choose a Career As a Bandleader?

Before you decide to pursue a career as a bandleader, you should take a minute to evaluate your reputation in the industry and assess your current and long-term professional goals. Becoming a bandleader can be the right decision for musicians who are extremely well known or less well known, who are at an advanced or beginning stage in their musical careers. The key reason to become a bandleader, of course, is that the advantages will outweigh the disadvantages for your particular situation.

The primary advantage to leading a band is that it places you in a stronger position in the marketplace than being a sideman. It also gives you the opportunity to aggressively market yourself; instead of waiting for someone to call you with a gig, you can pick up the phone and offer your services. These two benefits apply to midcareer musicians, like myself, who came of age during the 1950s and 1960s and who have had to learn some new tricks in order to survive in the current music industry. But they also apply to the thousands of young musicians who graduate from music schools each year without being taught the basics of how to find work. In reality, there simply aren't enough working bands around today to hire all of the emerging musicians as sidemen; so young musicians often have no choice but to start their own bands, sometimes before they feel that they are ready.

A number of things could factor into your decision to choose a career as a bandleader. Perhaps you've moved up through the apprenticeship system and have reached a level of notoriety where you feel that you can strike it out on your own. Maybe your artistry has grown to such a degree that you need to have your own band to fully express your musical ideas. Possibly, as a longtime professional, you simply have become too expensive to hire as a sideman. Or maybe you're not working enough as a sideman and you want to create another way to make a living. Of course, if you've suddenly got a hit record, you've got to tour.

Can I Handle Life on the Road?

As the title of this book suggests, your workplace will be the road. Working on the road is unlike any other kind of work. It can take years of touring to learn how to survive on the road. It took *me* ten years just to learn how to pack my suitcase!

When you're touring, you visit interesting places, making new friends and fans along the way. You sample a variety of cultures, learn new languages and customs, and eat many strange and wonderful foods. However, not everyone is psychologically suited to road life. And there's no middle ground—you either love the road or you don't.

Unlike most people, the experienced road rat doesn't feel the need to be geographically grounded to one place to feel comfortable and secure. He or she enjoys changing environments and the illusion of freedom from everyday concerns.

The conditions of life on the road are unusual, and sometimes stressful. You must endure such things as isolation from familiar surroundings, fatigue, substitution of your normal language, and unstructured time. In his book *Battle for the Mind: A Physiology of Conversion and Brainwashing,* English psychologist Dr. Robert Sargant, who worked with Ivan Petrovich Pavlov, the famous Russian physiologist and experimental psychologist, cites these same conditions as the four basic prerequisites for brainwashing.

The only way to cope with these conditions is to establish healthy routines and stick to them. Some people view the road as an excuse for a life of excess. But I've found that, to be successful over the long haul, you have to stay centered on the reason you're on the road—to make a living playing your music. It's your job. Everything you do on the road must be guided by this reality.

Unstructured time, as pleasurable as it may feel, is potentially self-destructive. Although some of your time on the road will be structured by your travel and work schedules, you'll still have plenty of free time at your disposal. Set your own routines. Plan ahead. Study your itinerary to see when you're going to have free time. Do some sightseeing or schedule your domestic chores for those blocks of time—things like doing your laundry or buying toothpaste. Plan to work on a tune or arrangement, schedule a band meeting or rehearsal, or even warm up on your instrument. These everyday tasks add form to your free time. Balance these activities with rest and relaxation.

Everybody needs a certain amount of stability in his or her daily routine. Most people live their lives in one locale and travel for pleasure. A lot of stability is built into these circumstances. However, the reverse is true for road rats. We travel to work and go home for pleasure. Consequently, as road rats we have to create our own sense of stability when we're on the road. Continuous isolation from familiar surroundings—such as home, family, and friends—can create a kind of "floating" feeling that is, simultaneously, pleasurable and disconcerting.

Psychologists report that messy hotel rooms, which are often the mark of the frequent traveler—with towels, clothes, and personal items strewn about—are the result of an unconscious attempt on the part of the traveler to create a sense of ownership of the space they're occupying. We're not slobs—it's man's inbred territorial instinct at work! Keeping in mind that you don't want to overpack, you'll feel more at home in hotel rooms if you have items that give you a sense of place: a CD or tape player with your favorite music, family pictures, your old, beat-up bunny slippers, or whatever.

Having not seen much of the world, young musicians tend to view each place as new and different. Experienced musicians, especially those who did a lot of sightseeing in their early days on the road, tend to perceive every place as the same. Although different places can be interesting, many musicians find that it's the rarely seen friends they have made in each town who keep them grounded and feeling less isolated when they're traveling. Establishing personal relationships on the road can be difficult because your contact with people is limited to your audience and people associated with your work Most of the time, you're inside a taxi, van, airplane, hotel room, band room, or clu These days, gigs where you spend up to a week playing in one place are the except

Moving from town to town playing one-nighters is often the norm. Consequently, it is especially important to leave yourself open to meeting new people—and to make an effort to keep in touch when you're in town. Likewise, it's important to keep in touch with your roots. And since modern communications are so accessible and inexpensive, it is easy to call home at least every other day.

Traveling is hard work. Though you spend most of your time in cars, planes, and buses, concerns about weather conditions, jet lag, not having enough time to eat or sleep, carrying suitcases, and packing and unpacking add up and take their toll on your mind and body. Energy is currency and it's one of your most valuable resources. You've only got so much, so don't waste it. In a sense, as a performer, your energy is part of what you're selling. Get as much rest as you can—wherever and whenever possible.

A case in point is bassist Bob Cranshaw, one of New York's busiest studio musicians. Bob would go from one recording session to another, from early in the morning until late at night. I often marveled at his ability to find a quiet corner and sit down and grab a few minutes of sleep whenever he had a five- or ten-minute break. I asked him about it once. He said it was a trick he'd learned in the army that kept him fresh all day, so the quality of his work wouldn't suffer from fatigue. You can't play well if you're tired. Conversely, you'd be surprised by how often—even after a hard day of traveling—you will get on the bandstand and feel a tremendous release of energy as soon as you start playing, as if you were working off the dues you'd paid getting to the gig.

Every occupation has "trade talk," and this is certainly true of musicians. Because they spend so much time together, musicians from every traveling band tend to develop their own language and codes that reinforce the band's sense of togetherness. This has happened to me with every road band I've been in. For two years (in 1972 and 1973), I toured fifty weeks out of the year with the Cannonball Adderley Quintet. We were often invited out to dinner and it was the band's philosophy never to refuse a free meal—either before a performance or on our way out of town the day after a gig. At the end of the meal, Cannonball would mutter "the half is in" and, much to the surprise of our hosts, we'd all get up from the table at the same time, offer our thanks, and leave.

Some jazz history is in order here.

The backstage dressing rooms at Harlem's Apollo theater are five stories high and when you're back there you can't hear what is happening on stage. To give musicians a half an hour's notice before their performance, a midget would run from room to room, up and down the metal stairs yelling: "The half is in, the half is in." Cannonball's use of this code is a good example of the way jazz tradition is carried on from generation to generation. To this day, I still use this phrase with my band members.

When I played with Phil Woods, from 1980 to 1990, everybody in the band was a jokester. After a few years together, we had developed such a strong rapport that we often spoke to each other only in punch lines. It was a very private way of communicating and anyone who overheard us had no idea what we were talking about. After each tour, I returned home still speaking in punch lines, and received uncomprehending stares from the people around me. It would take me a day or two to adjust to life at home.

As these anecdotes reveal, it's easy to develop two mind-sets—one for the road and e for home. The road has its own reality, but it also has elements of fantasy. There is nsitional period, a "crash," that happens when the fantasy elements of being on the road are replaced with the mind-set of being at home. Accordingly, you should give yourself time to decompress and take a day or two off to rest before you begin dealing with the realities of life at home.

Physical and mental constitutions vary. With time and experience you'll learn how much your mind and body can take and how long you can stay on the road before it begins to affect your well-being. Until you've made this judgment, assume that six weeks is the maximum length for a healthy tour.

This brings up a subject that you should consider very carefully before you begin your career as a touring musician: the quality of your life at home.

Touring can put excessive strains on personal relationships. Don't go on the road without first having fully discussed with your spouse or significant other the weight that constant travel can put on a relationship. Even after this discussion, the pressures of life apart will be felt and will have to be dealt with on a day-by-day basis, especially if you have children. You may not be around to help out with family crises, and you'll miss birthdays and anniversaries. It takes special care and understanding from both partners to keep a relationship firmly grounded under these circumstances.

Your relationships with your band members can also be affected by the whims of the road. Because of the inordinate amount of time you'll spend together while traveling and the extreme intimacy of playing together, you'll need to make a point of creating your own space and time alone. The combination of fatigue and intimacy can create disastrous personality conflicts and needs to be handled with delicacy and sensitivity.

As was mentioned earlier, musicians with a lot of road experience are called "road rats." The ultimate road rat, Dizzy Gillespie, spent a week as a guest with Phil Woods's band during one of our European tours. Often rising at five in the morning, traveling for long hours, and dealing with the vagaries of the road, he maintained his sense of humor and didn't complain once! I learned an important lesson from working with him: The best survival tools are a pleasant disposition, a good sense of humor, and a positive attitude.

Is There Enough Work Out There?

Most jazz musicians are convinced that there aren't enough places to play to support a performing career. This idea has permeated the jazz community from time immemorial and, in reality, has no basis in fact. The truth is that there are so many gigs out there, with more being created every day, that it would be impossible for any musician to play them all in a lifetime. Many would question the veracity of this statement. There are no hard-and-fast figures for the total of the gross product for music performances. There is, however, some pertinent research data that bears scrutiny.

According to a recent Reuters news agency release, music sales worldwide are slated to increase by 60 percent by the year 2002. The research company Market Tracking International estimates that the music market will be worth $62.1 billion at this time. A Recording Industry Association of America (RIAA) report released in February of 1998 showed the sound recording gross in 1997 to be $12.2 billion in the United States alone, with jazz sales at 2.8 percent of the total. Over the last ten years, jazz has accounted for an average of 3.7 percent of music sales in the United States. If these figures prove true and are applicable globally, sales of jazz music in 2002 will be worth $2.3 billion. There's no guarantee, but isn't it conceivable that you could eventually share a piece of that pie?

A recent National Endowment for the Arts demographic survey of the U.S. jazz audience estimated that there are more than fifty-five million jazz fans, almost 20 percent of the country's population. Although there are no actual figures on this, it would be safe to assume that there are *at least* a similar number of foreign jazz fans, bringing the total worldwide figure to about one hundred and ten million jazz fans. Isn't it possible that a good number of those fans might be waiting to hear your music when you come to their town?

The second edition of the international jazz directory *The Euro Jazz Book* lists 2,000 venue contacts in Europe alone. Just 2 percent of those venues could keep you on the road for a month.

The International Association of Jazz Educators has a mailing list of more than 2,500 jazz music departments in colleges and universities in the United States. Add to that the burgeoning number of jazz departments in countries outside the United States and you have an abundance of additional potential locations for clinics and concerts.

The American Federation of Jazz Societies has ninety-one member organizations. If thirty of those organizations enjoy the music of your particular genre, you could play three jazz societies a year for ten years.

The Jazz World Database boasts a collection of more than 20,000 performance contacts worldwide. Ten percent of those venues could keep you on the road for more than five years.

There are also countless nonprofit arts presenters and a variety of other venues that might be potential employers. If you add to that the repeat venues you will have collected after a few years of touring, there's no reason to ever be out of work. The only real limitations you'll have are finding the time to look for work and your expertise at getting it.

Where Do I Fit I into the Scheme of Things?

Most jazz musicians fit into one of the three following general categories: an entry-level musician who is at the beginning of his or her working career; a midcareer musician who has toured and recorded for years as a sideman; an established artist who has a recording contract with a major label and an agent. Naturally, if you're an established artist, you probably won't be reading this book—as you already have the benefit of recording, touring, and promotional support of a big record company.

The first thing to assess is your "marquee value"—in other words how much of a "name" you have in the industry. In estimating your marquee value, you're trying to determine how many of your clients believe they can make a profit from hiring you. This estimation is based on the number of paying customers you can attract to a particular venue or how good you make the venue look by performing at it. Although not an exact science, determining your marquee value involves assessing the length and visibility of your musical accomplishments, how many fans and industry people are aware of these accomplishments, how many recordings you've made and sold, and the category of venues that will hire your band. The bottom line of this evaluation is a matter of predicting how well your gigs will draw as well as categorizing your image.

Once you've considered the factors listed above and determined which of three categories you fall into, you can start researching the venues that feature musicians of your level. Setting obtainable goals is important. There's no point in trying to get into the best-known club in town, one that features only established artists, if you're an emerging musician and your name isn't well known yet. That would be a waste of your time. And it isn't necessary—since there are lots of venues that feature musicians in each of the three categories. (This subject is further explored in chapter seven.)

Why Can't I Get a Gig?

Everyone in the first two categories discussed above wants to know the answer to that one. The answer is probably a result of several factors that are working together to keep emerging and midcareer musicians out of the music market. The most obvious factor is the subject of this book—you don't have the know-how to get a gig.

When I first started in this business, musicians would play around town, the word would get out, and the phone would start to ring. Players in those days spent years on the road getting experience with great bands, performing and recording as sidemen. At some point, a longtime sideman would get a solo record date and then an agent would help him or her get started leading his or her own band. All you needed was one record to get started as a bandleader.

Back then, jazz musicians knew very little about their own business. It was as if it were unseemly or inartistic to do so. Musicians' careers were controlled by agents, managers, and record company executives. The musicians didn't need to learn anything about their business because someone else was always handling it for them. This bias kept musicians dependent, passive, and ignorant about the business in which they worked. And in the end this attitude proved to be problematic. This lack of empowerment is not pertinent to the realities of the climate of today's music business.

For a number of reasons the music business has changed radically during the last fifteen years. The traditional means for career advancement has changed, yet this change has gone unrecognized by some of today's musicians. A partial listing of these changes would include:

- the growing influence of major record companies in the marketplace;
- the media, which virtually excludes the independent musician from exposure to the public;
- over-commercialization of the music;
- most recently, the accelerated growth of independent record labels, which has created intense competition for radio airplay and shelf space in retail record store chains.

In response to these changes in the industry, many musicians have finally started to take control of their own careers. In the last ten years, there's been a phenomenal increase of self-determination that has revolutionized the music business. Musicians have been especially empowered by the following phenomena:

- the availability of affordable computers and business-based software;
- expanded possibilities for both research and promotion created by the Internet;
- technological advances in home recording;
- the increasing number of music-business courses offered by music schools;
- the proliferation of nonprofit local, regional, and national arts support organizations.

The last item on this list—the proliferation of nonprofit support organizations—has had a far-reaching impact. Funded by government, private, foundation, and corporate grants, these organizations offer self-help publications that encourage career independence, workshops that teach techniques for funding, and resources so that you can research venue contacts. These organizations also frequently work with individual musicians to increase their performance opportunities. The state of the current industry makes it challenging for musicians, but if we take the time to understand the current state of affairs, take responsibility into our own hands, and master the tools available to us, we *can* get gigs.

DEVELOPING A POSITIVE MENTAL ATTITUDE

No matter which career path you choose, you have to pay your dues. Choosing a career in music is no exception. And in many ways it can be even more challenging than a more traditional career path—especially since so much of the success of a career in the music industry rests on the individual's shoulders. Having a positive attitude can help you ride through the periods when you're paying your dues and achieve the goals you've set for yourself.

A Positive Mental Attitude (PMA) is rooted in your belief system. Whether you are aware of it or not, you have your own unique belief system. This system permeates and dictates your thoughts and actions. How well your belief system works for you depends on how much you believe in yourself. Accurate information and common sense are the basis of any healthy belief system. The more you know about yourself, what you are trying to accomplish, and how the world works, the more you can accomplish.

Identifying the Four Components of PMA

Don't underestimate the power of the mind. A positive attitude is a dynamic tool that can transform mental processes into higher and more complex forms of action. A Positive Mental Attitude has four basic components. You need to recognize that problems are a part of life; know that you have to give up something to get something; keep the odds in your favor; and harness the power of your imagination. Each of these four components needs to be digested and understood on a gut as well as an intellectual level. To make PMA more than just a philosophy, to implement it to create a living and actively functioning modus operandi, you'll need to practice its basic components every day. If you work at it, it will work for you.

RECOGNIZING THAT PROBLEMS ARE A PART OF LIFE
If you accept the fact that problems are a part of life, you won't see yourself as a victim when you encounter challenging circumstances. Victims don't do anything to improve their situations. Instead, they complain about their fate and use their bitterness as an excuse for inaction. Victims never resolve their problems. *winners go home and fuck the prom queen." Sean Connery*

When you realize that problems are a part of life, you open yourself up to a point of view that allows you to turn problems into solutions. Every problem has a solution. And the problem is often not the problem itself, but an inability to perceive its solution. These kinds of problems are perceptual, a matter of point of view. By shifting your point of view, you see the problem in a different light and often discover a solution that you hadn't thought of before.

KNOWING THAT YOU HAVE TO GIVE UP SOMETHING TO GET SOMETHING Simply put, there's no free lunch. Every achievement in life costs something. This idea assumes that every negative element has its positive side and every positive element its corresponding negative side. People who accomplish things in life tend to perceive the former view, those who fail tend to see the latter. But every situation has both.

You're in big trouble if you can't see both the positive and the negative aspects of any given situation. If this does happen to you, you'd better take a minute to step back and reappraise what you're trying to accomplish. That's part of PMA—having the ability to see both sides of the coin.

KEEPING THE ODDS IN YOUR FAVOR Keeping the odds in your favor is simply a matter of statistics. The more often you repeat a positive action, the more likely the odds will be that you will succeed. If you make twenty phone calls, the odds of getting a gig are twice as good than if you only made ten calls. If you make forty calls, the odds are four times better than if you only made ten calls. Las Vegas was built upon the science of the law of averages.

HARNESSING THE POWER OF YOUR IMAGINATION Anything the mind can conceive and believe, it can achieve. Motivational guru and author Napoleon Hill states: "When you're ready for a thing, it will make its appearance."

Everything in life is a product of man's imagination. This book is. The chair you're sitting on, the building where you reside, the club where your music is played—all are products of the imagination. So you imagine you want to lead a band. You then imagine the actions needed to make the band a reality. To make these actions work, you will have to imagine intermediate actions, each of which in turn contains more refined steps. Every one of these steps needs to be imagined—and then implemented.

Dr. Karl H. Pribram of Stanford University contends in *Theory of Holographic Memory* that "...there is nothing at all mystical about the power of the mind and its ability to control its owner's destiny. On the contrary, it's a phenomenon that is scientific in nature." If you take Dr. Pribram's assertions to heart, then it's more than a manner of speaking to assert that you are an invention of your imagination embarking on a course of reinventing yourself anew! Once you've begun to absorb a new mind-set, your feelings about yourself and your relationship to the music business will be transformed into a vigorous and positive attitude. Instead of waiting for the phone to ring, you'll realize that you have a product to offer—your music. And you'll have a powerful incentive to pick up the telephone—you have to offer your clients your valuable services.

Coping with Rejection

Rejection can cripple your best efforts. It's natural to feel that everyone should hire you, but it's unrealistic to expect everyone to do so. The problem is that many musicians take rejection personally, when it is really just a normal part of doing business. No business sells all of its products or services to everyone. Businesses work on percentages.

It's a given that you'll be rejected at least 60 percent of the time, if not more. It's part of the process. In chapter seven you'll learn that you need to have at least three venue leads for each day you're trying to book. So for a month-long tour, you'll need about ninety leads. If one of those leads confirms for each day, you'll have experienced sixty rejections.

However, a "no" now can often be a "yes" later—but perhaps not until the third or the fourth time you ask. Also, for all kinds of reasons, a "yes" now could turn into a "no" later. Think of every "no" as a delayed "yes." Depending on the type of rejection you get, keep the venue's name on file for later reference. You don't want to waste your valuable time calling clients who will never give you a gig, but the contact could come in handy at a later date when trading contacts with other musicians.

There are a multitude of reasons why a client will reject an offer. These reasons run the gamut—from common to bizarre. Learning the reasons for that rejection, not focusing on the rejection itself, is what's important. Most clients will tell you why they don't want you for a gig. But if they don't, ask! At best, they may be giving the very information you need to counter their refusal. At worst, you'll reinforce your professional image with the client by showing that you're confident enough to ask the question as well as learn what you need to accomplish to make your business stronger in the future.

Clients will give you either a "long no" or a "short no." If a client is a true professional and, for whatever reason, is not interested in booking your band, he or she will give you an immediate and polite refusal (the short no). Be equally polite in accepting it. A short no is better than a long no. You don't want to waste your time going after a gig that you're not going to get.

A long no is the least desirable response you can get. It shows a lack of respect for your talent, hard work, and commitment, wastes your valuable time, and does not benefit you at all because you learn nothing from it. A long no can take many forms. For instance, the contact may say, "Oh, man, we really would love to have you play for us, but you called too late and we're all booked for the period you'll be in our area. Why don't you call us about three months before the next time you're in the area." You make notes in your calendar and in your contact file to call him or her three months ahead the next time. When that time comes you call again and the contact says, "Oh, man, you called too late. We're already booked for that period. Call us the next time." Even if you swallow your pride and ask your contact why he or she told you to call so late, he or she will tell you, "Oh, man, some of the bands we really wanted were going to be in the area, so things got booked earlier this year than last year." If you get that kind of response, don't bother calling that contact again unless you find out at a later point that the venue has changed representatives.

Some of the most common reasons for rejection are:

- You're trying to get a gig where you can't get one. If you're an emerging or mid-career artist and your venue research shows that the venue only hires musicians with the highest marquee value, you're wasting your time and theirs trying to compete in a market area into which you don't fit.
- Your band is too big and/or too expensive (i.e., your fees may be unrealistic). Many venues have high overheads. In order to survive they have to be hard-nosed about their booking policies.
- The client doesn't recognize your name or isn't aware of your reputation. It's not possible for every client to know every musician.

- Your genre of music doesn't appeal to a venue's clientele. Many venues succeed by catering only to a particular musical genre.
- You called too late or too early, usually a result of having the incorrect lead time. Lead times, the amount of time you need to call ahead to book a performance date, can vary between a month to two years in advance.
- The client was turned off by the attitude you projected over the phone or your selling rap. Potential clients can be just as sensitive as you are.
- The client loves to insult musicians because he or she is insecure and enjoys abusing the position of power. Not everyone is in the business because of his or her love for the music.
- You didn't make a counterproposal. A client may believe that you're not flexible.

We'll go over these reasons again, analyze client psychology, and suggest counter-strategies for the above in chapter eight. You can't function effectively if you let rejection get you down. You'd be surprised how many times you can turn a "no" into a "yes" by maintaining a creative outlook and a positive attitude.

Creative Mistake Making and Decision Trees

Learning and implementing the techniques suggested in this book constitutes a continuous decision-making process. Not all of your decisions will be correct. Everybody makes mistakes. The Korean symbol for "mistake" also means "opportunity." Every mistake contains tremendous potential for learning something new. What's important is that you only make a particular mistake once. If you repeat the same mistake over and over, you have a blind spot that needs to be examined. Avoid repeating the mistake again by scrupulously reexamining the thought processes that led up to it.

Every decision you make branches off to a series of other decisions that then branch off to others, and so on. An unrealistic decision will make your decision tree branch off into unproductive actions and its subsequent decisions will be faulty.

As soon as you've made a decision of any kind, you've set a goal to be achieved. As soon as you set a goal, you create the possibility of both success and failure. Every action you take to reach your goal will not be successful. Your attitude toward failure is a crucial element in the success of your action plan. (Action plans will be discussed at length in chapter two). Failure does not invalidate your self-worth, but the lack of trying does. If you try for 100 percent of everything you plan for and achieve 51 percent of it, consider yourself successful. Jazz pianist McCoy Tyner once said, "Some nights you've got 100 percent available and some nights only 60 percent. What's important is that you give 100 percent of what you have available at any given moment."

The road to independence can be rocky. Some days everything will work in your favor, and other days nothing will. Some nights the music will take you to the heights and other nights, into the cellar. There is no endeavor in life that doesn't require paying some kind of dues. More often than not, the dues that life imposes on us are imposed by others. We do, however, have the freedom to select the direction in which we want to take our lives and the dues we are willing to pay for that decision. It will make a difference, on those bad days, to be able say: "These are the dues I've picked, and they're worth it!"

Chapter 2

Evaluating Your Assets and Creating Your Action Plan

Certainly, objective self-evaluation is one of the most difficult of all human endeavors. However, it is very important—especially if you're thinking about starting your own business. If you underestimate your capacities, you won't realize your full potential because underestimating yourself leads to setting low goals. While you may achieve these goals and receive a sense of accomplishment from this, ultimately your achievements will be less substantial than what you are *capable* of accomplishing.

On the other hand, the reverse occurs if you overevaluate yourself. If you reach for goals that are beyond your capabilities, you are doomed to be disillusioned. Accordingly, the most important decisions are the first ones, the decisions on which you base the foundation of your business. In other words, an accurate answer to the question "Do I have what it takes to begin this venture and carry it through to success?" is crucial to the prosperity of your potential business.

DETERMINING IF YOU CAN RUN A SMALL BUSINESS

Determining if you have what it takes to run a small business starts with an accurate evaluation of your personal assets. To author and marketing educator Jay Abraham, the word *assets* means those personal attributes that can be developed and organized to achieve the goals you set for yourself. He believes that self-knowledge is the most valuable knowledge of all, and that you gain this knowledge by evaluating yourself objectively. The following self-assessment questionnaires are designed to help you begin this process of self-discovery.

Your Self-Assessment Questionnaire

The questions in this section function in two ways. First, they evaluate your current mind-set. And second, they create the mind-set that is necessary for establishing a realistic decision-making process. Don't worry if you don't score well. The function of these questions is to help you gain an objective understanding of yourself at this time and to help you assess where you stand in relation to achieving your goals.

This questionnaire is designed to help you assess the *probability* of whether or not you will be successful in small-business ownership. It is not scientifically valid—nor does a high score on this test guarantee success in future business ventures. Rather, the test is meant to serve as a reflection of whether you have the characteristics that research has shown to be important for a small-business career. You will grade yourself, so answer the questions honestly and objectively. The results of this test may lead you to make changes in your life—and these changes may ultimately make the difference between winning and losing in the world of business.

1. Are you willing to work long hours with few vacations and irregular time off in order to achieve your goals?
   Yes __
   No __
   Uncertain __

2. Are you prepared to place the needs of your business before your own needs and those of your family, if this is necessary to preserve the health and continuity of your business?
   Yes __
   No __
   Uncertain __

3. Does your need to be independent and in control of your work environment make it difficult for you to be satisfied when you're working for others?
   Yes __
   No __
   Uncertain __

4. Are you willing to take full responsibility for the mistakes you make, without looking for others to blame? Can you learn from your mistakes to improve your performance in the future?
   Yes __
   No __
   Uncertain __

5. Are you able to sustain your energy and motivation in an uncertain or unstable working environment?
   Yes __
   No __
   Uncertain __

6. Are you willing to take a fair amount of risk in the hope of achieving something you want?
   Yes __
   No __
   Uncertain __

7. Do you feel that you have a high degree of self-discipline? Can you apply yourself to a job that needs to be done even when you don't feel like doing it?
   Yes __
   No __
   Uncertain __

8. Are you willing to "be on stage"—to know that others are watching, evaluating, and counting on you?
   Yes __
   No __
   Uncertain __

9. Do you believe that you are able to show grace under pressure?

    Yes __

    No __

    Uncertain __

10. Do you have excellent problem-solving abilities, particularly in crises when others are not thinking clearly?

    Yes __

    No __

    Uncertain __

11. Are you willing to go against the mainstream, to persist on a course you believe in, even when others disapprove?

    Yes __

    No __

    Uncertain __

12. When things go wrong, do you pick yourself up promptly and move to another challenge instead of brooding for a long time and feeling a lot of self-pity?

    Yes __

    No __

    Uncertain __

13. Do you empathize well with others?

    Yes __

    No __

    Uncertain __

14. Do you have an ability to lead others, even when you're in a confused or chaotic environment?

    Yes __

    No __

    Uncertain __

15. Are you willing to spend a great deal of time, as long as you are in business, learning about things that are required or will be helpful in the business?

    Yes __

    No __

    Uncertain __

16. Do you enjoy most other people?

    Yes __

    No __

    Uncertain __

17. Do you enjoy working?

    Yes __

    No __

    Uncertain __

18. Do you have (or are you willing to work hard to acquire) a broad range of business-management skills?

    Yes __
    No __
    Uncertain __

19. Do you possess a high degree of "information consciousness"? That is, do you usually, before starting off on a new course, go to considerable lengths to gather and use extensive information and data to assist you in planning and decision making?

    Yes __
    No __
    Uncertain __

20. Do you rely extensively on feedback to test the results of a course of action and make corrections or adjustments as a result?

    Yes __
    No __
    Uncertain __

Check the answer that most accurately describes how you feel about each statement.

21. You don't have to "cut ethical corners" to be successful in business.

    Agree __
    Disagree __
    Not Important __

22. People need a "sense of mission" in order to be fulfilled in their work.

    Agree __
    Disagree __
    Not Important __

23. It is very important for a business to provide a service that is worthwhile and useful to others.

    Agree __
    Disagree __
    No Difference __

24. I want the credit for my accomplishments and am willing to take full responsibility for my mistakes.

    Yes __
    No __
    No Difference __

25. I have a better chance of reaching my goals by working for myself than by working with others.

    Yes __
    No __
    No Difference __

26. It is important for a person to have the freedom to be creative in his or her work.

 Agree ___
 Disagree ___
 Not Very Important ___

27. It is more important to accomplish something worthwhile than to earn a great deal of money.

 Agree ___
 Disagree ___
 Don't Know ___

SCORING THE SELF-ASSESSMENT QUESTIONS

Questions 1–20

 _____ (Number of yes or agree responses) $\times$ 5 = _____

 _____ (Number of uncertain responses) $\times$ 5 = _____

Questions 21–27

 _____ (Number of yes or agree responses) $\times$ 5 = _____

 _____ (Number of other responses) $\times$ 2 = _____

 Total _____

A score that falls between 120 and 135 indicates a person who is likely to thrive in small-business ownership.

A score that falls between 80 and 120 indicates a person who has a tendency toward small-business ownership, but will have some areas of conflict to overcome.

A score that falls below 80 indicates a person who is probably not suited for small-business ownership.

INTERPRETATION

The "yes" answers define the profile of a person who will have a high chance of success in most small-business ventures. The characteristics reflected by the "yes" or "agree" answers indicate an individual with high independence needs, self-control, and self-direction, a willingness to face a moderate degree of risk, and an ability to make a high level of commitment to the success of a venture. Various studies have identified these characteristics in successful small-business owners.

No single person is likely to answer "yes" or "agree" to all questions. Successful owners have as much individuality as any other class of person. However, a preponderance of "yes" or "agree" answers is a good indication of someone who has the qualities that are required for a small-business venture.

Listing Your Abilities and Limitations

On separate sheets of paper write the headings: "attributes" and "limitations." Underneath these headings, list as many of your attributes and limitations that you can. Be as honest as possible. And don't try to do it all at once. If you run out of things to list, think about it for a while and come back later to add more. Expect to be adding new things as they come to you, over a period of several months. If your lists aren't ten to fifteen pages, you are not done yet. If you're not sure about an item, put a question mark beside it. You'll find it interesting to come back to this list a couple of years later to monitor and assess your growth. You might even want to do it again.

On a separate sheet of paper list your personal, musical, and business attributes.

On a separate sheet of paper list your personal, musical, and business limitations.

On separate sheets of paper list all the reasons you can think of that will answer each of the following eight questions:
1. Why will people come to my performances?
2. Why won't people come to my performances?
3. Why will people like my music?
4. Why won't people like my music?
5. Why should someone hire me?
6. Why shouldn't someone hire me?
7. Why will I be successful?
8. Why won't I be successful?

After you've written down the answers to these questions, then ask yourself the following twenty-six questions:
1. Am I aware of my own character and know how to use, improve, or compensate for my natural traits?
2. Can I inspire confidence in and command respect from other people without asking for it?
3. Do I have clear goals?
4. Am I willing to shoulder the responsibility of meeting a payroll and paying my debts on time?
5. Do I like to sell?
6. Do I understand that a business is a speculation, and am I willing to take the risks involved?
7. Do I like to make my own decisions?
8. Do I enjoy competition?
9. Do I have willpower and self-discipline?
10. Can I plan ahead?
11. Can I take advice from others?
12. Am I adaptable to changing situations?
13. Do I have the physical stamina to handle a business?
14. Do I have the emotional strength to stand the strain of running a small business?

15. Am I prepared to lower my standard of living for several months or years?
16. Do I know which skills and areas of expertise are critical to the success of my project?
17. Do I have these skills?
18. What are my career expectations?
19. Do I know what my expenses will be (i.e., rent, wages, insurance, utilities, advertising, interest, etc.)?
20. Do I need to know which expenses are direct, indirect, or fixed?
21. Do I know what my overhead will be?
22. Am I aware of the major risks associated with my business?
23. Can I minimize any of these major risks?
24. Are there major risks that are beyond my control?
25. Can these risks bankrupt me?
26. Am I aware that there is less than a fifty-fifty chance that I will be in business two years from now?

Now list any other talents, abilities, and faults you may have that are not included in the answers to the above questions.

Finally, list all of your reasons for starting your project as well as your musical and financial goals.

At this point you should have a good idea of your strengths and weaknesses, which characteristics you can or can't change, and what you do and don't know. Now you can begin to improve those areas that can be improved, find ways to work around those aspects of yourself that can't be changed, and start educating yourself about how to become a successful small-business owner.

Before I started making my own action plan, I took a similar self-evaluation test, and, at the end, I started to worry about whether I could achieve the goals I'd set for myself. One night I was standing at the bar of a club in New York City, expressing these concerns to bassist Ray Drummond. He said, "Hal, there are musicians out there who can play and musicians who can't. There are smart musicians and dumb musicians. Who do you think is working?"

That cleared things up for me. I figured, I may not be the greatest piano player in the world, but I'm certainly not dumb and I can play! With patience, study, and intelligent planning anyone can accomplish whatever he or she sets out to do. You can, too.

CREATING YOUR ACTION PLAN

An action plan is basically a big to-do list that is divided up into smaller to-do lists. An action plan is comprised of many different action steps. Action steps are the actual moves that bring each stage of the plan into being. Expect to waste a lot of legal-size paper when you're creating your action plan. If you don't like using paper and you're computer savvy, consider investing in one of many inexpensive business software project planners that are available. At some point you'll need to be able to visualize the total plan in your head. Be careful not to forget something crucial to the success of your plan. Otherwise, you may miss an opportunity to take advantage of something that could complete an action step. Imagine as many ideas as you can and put them into your plan.

A well-drafted action plan alters your perceptions so that previously meaningless events suddenly appear significant. With these new perceptions, you will readily comprehend how to utilize your previously unrealized assets and abilities and organize your thinking into logical actions that will ensure that you will reach your goals. The first move you need to make toward realizing your final goal is to create an action plan of intermediary goals, or action steps. Each action step has within it sub-action steps and each of these sub-action steps will contain sub-sub-action steps, and so on. Like limbs on a large, fully formed tree, actions will branch off from each other, working symbiotically toward your goal.

I had my first experience creating an action plan when I wanted to start a working quintet with Mike and Randy Brecker in the late 1970s. The key to the success of this plan was an appraisal of the assets I'd gained working for years as a sideman in various bands on the road and in New York City.

Contacts are the currency of the music business and one of my primary assets was the fact that I was on a first-name basis with a number of club owners. My career as a performing and recording artist was another asset. The fact that the musicians I knew felt the same way as I did about the music was a third asset. I didn't have the fourth asset yet, but I knew that I needed it to carry through with my plans for a new band: seed money.

So, using the best musicians I knew, I made a demo tape of my music. Armed with recommendations from Phil Woods and Lee Konitz, I applied to the National Endowment for the Arts and received a grant of $2,000. The challenge was how to maximize the money from this grant. Two thousand dollars isn't very much when you consider the cost of renting a venue, paying the musicians, and promoting a concert.

The weekly New York newspaper *The Village Voice* advertises weekly schedules of artists' appearances for every jazz club in the city. Reading these advertisements was a weekly habit. When I created my action plan, something I'd seen but never thought of before took on new meaning and jumped right out of the pages at me. Both the Village Vanguard and Sweet Basil are idle on Sunday afternoons.

With grant in hand, I spoke with people at the Vanguard first. They refused. Then I approached Sweet Basil with an offer they couldn't refuse—free music. My proposal was to put our band in their club for a series of four consecutive Sunday-afternoon concerts. Their only commitment was to pay for the promotion. I'd pay the band's salaries. The management of Sweet Basil accepted the offer. By the third week, thanks to word of mouth, we had lines around the block.

Consequently, we worked that club on and off for two years, sometimes for a week at a time, sometimes on off nights, or sometimes at the last minute when they had a cancellation. Taking advantage of our growing profile, we eventually worked every jazz venue in New York City, including a triumphant week at the Village Vanguard. Later, the band branched out and toured internationally. Working part-time, we played together more than two years, recorded three albums, and grossed $90,000. All of this because I put together an action plan that worked.

To maximize the potential of every action, whenever possible, avoid thinking linearly and doing only one thing at a time. It's most efficient to combine action steps, but only if you're able to do it without making the success of any one step dependent on the success of another.

Here's an example of a successful combination of action steps. When I started my trio in 1990, I had no promotional photographs for my press kit. Seeking a title for the trio's soon-to-be-released debut album, I put two and two together to make five and decided to call the album *Portrait*. It's standard procedure for record companies to pay for the expenses of creating an album cover as an advance against the band's future royalties. Approving the title suggestion, the company arranged for a photographer to take a portrait-style photograph of me for the cover of the album. I also convinced the company that it was in its best interest to have the publicity picture coordinated with the album cover. Then, I made two hundred quality black-and-white promotional pictures from the negative they sent me of the publicity picture. I saved at least $300 by combining action steps.

A SAMPLE ACTION PLAN

You can control and coordinate all the elements of your action plan by creating a planning schematic. (See pages 27–30 for a sample action-plan schematic.) Start at the top of a sheet of paper and list your short-term, intermediate, and long-term goals. Leave a lot of room in between each of your goals. And remember that you will add and subtract from the plan as its details progress. After each of your goals list the things that you need to do in order to accomplish that goal. Within each general to-do list, you may need to add several, more detailed to-do lists. For instance, in order for you to set up your office you may need to buy a new computer, but before you decide which computer to buy you may need to take a computer course.

Each of the actions in the above example are considered action steps. Draw a box around each of the action steps in your action plan. Each box will have sub-boxes that contain to-do lists of things that you will need to do before you can accomplish the larger action step. These sub-boxes in turn will have sub-sub-boxes that contain to-do lists that have a finer level of detail, and again, that you will need to do to support the larger action step. However, be aware of the fact that the tasks in any to-do list are rarely ever accomplished in the order in which they are listed. Life can be inconvenient. It's normal to complete these tasks when it is possible and practical for you to complete them—and not according to some abstract order. There may be some tasks that you can only do one at a time; however, there may be others that you can accomplish all at the same time.

The action plan on the following pages gives you an overview of some of the tasks you may need to accomplish in order to start your business. As you start to break down all of the steps that are required it will quickly become apparent that you have a lot to accomplish just to get your business started—let alone before you begin to book and tour with your group. Each step that is featured in the plan is discussed in detail in the chapters that follow. Although a book moves from chapter to chapter in a linear fashion, an action plan is nonlinear and functions simultaneously on many levels and therefore you will work on multiple stages of the action plan simultaneously.

Sample Action Plan: Stage One When I decided to form my own trio and take my band on the road, I started brainstorming about the things that I needed to do to get myself ready to run my own business. Here are some of the things I knew I needed to do to prepare myself.

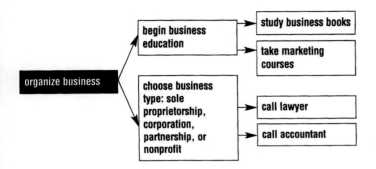

Sample Action Plan: Stage Two Once I had begun organizing some of the practical and legal components of getting a business together, I needed to think about how I was going to finance my venture. At this point I also started to think about the practical things that I could do to set up my office. Here are a few of the things that I anticipated that I would have to deal with to get it all together.

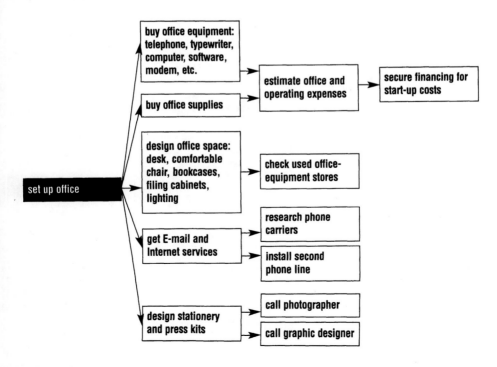

Sample Action Plan: Stage Three In many ways, I had been working on putting together my band for a long time. After I had made the decision to officially start this business venture, I needed to systematically work through the process of organizing my band. Here are some of the things that I knew I needed to work through.

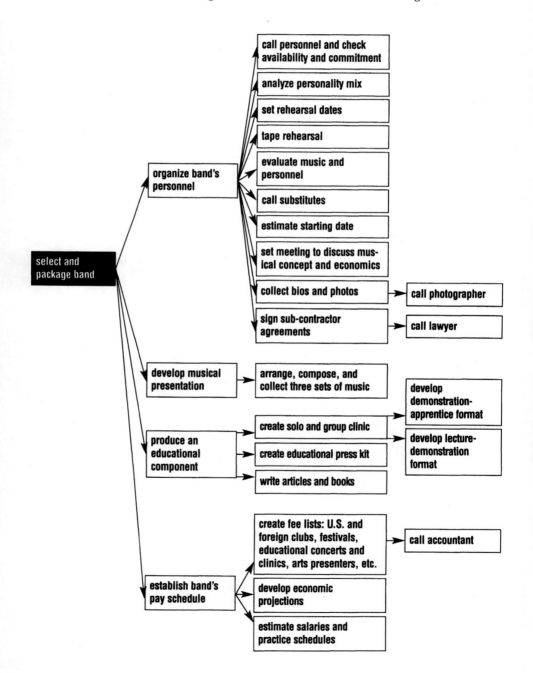

Sample Action Plan: Stage Four Once the group was organized and the business side of things was more or less up and running, I could begin to start researching and collecting venue contacts. Here are a few of the things I thought I should get together.

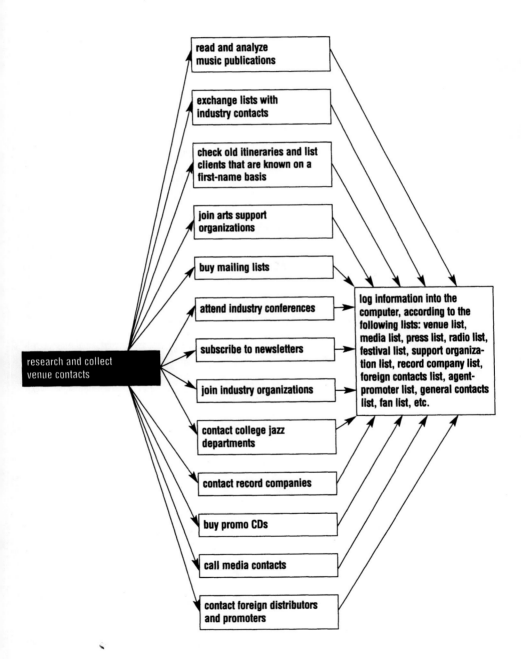

Sample Action Plan: Stage Five Finally, I was ready to start booking the band's first tour. Here are some of the things I wanted to do to get myself organized for the booking and the routing of our first tour.

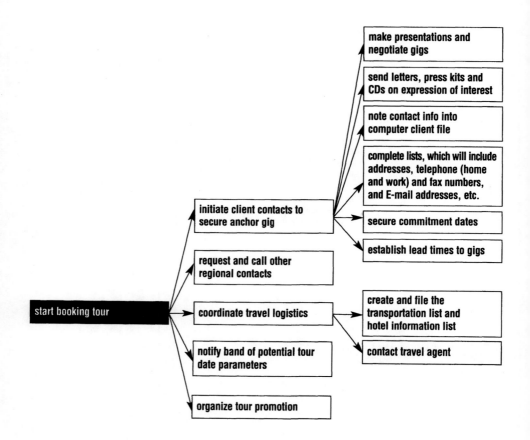

Chapter 3
Organizing Your Business

A good business sense is not an attribute with which everyone is born. However, with a little application and study anyone can learn the basic skills and develop this sense. Literature on the subject is endless and even just deciding *what* to read can be a daunting venture. This chapter will help you organize your business; it also includes a short list of books that most people can handle. As you immerse yourself in these recommended books, you're bound to start thinking of things that aren't specifically in them. Keep in mind that—no matter what the subject—if you have a business-related question, *somebody* has written a book that will contain the answer. The books recommended here, however, will go a long way toward heading you in the right direction.

As you begin your business education (and especially as you work your way through this reading list), you'll have to think about which business format best suits your current needs—and which will best maximize your circumstances. There are four types of businesses—sole proprietorship, partnership, corporation, and nonprofit organization. Each of these has unique requirements as well as unique benefits and limitations. Choosing which of these four types is right for you is the first major step you need to take to get your business started. The basic distinctions of each of these business types are listed in this chapter—as are some tips about how to get the maximum benefit from each of these types. By the time you finish this chapter, you'll be ready to start thinking about answering the question: Which business venture makes the most sense for my circumstances right now?

BEGINNING YOUR EDUCATION

One of the things that tilts the odds of success in this industry in your favor is that musicians are not generally good businesspeople. The fact that you're reading this book is a good indication that you at least recognize the need for these skills (even if you don't possess some already). So, without even picking up a single book listed below, you're already ahead of the game.

As a bandleader, you will regularly be talking to hundreds of potential clients. Your experience and grasp of the realities of business are necessary to earn their respect. To become a good businessperson, you need to familiarize yourself with some basic business precepts as you begin to put your action plan into motion. The following five books are recommended reading:

- *Getting Noticed: A Musician's Guide to Publicity and Self-Promotion* by James Gibson (Writer's Digest, 1987)
- *Million Dollar Habits* by Robert J. Ringer (Fawcett, 1991)
- *Guerrilla Marketing Weapons: 100 Affordable Marketing Methods for Maximizing Profits from Your Small Business* by Jay Conrad Levinson (NAL, 1990)

- *Making Money Making Music: No Matter Where You Live* by James Dearing (Writer's Digest, 1982)
- *Your Own Way in Music: A Career and Resource Guide* by Nancy Uscher (St. Martin's Press, 1993)

Once you've read these books, turn to the business reading list located at the end of this book and start reading the titles listed there. During the first phase of your action plan you're going to be doing a lot of self-study. And this process of evaluation won't stop when you pursue the later goals on your action plan; most of the books that you read now, you will refer to later from time to time. Once you begin your booking process, the type of material you'll be primarily reading will change from basic business books to music-industry magazines and newsletters.

Once you read these recommended books, your mind will not be the same. New information breaks down old ways and establishes new ways of thinking. This process is called catharsis. During a period of catharsis your imagination takes flight. Let it happen. Go with it. Mental readjustments will occur as your mind absorbs and catalogs new information and begins to relate it to the goals you've set for yourself. Be patient. Don't waste your time with premature actions. Review your action plan and prioritize your actions. Rate them according to what you can do and when you can do them. Schedule extraordinary purchases according to your personal budget. Think in the long term.

About a year after I formed my trio I experienced the following catharsis. In my enthusiasm I began a multitude of projects simultaneously. And then, having overextended myself, I became totally stressed out. As a result, I had to stop working for eight months in order to step back, refocus, and readjust my priorities. I had a serious case of having too many hats and not enough heads! Eventually I learned how to manage my time more efficiently and how to put some of the projects I had started on hold until a later date.

If you really want to change the way your brain works, enroll in a minimarketing seminar. It will radically change your perceptions. Things that you never noticed before, or that you took for granted, will take on new meaning. Minimarketing seminars are offered many places, often for as little as $200, and are an investment that will be returned to you tenfold. Community colleges frequently offer these seminars, as do many colleges and universities—especially those with strong adult education divisions. You may also find these classes advertised in the business section of your local newspaper. The classes are out there; make a few phone calls and find the course that will work best for you.

CHOOSING YOUR BUSINESS TYPE

Deciding which business type fits your current business goals is the first major decision you need to make as a small-business owner-to-be. There are four different ways to organize your business. Listed from the simplest to the most complex they are: sole proprietorship; partnership; corporation; and nonprofit organization. Each of these types has its own pros and cons. As you read through the summaries of the various types, one might jump out as the type that's right for you. However, it is important to stay open-minded and learn a bit about them all—if for no other reason than to prepare yourself for your future successes and the future growth of your business.

Your choice of business organization should be based on the following considerations. Each type of business organization:

- has legal restrictions, so you'll need to make sure that the restrictions of the type of business that you choose do not inhibit the success of your business goals;
- has unique administrative parameters, so you'll want to be careful to choose the type of business that is most suited for the assets that you have available to you now as well as what you are trying to accomplish;
- has different needs for capital;
- has tax advantages as well as disadvantages;
- allows for liabilities to be assumed in slightly different ways;
- is designed for a different number of people to be associated with the venture;
- has different guidelines concerning the perpetuation of the business.

Before you choose the type of business organization that is best suited to the situation that you want to create, it is advisable to consult with both a business manager and an entertainment attorney.

Business managers are in charge of handling your money. For this reason, you should be extremely cautious in selecting the person for this job. A business manager should be a professionally qualified accountant who has specialized knowledge of the music business. Payment can generally be arranged as a percentage of the earnings of the business, by the hour, as a flat rate—or as any combination of the three.

Entertainment attorneys have to be specialists in the music business and have experience with copyright law, licensing, and contracts. When choosing an attorney check his or her references carefully. You can contact your Secretary of State's office or the Better Business Bureau (http://www.bbb.org) to see if any complaints have been filed against the lawyer you're considering. Your lawyer may be paid by the hour (for a short-term job) or by a percentage of your income (for long-term work). Free or inexpensive legal advice can also be found through your local office of Volunteer Lawyers for the Arts. Check the Artswire Web site at http://www.artswire.org/artlaw/info.html for more information.

Sole Proprietorship

Of the four types of organizations, the most common is a sole proprietorship, a business with one owner. Almost two-thirds of the businesses in the United States are set up this way. A business that is organized as a sole proprietorship is not separate from its owner, but is merely a name with which the owner represents him- or herself to the public. The business is the owner and the owner is the business.

Because of this relationship, a sole proprietorship is known as a pass-through entity. All expenses and income pass through, and are filed as part of, the owner's personal tax return. If the business makes a profit, the owner is liable for any taxes due. However, if there is a business loss, the owner can deduct it from his or her personal income.

Sole proprietorships are inexpensive to form and easy to operate. In most cases, all you have to do is get a d/b/a (doing business as) certificate and start operations. You also have the option of starting out as a sole proprietor and, if you're wildly successful, changing to a corporation at a later date.

Although simple to set up and operate, sole proprietorships have one major disadvantage: The business and the business owner are inseparable. So, if someone sues the business, he or she actually sues the owner. The owner's personal liability is unlimited. The owner is liable for the company's debts and the owner's personal assets can be taken to pay for company obligations. In addition, owners of sole proprietorships can lose profitable tax-free fringe benefits because they cannot take part in company-funded employee-benefit plans like medical insurance and retirement plans. This, however, is not a big concern for bandleaders whose bands have high employee turnover rates.

These are the advantages of a sole proprietorship:

- It is simple to organize.
- It allows the owner the greatest freedom of action.
- The owner receives all of the company's profits.
- It grants the owner the maximum authority that can be granted in any of the four business types.
- It is easy to discontinue the business.

These are the disadvantages of a sole proprietorship:

- The owner assumes unlimited liability.
- The proprietor has only a limited ability to raise capital from outside investors.
- The company's growth is limited to the owner's personal energies.
- The personal and business affairs of the owner are mixed.

Other than the price of printing business checks and the nominal legal fees involved with acquiring the d/b/a certificate, there are no start-up costs for a sole proprietorship. Maintaining a business checking account costs nothing except for the monthly account service fees that are applied to any checking account. To avoid being charged the extra bank fees that are charged when your account is underfunded, ask the bank what the required minimum balance is and reserve that amount (which is often as little as $200–$250) to keep in your business account. As a sole proprietor, you can cash checks that are made out to you in your personal name and that have your Social Security number. However, most musicians (who are traditionally distrustful of taking checks for services rendered) prefer to be paid in cash—as cash doesn't bounce. Likewise, band members' salaries are usually paid in cash from income collected while on the road.

If you're thinking about becoming a sole proprietor, here's a tip: Don't use your bank to order your business checks. They're too expensive. Banks farm out the work to a check-printing company and then add a service charge to the cost. You'll save money by contacting Designer Checks, which can be reached at P.O. Box 9222, Anniston, Alabama 36202-9222. The company can also be reached at 1-800-239-9222 or on the Web at http://www.designerchecks.com.

Partnership

Co-leading with another musician as well as creating a cooperative band are both practical formats for organizing a musical group. Both scenarios fall under the partnership category. As a member of a partnership, you'll maximize your effectiveness by sharing the tasks of booking and running a group with one or more people. By officially pooling your physical, psychological, emotional, and financial resources on the business side of the collaboration, partners often find that day-to-day operations come together more quickly and thoroughly than they might in a sole proprietorship situation.

You can form a partnership by making an oral agreement with your partner(s), but this is not recommended. It is advisable to form a partnership officially, by having each partner sign a partnership agreement. This is a quick and easy process that can be worked out with your attorney, and involves relatively minor fees. A partnership agreement should include the following information:

- the type of business that you're forming;
- the amount of money that is being invested by each partner;
- instructions for how profit and loss are to be divided among the partners;
- the amount of or percentage of compensation that each partner will receive;
- instructions for how the assets will be distributed, should the partnership be dissolved;
- specifications of the duration of partnership;
- provisions for how or when the partnership will be dissolved;
- provisions for how new partners will be added or withdrawn;
- a dispute-settlement clause;
- any restrictions of authority that may apply, particularly concerning expenditures;
- stipulations for settlement in the case of death or incapacitation of one of the partners.

These are the advantages of a partnership:

- It benefits from the combined management skills of the partners.
- The possibility for financial strength is greater than in a sole proprietorship.
- Each partner has a personal interest in the partnership, and therefore more collective energy is invested in the success of the partnership.

These are the disadvantages of a partnership:

- The authority for decisions is divided, which creates the potential for disputes.
- Each of the partners is subject to unlimited liability.
- It may be difficult to find suitable partners.

A partnership is similar to a sole proprietorship, except that it has two or more owners. Like a sole proprietorship, a partnership is not a separate legal entity from its owners. Unlike a sole proprietorship, however, a partnership can hold property and incur debt in its name.

In general, a partnership shares the same advantages and disadvantages as a sole proprietorship (see pages 33–34 for details), but a partnership has an additional drawback: A partner can be held liable for the acts of the other partners. This increases the potential for personal liability of each of the partners. The general rule of a partnership is that all of the partners' personal assets are on the line for any business debts that are incurred by any of the partners. If you have more money than your partner(s) and your partnership incurs business debts, you may have to bear the brunt of those debts, even if your partnership agreement says you will split debts fifty-fifty. A partnership agreement does not bind third parties who are unaware of the agreement. Also, one partner cannot sell his or her share in a partnership without the consent of the other partners. Death of one of the partners dissolves the partnership automatically. Heirs of a partner inherit his or her share of the partnership assets as well as the debts of the partnership. If partners have an oral agreement but haven't signed an official partnership agreement and one of the partners dies, the heirs of that partner often have to sue to enforce their legal rights and gain their fair share of the assets of the partnership.

Tax treatments for partnerships are slightly different than they are for sole proprietorships. Although, like a sole proprietorship, a partnership is a pass-through entity and therefore doesn't pay its own income tax, members of a partnership are required to file an information tax return with the Internal Revenue Service. The pro rata share of the income and expenses of the partnership are shown on each partner's personal tax return forms, and any taxes that are due are paid by the individual partners.

Corporation

The corporation was created to solve the problems that are typical of the partnership. Forming a corporation allows a group of entrepreneurs to act as one unit, as in a partnership, but it has one important advantage: Since the corporation is a legal entity that is separate from its owners and is capable of being sued, it can protect its owners by absorbing the liability if something goes wrong.

A corporation is essentially an artificial person that is created and operated with the permission of the state in which it is incorporated. A corporation is like a person, except that it exists on paper only. A corporation is brought to life when the incorporator files a form known as the Articles of Incorporation with the state. An owner of a corporation is called a shareholder, and a corporation can have an unlimited number of owners/shareholders. The corporation owns and operates the business on behalf of the shareholder(s), but it is under the shareholders' total control.

These are the basic advantages of a corporation:

- Shareholders assume only limited liability.
- The continuity of ownership is assured.
- It is easy to transfer ownership of a corporation from one shareholder to another.
- It is easier to raise capital for a corporation than for either a sole proprietorship or a partnership.
- The potential for efficiency of management is greater in a corporation than in either a sole proprietorship or a partnership.

And these are the three most important advantages of a corporation:

- It allows you, the owner, to hire yourself as an employee and then participate in company plans like medical insurance and retirement benefits.
- Since you and your company are two separate legal entities, lawsuits can be brought only against your company.
- When debt is incurred in the company's name, you're not personally liable and your personal assets cannot be taken to settle company obligations.

These are the disadvantages of a corporation:

- It is subject to special taxation.
- It is more difficult to organize than either a sole proprietorship or a partnership.
- The charter of the corporation restricts certain types of activities.
- It is subject to state and federal controls.

Small-business corporations should have liability insurance. Otherwise managers and corporate officers could be held personally liable for the activities of the corporation. Consult your lawyer for the amount of insurance your corporation should have and shop around for the best price.

The legal fees involved with setting up a corporation can be costly. However, if you decide to set up your business as a corporation, you can fill out a simple and relatively inexpensive do-it-yourself corporate application kit. This kits cost approximately $250, though prices vary from state to state. A more expensive option is to have your lawyer set up a standard Sub-Chapter S-Corporation for a fee of about $150 to $250, which is in addition to the application fee.

The major drawback of a corporate setup is that it is subject to more regulations from state and federal authorities than either a sole proprietorship or a partnership. As a shareholder, your personal Social Security tax will be somewhat more, as well. And you must pay unemployment taxes, which cover you as an employee of the corporation, to the federal and state government. Accounting procedures are somewhat complicated, too, and personal and corporate funds cannot be intermixed. Your salary will be watched closely by the tax offices.

The major benefit of setting up a corporation is that you, as owner/shareholder will enjoy certain significant tax advantages. You can also be set up and included in such employee benefits as health insurance, tax-sheltered pension plans, profit sharing, and bonus plans.

Nonprofit Organization

The nonprofit organization (which is also called a nonprofit *corporation*) is the last of the four alternatives that you can consider as a legal framework for your business. You may have heard the expression that a company "has 501c3 status." This simply means that it is a nonprofit corporation. As was mentioned earlier, the nonprofit corporation is the most complicated of the four options—both to establish as well as to maintain. However, it also has many advantages that are unique to this business type.

These are the advantages of a nonprofit organization:

- It is eligible for state and federal exemptions from payment of corporate income taxes; it is also eligible for other tax exemptions and benefits.
- It can receive both public and private funding.
- As with a corporation, it is subject to only limited liability.
- As with a corporation, separate and legal perpetuity exists.
- Its principals can be eligible for employee fringe benefits that are generally not available to self-employed business owners and operators.

- It is eligible for lower postal rates on third-class bulk mailings. (A book detailing the various fees for nonprofit, commercial, and bulk mailings can be obtained free of charge from the post office.)
- It is eligible for discounted classified advertising rates at many publications.
- Unlike the other kinds of business organizations, it is the beneficiary of free radio and television public service announcements (PSAs) that are provided by local media outlets.
- Employees of nonprofit organizations can be eligible to participate in job training, student internships, work-study programs, and other federal, state, and local employment incentive programs at which salaries are substantially paid out of federal and state funds.
- It is eligible for checking accounts that don't have monthly service charges or minimum deposit restrictions.

These are the disadvantages of a nonprofit corporation:

- A fair amount of paperwork is required to form and maintain it.
- There are many costs and fees involved with processing this paperwork.

Although the list of *disadvantages* of having a nonprofit corporation appears relatively short (especially in relation to the list of advantages), each of the two items listed above has many facets. First of all, *a lot* of time, energy, and (generally) money is required to obtain nonprofit status. Lawyers' fees for doing the paperwork and filing an application for 501c3 status with the IRS can cost between $2,000 and $2,500. And it may take up to a year for your application to be approved. However, the good news is that you can function as a nonprofit while your application is being reviewed.

If you are willing to put in the time and effort to learn how to apply for nonprofit status, you can prepare the incorporation forms and tax exemption applications yourself that are required for the 501c3-status application process. Look for 501c3 how-to books at your library or bookstore. You will be preparing a number of documents, including the Articles of Incorporation, Bylaws, and Minutes of the First Meeting of the Board of Directors. If you prepare the paperwork yourself, you will then be required to pay only the actual cost of incorporation, which, in many states, is less than $200.

In addition to the paperwork that is required when applying for 501c3 status, a fair amount of paperwork is also required to maintain this status. Articles, bylaws, and minutes of ongoing meetings will need to be amended, and annual reports of your activities will need to be written. In addition, a lot of accounting and financial record keeping are required to maintain nonprofit status.

Given the right circumstances, of course, all of this paperwork is worth the effort. Nonprofit companies enjoy many benefits. As was mentioned above, nonprofit corporations can receive private as well as public funding. When a company has nonprofit status, its funding contributors—either public or private—can take tax deductions for their gifts. In addition, having 501c3 status allows the company to receive grants of all kinds— including technical assistance, emergency assistance, and support services—from corporations, foundations, state and/or federal government agencies, and individuals.

Another major advantage to forming a nonprofit company, is that the principals of a nonprofit group can be employed and, therefore, can be eligible for employee fringe benefits that are, for the most part, not available to self-employed business owners and operators. These benefits include sick pay, group life insurance, accident and health insurance, payment of medical expenses, and coverage by an approved corporate employee-pension or retirement-income plan. In addition, the nonprofit corporation's contribution to these employee plans is deductible from its unrelated business income, should it have any.

If you decide to establish a nonprofit company, the book *Your Own Way in Music: A Career and Resource Guide* by Nancy Uscher (St. Martin's Press, 1993) is a valuable resource book, as it contains an extensive list of nonprofit support organizations.

Many nonprofit groups rely on the Foundation Center, which is located at 79 Fifth Avenue, New York, New York 10003, and its comprehensive listings of funding organizations. As a member of the Foundation Center, you can receive discounts on the purchase of the center's funding resource books (which otherwise generally sell for around $125) or do research at the facilities free of charge. Call the Foundation Center at (1-212) 620-4230 to determine the closest branch location. Or check out the center's Web site at http://www.fdncenter.org.

Membership of the American Music Center, which is located at 30 West Twenty-sixth Street, Suite 1001, New York, New York 10010-2011, offers additional resource benefits for nonprofits. You can call them at (1-212) 366-5260 or check out the center's Web site at http://www.amc.net. One of the benefits of being a member of the American Music Center is that the center will host your Web page; another benefit is that you will receive automatic membership in Support Services Alliance (SSA). SSA can be reached at P.O. Box 130, Schoharie, New York 12157, or by telephone, at 1-800-322-3920. SSA's Web site address is http://www.ssainfo.com. SSA has a monthly newsletter that offers valuable advice to small-business owners and entrepreneurs and, most importantly, can arrange low-cost health insurance for you and/or your employees for less than 50 percent of the cost of most health-insurance plans.

The nonprofit sector is incredibly vast, and receives billions of dollars of support funding annually. Likewise, the amount of resource information that's available can be mind-boggling. Booking and managing a band is, in itself, labor intensive and the process will leave you with little time for the additional work that is required to administer the business and write grants. Professional nonprofit managers and grant writers are available and can help with this aspect of the business, but most will not work "on spec" (i.e., for a percentage of the monies that will be received if the grant is awarded), and instead will charge a fee in advance.

There's also a catch-22 involved with funding a nonprofit company: You need to have received a grant to get a grant! Large, well-staffed, and long-standing nonprofit organizations that have extensive grant histories are the most successful groups to receive grant funding. Often the smaller mom-and-pop nonprofits are less successful.

I once asked an associate—a man who had a long-term contract with a city government to supply a jazz music education course to elementary schools kids—whether or not he had received many grants from filling out applications. His answer was: "No!" When I inquired further as to how he obtained his grant money, his response was: "Mostly through political connections." If you don't have any political connections or abilities in this area, your task is that much more difficult. Create your own grant history by looking for small, local nonprofit organizations that offer grants for local arts presentations. The more grants you get, the more grants you can get.

The legal restrictions for maintaining nonprofit status are complex. One of these restrictions is the IRS's formula that dictates how much of the income from your nonprofit needs to be self-generated by its own programs as opposed to how much can be received from outside funding sources. Without the proper ratio, your company can have its nonprofit status suspended by the IRS. There is another restriction that is imposed by the government: If at a later date your organization is financially successful and you want to opt out of the nonprofit sector, you cannot take your organization's money with you. According to the IRS, you would then be making a profit. Any monies that remain in a nonprofit's account at the time that it is dissolved must be donated to another nonprofit.

Although the IRS may frown upon it, it is possible for a sole proprietor or nonprofit organization to work with another nonprofit organization to use some of its services. For example, you can use a nonprofit's metered postal registration number to mail your newsletters as long as you use the return address of the nonprofit organization that maintains the postal account. Also, as long as you fill out the application in the organization's name, you can filter grant applications through a nonprofit; the only stipulation is that you give the organization a percentage of any grant money received. Nonprofits always need funds.

One drawback of being either a corporation or a nonprofit organization occurs when you're doing business with venues whose normal business procedure is to pay performance fees using business checks. Your contract will be signed under your corporate name, and will have your Employer Identification number. And so, the venue will be obligated to write out your check in the same manner. While checks made out in your name can be easily cashed at a venue's bank, corporate checks cannot be cashed on the road. They must be deposited in your corporate checking account for collection.

Chapter 4
Setting up Your Office

Every businessperson needs an office in which to work. Most small-business owners will fall into the home-office category. Home offices are generally out-of-the-way corners of our homes where we can work without distraction. An unused bedroom, an attic, or even a barn can be converted to a home office. The basic considerations for setting up a well-functioning office are expense, comfort, and efficiency. Unlike the office worker, the home-office worker is able to customize his or her working conditions and control his or her office expenditures.

There are other benefits of setting up your own office, too. You can play your own music, sit in a comfortable chair, and decorate your office with flowers, for instance. You can also set your own work schedule, eat snacks while you work, and work in your jammies if you so desire. You also have the freedom to decide what office machines you want to use, when you want to buy them, and how much you want to spend on them. You can schedule your purchases according to your flow of income. Before you begin to build an efficient office you should have some idea of what you're getting into and how much an office setup might cost you.

ESTIMATING YOUR OFFICE EXPENSES

You can't run a small business without an office and you can't work efficiently in your office without the proper tools. Generally small-business owners who are just getting started are able to create a suitable office space within an area that they already occupy; so creating the office itself doesn't have to add costs to the venture. However, obtaining the tools to run the business requires a certain amount of money. One of the tricks to starting a business is planning how much money you will need to get the business started. How well you plan up front will largely determine how smoothly the financial aspect of your business will run during its initial stages.

The costs of the key items required to run an office—a computer (plus all of the necessary software), printer, telephone/fax/answering machine, and personal copier—will determine the majority of your start-up expenses. You may be lucky enough to own some of these items already. If so, your initial start-up expenses will be considerably lower than if you're starting from scratch. However, if you don't own these items, you'll need to start shopping around—learning about the equipment and where you can buy it most easily and at the best price. As you begin to make your preliminary phone calls, read through catalogs, and check out company's Web sites, you may start to wonder how you're going to pay for it all. Don't worry. If you're short on start-up money, you can stagger the purchase of the big items. The most important thing is to try—as best you can—to accurately estimate the amount of money that you are going to need to get yourself up and running.

You can keep expenses down by buying used equipment. Small Dog Electronics is a good source for refurbished computers that have warranties and service contracts. You can access their Web site at http://www.smalldog.com. Penton Publications also compiles a monthly directory that lists used business machines that are for sale as well as secondhand equipment dealers throughout the country. Write for a complimentary issue at Penton Publications, P.O. Box 823, Hasbrouk Heights, New Jersey 07604; you can also reach them by phone at 1-800-526-6052 or by fax at (1-201) 393-9553. You can also access their publications on the Internet at http://buyused.hsix.com.

The best deals for *new* Apple computers and software are often found in mail-order catalogs. MacMall has a comprehensive catalog. You can reach them at 1-800-222-2808, or on the Web at http://www.macmall.com. MacWarehouse also has a good catalog. You can reach them at 1-800-255-6227, or on the Web at http://www.warehouse.com. Mac Connection can be reached on the Internet at http://www.macconection.com or by telephone at 1-888-213-0260. Multiple Zones International can be contacted via the Internet at http://www.zones.com. Multiple Zones International deals with both IBM as well as Mac computers within two different branches of the company, PC Zone and Mac Zone respectively. PC Zone can be reached by telephone at 1-800-408-9663 and Mac Zone can be reached by telephone at 1-800-454-3686.

Now that you know where you can get good deals on the *big* items, here's a list of the basic office equipment and supplies you'll need to have a fully functioning office. Prices are approximate, rounded off, and subject to change. Quotes for business machines are based on the least expensive models of new items. Using this sample expense list as an example, you'll want to create your own cost estimate—paying particular attention to the costs of the larger, more-expensive items that you need.

In addition to the essential materials that are required to set up an office, there are other items that are optional, but can make your office work a lot easier. Below is a list of reference books and material that I have found to be helpful:

- *Rand McNally Road Atlas* (Rand McNally, 1999), which costs $10.95.
- *The Random House Compact World Atlas* (Random House, 1999), which costs $15.95.
- *The Trucker's Atlas for Professional Drivers* (American Map Corporation, 1999) is an excellent book for U.S. city maps; it costs $19.95.
- *Michelin Guide No. 703: Europe, Main Cities* (Michelin Red Guides, 1993) is a great source for European city maps; it costs $24.95.
- AT&T 1-800 phone book, which you can receive free of charge by calling AT&T.

In addition, the following items can be downloaded free of charge from the Internet:

- State abbreviations can be found on the Georgia State University site at http://www.gsu.edu/other/st-abbr.html.
- Free maps and point-to-point directions can be found both on the Maps On Us site at http://www.mapsonus.com and on the MapBlast! site at http://www.mapblast.com.
- Zip codes can be found on the United States Postal Service site at http://www.usps.gov/ncsc/lookups/lookups.htm.
- American area codes as well as European country and city codes can be found at the AT&T site at http://www.att.com/traveler/tools/codes.html.

SAMPLE OFFICE EQUIPMENT AND SUPPLY LIST

computer	$ 1,000
ink-jet printer	$ 200
contact manager program	$ 100
telephone/fax/answering machine	$ 300
personal copy machine	$ 300
calculator	$ 10
digital diary	$ 200
printer ribbon	$ 25
computer paper	$ 11 /box
fax paper	$ 9 /roll
copy paper	$ 4 /package
legal pads	$ 3 /dozen
manila file folders	$ 3 /package
paper clips	$ 1 /box
Post-it Notes	$ 6 /dozen
ballpoint pens	$ 5 /dozen
stapler	$ 12
staples	$ 1 /box
tape dispenser	$ 5
tape	$ 1 /roll
rubber bands	$ 2 /box
business envelopes	$ 6 /box
clasp envelopes	$ 6 /box
return address rubber stamp	$ 7
business cards	$ 25
mailing labels	$ 8 /box
scissors	$ 4
wall calendar	$ 4
surge protector	$ 20
diskettes	$ 1 /each
diskette storage tray	$ 7
two-drawer filing cabinet	$ 50
CD mailers	$ 4 /package
wastebasket	$ 4
blank audiotapes	$ 10 /package
blank videotapes	$ 7 /package
business books	$ 250
magazine subscriptions	$ 250
(add 10 percent for unknown costs)	$ 286
TOTAL START-UP COSTS:	**$3,147**

If you don't have access to the Internet, you can find state abbreviations, U.S. zip codes, and U.S. area codes in the back of your *Rand McNally Road Atlas*. I've found it helpful to either tear out or photocopy these particular pages from the atlas and keep them handy—either by storing them on my desk or in a separate file folder. I also like to keep a photocopy of the U.S. map in this folder—for ready reference. This comes in handy when I'm organizing the travel details for a tour.

The estimate above doesn't include the cost of creating your press kits, promotional pictures, brochures, and either special or custom paper products. Depending on the quality of the image you wish to project to your future clients, you may find that you want to invest in high-quality paper goods and matching stationery, envelopes, mailers, and business cards that will enhance your presentation. They can be purchased at any good stationery supply house. Once you've decided what image you would like to present with this material and you've estimated how much it will cost to create these items, you'll want to add these expenses to your own start-up expense list.

I designed the press kit for my trio with advice from a media professional. I also hired a graphic artist to design my brochures, business cards, envelopes, stationery, and mailers. I even went so far as to buy a book on the colors and textures of paper and its psychological effects on people. All of this added another $2,500 to my start-up business expenses. However, I felt the cost was worth it, since these materials put the odds of success in my favor by creating the best first impression I could with potential clients. My strategy paid off: I acquired one concert just on the strength and quality of my brochure alone.

PREDICTING YOUR OPERATING EXPENSES

As with most new businesses, your first year will be the most expensive. Since you'll be booking your band from six months to a year in advance, you won't be able to count on any immediate income to offset these initial expenses. And so, you will need to have saved or acquired enough money to fully finance your start-up and operating costs through the first year. It's not good business policy to be either under- or overfinanced. If you're underfinanced, you'll run out of money before you can do your first tour (and earn your first income with this new business). If you're overfinanced, you'll be overburdened with debt you simply can't handle. Both situations make it impossible to follow through on your action plan. A new business must have realistic financial projections of its future income and expenses or the venture is sure to fail. Assume you'll spend between 10 and 15 percent of your gross income per year on your business operating expenses.

The following is a list of expense categories and average ballpark estimates of your office operating costs per year:

- telephone: $4,000–$6,000
- office expenses: $1,000–$2,000
- postage: $800–$1,500
- tax preparation and legal fees: $300–$3,000, depending on your business setup
- association memberships: $200–$300
- estimated taxes: $600–$1,200
- union dues: $50–$150
- subscriptions to professional journals: $100–$250

TOTAL AVERAGE OPERATING COSTS: $7,050–$14,400

The above list doesn't include tour expenses, such as transportation, band members' salaries, and hotels. It also doesn't include personal expenses, such as rent or mortgage payments, food and health costs, auto insurance, etc. So, in addition to estimating the start-up costs for getting your office set up and keeping it running for the first year, you'll also need to estimate how much money you personally will need to have in order to keep your life running while you start this new business venture.

Once you've established what equipment and supplies you need, estimated the costs of acquiring these items, and estimated the costs of operating your business for its first year, now you should add your start-up costs and your operating costs together. This will give you an idea of what it will cost to run your business for the first year. Now, you're ready to think about how to get the money to set yourself up so that you can begin the process of booking your band. Fortunately, there are more ways to finance your start-up costs than you probably have imagined.

FINANCING YOUR START-UP COSTS

Every new business begins in debt and much of this debt is incurred by the costs involved with starting a business. It can take years to recoup your start-up costs. Be judicious in your debt management. Carry only the amount of debt your monthly budget can tolerate. Also, consider the emotional effects that this debt may have on you and the other members of your family. An individual's ability to tolerate debt varies from person to person. Psychologists rate beginning a new career as being as high on the stress scale as a death in the family, divorce, or bankruptcy. You don't want to add more stress to what will already be a challenging situation by incurring more debt than necessary. Even if you don't recoup your start-up costs early on, remember that these expenses are investments in your future. Keep receipts for everything—as the expenses are tax deductible as capital business expenditures.

There are numerous ways that you can obtain start-up money. Possible sources of financing include: savings accounts, bank loans, loans against investments, credit cards, time-payment plans, family members, barter arrangements, and contributions. These sources can be used either individually or in combination with one or more of the other sources on this list. Each of these options is discussed below.

Savings Accounts

You're ahead of the game if you have money in a savings account. But if you don't, you can start now. You'll probably be surprised by how quickly you can build a start-up nest egg simply by putting aside 10 percent of your income. If you are making $25,000 annually, you can save $2,500 in a year. That's enough to get started with the right equipment and a minimum of office supplies. You may find it helpful if you open a business account and then deposit 10 percent of your income directly into that account each time you get paid. This way the start-up money will be clearly distinguished from your personal funds.

Even though using your own savings may be the obvious way to start, it is often better, whenever possible, to use OPM (Other People's Money). The prime benefit to using OPM—i.e., investors' money if you've established a corporation or grant money if you've established a nonprofit organization—is that it personally costs *you* less money. There is a wide range of sources for OPM. The seven major sources are listed above and will be discussed in the sections that follow.

Bank Loans

If you're a homeowner, a small home-equity loan is a good source of financing. The interest may be tax deductible. If you don't want to use your real estate and you have a relationship with a local bank, you may be able to arrange for an unsecured loan of up to $2,500. The interest rates for this kind of loan can be competitive with those that are offered by credit cards, and monthly payments can be spread over a period of up to ten years or more.

Whatever kind of loan you're considering, be sure that it doesn't have a prepayment penalty. If, as sometimes happens, you receive a windfall (such as a big royalty check or a proposal to buy a master tape), you will want to prepay the loan—in other words, pay it off before the payment deadline. The benefit to prepaying, of course, is that it saves you from paying the interest on the loan that you would otherwise pay if you spread the payments out over a longer period of time.

Loans against Investments

Banks will often give you a loan, using your investments in stocks, bonds, and securities for collateral. However, if you default on the loan, the bank will sell your investments to recoup its losses and will return to you any unused portion from the sale. No matter what form of bank loan you choose, both the expense of the loan (i.e., the interest) as well as any purchases you make with the money from that loan (i.e., capital expenditures) are considered to be part of your normal business expenses and are tax deductible.

Credit Cards

The third way to finance your start-up costs is to use a credit card. The limit on a new credit card is often $2,500. Shop for the best deals on credit cards at the Bank Monitor site at http://www.bankrate.com. The best credit cards are ones that have low interest rates and low monthly payments. Use your credit card for your start-up costs only. If you use the card only for business purchases, then the purchases and interest payments are tax deductible. This, in effect, makes the interest rate significantly lower than what is stated in the cardholder agreement. If you do decide to use a credit card to purchase your start-up costs, it is imperative for you to stay disciplined and not mix personal purchases with business expenses. If you do mix business and personal purchases, you will have to pay your accountant to untangle the finances so he or she can figure out your deductibles at tax time.

You can upgrade your credit limit by borrowing the maximum amount allowed (which, on a new credit card, is usually around $2,500) and depositing it in your savings account for a month. It will earn a little interest for you while it sits in your account. Then, when your bill arrives, pay off the balance that is due with the amount you borrowed. There will be no interest charge if you pay it off by the billing date. Repeat the process every month. Within six months you can request an upgrade of your credit limit, or, in most cases, they will upgrade you automatically. Credit-card companies look for any good reason to upgrade you because they want you to borrow more money. If you continue to repeat this process, within a couple of years your limit will be about $10,000.

Time-Payment Plans

Many office-supply houses offer time-payment plans. For instance Staples, which hosts a Web site at http://www.staples.com, offers a credit card for home-office users. Call 1-800-378-2753 for the rates for the Staples personal credit card. Office Max, which hosts a Web site at http://www.officemax.com, offers a similar service. Call 1-800-767-1293 for more information. Although their rates may be higher than most regular credit cards, office-supply houses require no annual fee and offer free delivery when you order more than a certain amount.

Family

Your family members could conceivably help you finance your start-up costs. If you show them that your plan is economically feasible and that you're committed to working hard to make the project a success, they may be willing to lend you the money. Offer them a return on their investment at a rate that is equal to the return that they receive from their other investments. The interest on this kind of arrangement could cost you less in the long term than what you would pay for carrying the same debt with a credit card or if you took out a bank loan. Buy a loan-rate book at any business stationery-supply store that will help you figure mutually agreeable interest rates.

Barter Arrangements

Of all the methods that have been listed thus far, bartering for goods and services is the most powerful financing tool. However, it is also the option that people overlook most frequently. It requires creativity and imagination to recognize a barter situation—even when it's right in front of you. You can barter your talents and services (musical or otherwise) in exchange for many items and services you'll need in the course of running your business. But the best part about bartering is that you don't have to divert funds from your budget to receive these items and services.

Here's an example from personal experience: When I decided to start my first newsletter, I didn't have the talent or the time to develop it. Obviously, I needed the services of a designer and editor. I had a friend who had her own publishing consulting firm. Her child was enrolled in a school that was putting on its yearly fund-raiser. She designed and created my newsletter; in return I played a solo concert at the fund-raiser, gratis. It cost each of us only our time and talents.

In another instance, I struck a deal with one of my former students who was helping me with a book I was writing about how to practice to be a jazz improviser. He was transcribing and editing a full year of tapes and notes from my lectures at the jazz department in the Mannes College of Music at the New School University. At the time, I was working with a Tandy laptop computer, which was not compatible with his Mac. This was making my editing job impossible. In exchange for a credit in the book and 15 percent of the book's future royalties, he bought me a Mac computer and deducted it from his taxes as a business expense.

Barter agreements can be very creative. I live in the Catskill Mountains, where owning a pickup truck is a necessity. At the time that I moved to the Catskills, I couldn't afford to buy a truck, but I had a beautiful upright piano for sale for $2,000.

Our local PBS radio station ran a regular program of Sunday afternoon concerts, which were broadcast live from their studio, and they happened to be looking for a better piano. I offered to give the station the piano for free, if in response they would agree to give a local car dealership a year's sponsorship for *Car Talk,* their most popular Saturday morning show. (The sponsorship was worth $2,000.) The station agreed. The dealer needed the advertising, and so, because I had coordinated the sponsorship for him, he gave me a used pickup truck that was valued at $2,000. I only paid $800 for the piano, the car dealer had received the pickup truck as a trade-in, and it didn't cost the PBS station anything to give the sponsorship to *Car Talk.* Everyone won in the deal.

Books on the barter system can be purchased at most bookstores and will be among the best investments you ever made.

Contributions

Finding contributors is like finding people to barter with: It takes a little creativity and effort. And, as with bartering, you have to be able to recognize that you have a specific service or item that is valuable to another person or business. For instance, if you're playing a concert somewhere and need posters, announcement cards, and handouts, you may be able to make arrangements with a business—such as a restaurant or merchandiser that is near the concert hall—to pay for part or all of the printing of this material in return for advertising space on your printed material.

Likewise, if you create a band newsletter, you may be able to find an interested party that is willing to pay some or all of your printing and postage expenses in exchange for advertising space in the newsletter. When I was working on my first newsletter, I sold logo advertising space to my record company (my records were being offered for sale), my school (I was a faculty member), and a jazz music publisher (my books and play-a-longs were being offered for sale). The advertising amounted to enough money to print and pay the postage for the mailing.

In addition, consider applying for a grant from a local or national arts-support organization. That's how I got my quintet started. As you can see, there are many ways to get start-up funds for your project. Try them all, and think of new ones as well.

PURCHASING OFFICE EQUIPMENT AND SUPPLIES

Don't let the fact that you may not have all the money on hand to buy everything you need from the start hold you back from beginning your project. Start small, but start. Like many of us, you may have to begin your booking process working with the bare essentials. When it comes right down to it, if you have a pen, paper, and a telephone, you can start booking a tour. When you can afford it, you can graduate up to more sophisticated and expensive business machines.

Office Equipment

Even though, in a pinch, you *can* get away with bare essentials, there are about half a dozen items that you will need to run a professional and efficient small business. These few things will be immensely helpful in keeping you (and your information) organized—a valuable and timesaving quality that is especially useful when you're in the throes of putting together a tour. Your first business investment should be some communications equipment; personally I prefer a combination telephone/fax/answering machine, though you can purchase these items separately. If, when you're initially starting to build your office, you can't afford to buy a computer right away, your second purchase should be a typewriter. And your final purchase should be data management equipment—in other words a computer. After you've purchased these major items, you'll want to outfit your computer with the following three things: software, a modem, and a printer. These will be the most expensive office items you'll buy to get your office up and running.

TELEPHONE/FAX/ANSWERING MACHINE If you have to make a choice about which item to buy first, get the telephone/fax/answering machine. This equipment will be the cornerstone of your business. While you're making your selection, consider buying an inexpensive chin-shoulder rest for the telephone as well. It will leave your hands free while you're talking on the telephone—so you can make notes, access your files, move your chair around, or whatever. A more comfortable, but also more expensive, alternative to a chin-shoulder rest is a telephone headset. This can cost between $100 and $200; however a headset has a much longer cord than a telephone, and so it allows you greater freedom of movement.

Make sure that your telephone/fax/answering machine has a speakerphone. This is helpful for off-hook dialing, as well as for waiting in telephone queues when you're calling airlines or van-rental agencies and you get that bothersome all-of-our-operators-are-busy tape. However, because they're so impersonal, avoid using your speakerphone when you're making venue contacts.

Your fax machine can save you time and money, especially when you want to make sure that any information you have discussed with a client or travel agent is accurate. You can simply type up a confirmation letter that spells out the details of your discussion and fax it to your contact to review at his or her leisure. You can ask your contact to call you *only if* there is a mistake in the details; this will save both of you time. Likewise, sending a confirmation fax to foreign venues can help avoid problems that can arise from language barriers.

A fax machine can be used to make copies of documents. However, if you're using rolled fax paper, your faxes will eventually fade. A handy trick, if your computer is on a dedicated line, is to send a fax to your computer's telephone number. Then, from your computer, you can print out a hard copy on plain paper that will never fade.

You can also use your fax machine for "shotgunning" potential clients. You can print out form letters that have been personalized in the addresses and salutations only on your personalized stationery and stack them in the feeder of your fax. Some machines can be preprogrammed to send up to twenty faxes at a time—one right after the other. You can also save time during your workday and keep your fax number clear for incoming faxes by programming your machine to send large "mailings" automatically at a less active time of the day or at night.

As a bandleader, you will be a prisoner of the telephone as it is. Having an answering machine can free you from feeling like you can't leave the phone for fear of missing important calls. But remember that a depressing or desultory tone of voice can turn a client off. Your outgoing message should be businesslike, pleasant, and even humorous.

It's not advisable to speak with clients when you're fatigued. Your machine's call-screening function can filter calls from clients you'd rather speak with at a time when you're rested. However, if you're call-screening clients, don't pick up the phone when a client is leaving a message; it can leave a bad impression on him or her.

A high-quality telephone/fax/answering machine will have many additional features that can make your work time more effective. Be sure to read its manual and experiment with its various functions.

TYPEWRITER As I mentioned earlier, if you can't afford to purchase a computer right away, you'll definitely want to purchase a typewriter. My handwriting is almost illegible to anyone but myself, so I've found that an inexpensive electric typewriter is an indispensable office item. They cost about $200–$300. If you don't have a computer (and therefore don't have the capability of printing personalized stationery yourself), consider buying your own personalized stationery. It's well worth the small expense to ensure that your letters look good.

When I started, I purchased a Smith Corona word processor with diskette capability for about $300. Working with paper files was fine for the first year, but as the business grew working with paper became too labor intensive and I bought my first computer.

COMPUTER In the second year of running my own business, I purchased a Tandy laptop computer (which at the time cost about $500) and a compatible dot-matrix printer. However, after a year of coping with the DOS format, I couldn't wait to get rid of it and sold it at a loss. When it comes to a choice of whether to have an IBM or a Macintosh computer, I recommend the Mac. The Mac is more user-friendly and the software isn't as difficult to learn. But because Apple once again manufactures the Mac exclusively, expect to pay about 20 percent more for a complete system than you would if you bought an IBM.

The size and kind of computer you'll be able to get will depend on your start-up funds. Buying a computer is like buying a car. A smaller car will also take you where you want to go. You don't necessarily have to buy a Mercedes-Benz to drive across the country. Computers are marketed and sold by their "power"—the speed of their CPU, or central processing unit. The top-of-the-line computer is the one with the fastest processor. But the truth is, most people don't need that much power. The software applications you will be using don't require anywhere near that much firepower. Unless you're running a high-end graphics program, last year's computer model will more than meet your needs. If you buy a less powerful or "old" computer instead of a souped-up, new one, you can save as much as 50 percent.

When buying a computer, one factor that is particularly important is memory. As having access to the Internet is quickly becoming a necessity in the business world, your computer must have enough memory to handle the Internet's requirements. Accordingly, even though most computers are sold with thirty-two megabytes of RAM, or random-access memory, you must have sixty-four megabytes on board, otherwise your machine will crash with some degree of regularity when you start using the

Internet. Luckily, purchasing and installing additional memory is relatively easy—and not too expensive. (Information about where to purchase both new and used computers is listed on page 42.)

SOFTWARE Computers increase your capacity for work, making you more efficient, but it does take some time to get up and running. The more sophisticated a software program is, the greater its learning curve will be. If you're not mechanically minded, save yourself time by taking an inexpensive introductory computer course—in Windows 99, should you decide to buy a PC system, or in MicroSoft Word, should you decide to buy a Mac—at your local college or university. Time management is always a consideration when you're running your own business and you can't afford to spend excessive amounts of time learning how to use both a new computer and its software programs.

You'll need at least a year of lead time to put your action plan into motion, and during much of that time you'll be doing research and logging in venue information. However, once you've started booking your band, assume that you'll be spending about 25 percent of your time contacting potential clients and the other 75 percent of your time administering the business of the band and managing data. The data categories you'll be managing require specific software: a database for cataloging business contacts for venues, mailing lists (of fan lists, press contacts, etc.), lists of record companies, media contacts, etc.; a calendar program for logging tour dates, callback times, to-do lists, and memos; a word-processing program for writing letters as well as for designing stationery and fax cover sheets; a spreadsheet program for computing tour budgets, economic evaluations, and your personal financial accounts; and a simple graphics and desktop-publishing program for creating press kits and Web sites.

You'll also want to purchase a contact-manager program. *Macworld* magazine recommends Chronos's Consultant 2.56, calling it "probably the best all-purpose" and inexpensive Mac platform contact-manager program available. It's only sold via the Internet and costs less than $100. You can contact Chronos at (1-801) 957-1744 or visit their Web site at http://www.chronosnet.com. Another option is FileMaker Pro, version 4.1. Although FileMaker Pro is more expensive than Consultant 2.56, it is customizable. It costs approximately $200. This cross-platform database software program can be found on most on-line software marketers' Web sites and in software stores.

If you have the expertise and the time, you can also do your own desktop publishing. Rather than paying outside services to design and print your posters, handouts, postcards, brochures, and stationery, it's more cost effective in the long run to design them yourself. I recommend purchasing an inexpensive desktop-publishing program like the Print Shop Publishing Suite, which is made by Broderbund Software.

Computer map software programs come in handy for estimating travel times and inserting maps and driving instructions into your itinerary. AAA has an excellent CD-ROM program for North America and Canada that can be purchased through MacWarehouse, MacMall, Mac Connection, or Mac Zone (see page 42 for information about how to contact each of these four companies). You can also join AAA on-line at http://www.aaa.com. The Netherlands-based company Route 66 has a map program on diskette and CD-ROM that covers all of North America and Europe. They can be reached by phone at (011-31-318) 554724 or on the Internet at http://www.route66.nl or at http://www.magicroute.com.

Computer junkies love to talk computers. If you're a novice at computers, try to find a friend who has some computer expertise. Call upon this expert at those moments of computer frustration when you've accidentally hit a wrong key or don't know how to work a particular function. The instruction books don't have all the answers.

MODEM Having a modem facilitates two major things: access to E-mail and the Internet. Both of these are increasingly becoming requirements for small businesses. While the modem itself costs $150 and up, you can save an average of 30 percent on your monthly phone bills by using E-mail instead of the phone for some transactions. At this rate the modem will pay for itself within three months. A modem also can save you from wasting a lot of time dialing telephone numbers incorrectly and logging calls. Calls can be logged automatically when using a computer. Maximizing your work time is an important factor in running a small business (more time equals more calls, more calls equals more income).

E-mail is one of the fastest-growing aspects of the Internet. In addition to the money-saving attributes mentioned above, E-mail allows you to attach and send electronic documents along with your messages. Attachments can be written documents, color photos, or graphic design pieces—almost any kind of document that a computer can create. I once met a book publisher who told me that he'd never met his printer because he sent everything to him as an attachment. Sending attachments electronically instead of through the mail can also save you money.

Buy the fastest modem possible. The modem is your connection to the Internet. If you have a fast modem, you'll save a significant amount while accessing information on the Internet. You can find all sorts of material on the Internet: venue contacts, business information, other bands' itineraries, etc. Depending on your level of expertise, you may even want to design and maintain your own Web site.

PRINTER Color printers are becoming less expensive every year. You can buy a good quality color ink-jet printer for about $200 to $300. One of your most-used office machines, the printer will allow you to print customized form letters, contracts, faxes, promotional materials, as well as photos. If you decide to design your own promotional material, you'll probably want to invest in a laser printer instead of an ink-jet printer. With prices that range from $800 to $5,000, laser printers can be more expensive than other types of printers, however, the printing quality is higher and the speed is faster than other printers. When you're a desktop publisher, speed is of the essence.

Office Supplies

Save by shopping for desks, filing cabinets, in-boxes, lamps, etc., in secondhand business-supply stores. The Salvation Army, auctions, garage sales, and thrift shops can be cost-cutting sources for office supplies, too.

Most cities have organizations that, free of charge, collect office equipment from corporations that have gone out of business and distribute this equipment to nonprofit organizations. Ask some of the nonprofit organizations in your area if they are aware of this resource. Sometimes an individual or business needs a tax deduction and they will give you their used equipment for nothing. Or, they can buy new equipment and give the old equipment to you as a gift (these gifts are tax deductible if your company is set up as a nonprofit).

There are other supplies you'll need to have a fully functioning office. Save time and expense by buying your paper products and small-business machines by mail at discount prices. Three of the best mail-order houses that offer free catalogs as well as next-day delivery are: Viking Office Products 1-800-421-1222 (http://www.vikingop.com); Staples 1-800-333-3330 (http://www.staples.com); and OfficeMax 1-800-788-8080 (http://www. officemax.com).

Chapter 5

Selecting and Packaging Your Band

Once you have selected the legal framework for your business and have set up your office, you'll be ready to start working on the fun part: choosing your band personnel and developing the musical conception that you collectively wish to project to the public. On some level, a certain amount of this process will be intuitive. However, even though a lot of the steps will feel familiar, don't be fooled into making these decisions lightly. It takes time, extreme thoughtfulness, and foresight to decide your band's personnel and musical conception. When you get to this point, you personally will already have invested a lot of energy in your business efforts. The future success of your band will be based on the business foundations that you have established as well as on the quality of your band's musical presentation. This is the first step where you will be placing the success or failure of your business venture into other people's hands. It is, therefore, very important that you pull people on board who work well together and who are committed to achieving the same goals that you have set for yourself.

ORGANIZING YOUR BAND'S PERSONNEL

For your band to be truly effective, the band members must generate a synergistic effect when they're working together wherein the whole is greater than the sum of the parts. When I started each of my groups, I spent at least a year to a year and one-half planning its personnel. Fortunately, I worked in New York City for more than twenty years, so each time I put together a group I was able to select from a pool of excellent musicians, all of whom I knew personally. And because I knew and had some history with each of them, I was familiar with each musician's character and personality.

There's no rule of thumb that can be applied to how to go about selecting musicians for a band. It's a judgment call that you make by analyzing how each musician's character is expressed in his or her playing. After making my initial selections, I called the musicians and we rehearsed and then played a test gig, which I taped. Taping the session helped me to be sure that the mix was right and the magic was there. Only after analyzing the tape of the test gig and evaluating the feeling of the music, did I approach the musicians to see if they'd be interested in joining my band.

Key Factors to Consider During Selection

When selecting your band's personnel, you'll have to consider many key factors. You'll need to think about what size band you want to have, the chemical reactions among your musicians, and the quality of the band members' interpersonal relationships. You'll also need to decide whether you should use experienced or inexperienced musicians and whether or not you want to maintain consistent band personnel. And finally, you'll need to evaluate the commitment of your personnel to the band's long-term goals.

Each of these six factors is unique and independent. You'll want to think about each of the items separately. However, when you make your final decisions, you'll want to focus on the big picture. Individual musicians may have minor personal or stylistic differences that may not totally conform to your ideal vision; however, if the overall chemistry works and each of the members is committed to the band's success and is respectful of the other musicians, then the mix will most likely work.

BAND SIZE The size of your band has a direct bearing on its marketability. Add another person to your band and you'll have to factor in another salary, as well as additional costs for transportation and accommodations each time you go on tour. All of these things will increase your performance fees. Although you might believe that the only way you can express your musical concept is by going on the road with a ten-piece band, the economics of this approach may be nonproductive—especially if you have an unknown band without any marquee value. Depending on the situation, less is frequently more.

Pianist Lynn Arriale came up with a solution to the challenge of band size that works perfectly in her situation. She's a trio pianist with a budding reputation. Understanding that the drummer is the key to the success of any band, Lynn uses the same drummer whenever she tours. The third musician required for her trio is a bassist. To compensate for the fact that hiring a full-time bassist would add to the cost of touring and might price her out of a competitive market, Lynn has compiled a list of excellent regional bassists who she uses when touring and who, over time, have learned her music. By not hiring a full-time bassist, she has eliminated a potentially prohibitive salary and airfare. This keeps her performance fees within a marketable range for her level of marquee value.

This idea can work for larger groups as well. If you're a pianist with a quintet and your horn players are set, you can hire a local rhythm section wherever you go. Most areas have top-notch local players that can easily fit into your musical conception.

Given the intense competition in this business, you need a musical concept or instrumentation that works for you financially and musically as well as offers something different to your listeners. Although my trio has the standard instrumentation, I've worked hard to keep the same personnel since its inception. Because of this, we can offer music that benefits from a high level of rapport and interaction—a quality that is often missing from the pickup bands that populate the music scene today.

CHEMICAL REACTIONS The potential effect of a band's dynamics—in terms of the quality of the band members' chemical reactions with each other—has been demonstrated by the master of personnel selection: Miles Davis. His bands always had that electric, chemical reaction. Miles understood that when you're pulling together a band you're not just picking instrumentalists, you're choosing musicians by their character and personality—and that these traits create a combined effect when the group comes together to play.

This secret was brought home to me by one musical situation in particular. Guitarist John Scofield had a trio that was one of the most impressive jazz bands I'd ever heard. With Adam Neussbaum on drums and Steve Swallow on electric bass, the band's music appeared to be from another world. I went to hear them whenever I got the chance. No other combination of guitarist, bassist, and drummer could have created the magic they produced.

INTERPERSONAL RELATIONSHIPS It's also important to assess the quality of your band members' interpersonal relationships—both when you're at home and on the road. There will be times when the band members are tired from traveling or someone is late for a concert and feeling rushed. Road glitches are inevitable. In putting together the right personnel for your group, you'll want to consider how well the band maintains its equilibrium under these kinds of adverse circumstances. In my experience, well-conditioned road rats generally don't have any problems in this area. They've already spent decades on the road, have made all of the mistakes that young musicians make, and understand the value of working toward maintaining a smoothly functioning group.

EXPERIENCED VERSUS INEXPERIENCED MUSICIANS Whether you use youthful and inexperienced or older and more seasoned musicians is not necessarily an either-or question. Both have their advantages and disadvantages. In part, your decision will depend on your own standing in the music business.

Younger musicians have spirit and energy that can spark a band's music. Audiences take a particular delight in hearing younger musicians grow and stretch their wings. In addition, younger musicians generally earn lower salaries. As a result, if you hire young musicians, your band's performance fees will be more economical. This can be a real asset—especially when you're marketing a new band to venues. One of the difficulties involved with hiring younger musicians, however, is that their names may lack marquee value. Also, as the bandleader, you may find that you need to have a bit of patience and give a bit of guidance to the younger musicians in your band—as they can be less disciplined than seasoned road rats. It takes years of traveling to develop healthy and wise road habits.

Employing experienced musicians can help ensure that your band will deliver a quality musical product. Plus, the additional marquee value that a band gains from bringing on a well-known talent can only improve its selling position. However, experienced musicians may not be as available to work with you as younger ones. They're more in demand and more expensive to hire. So by using them, you can raise your performance fees to a point where venues may not be able to afford your group.

Additionally, if you decide to pursue experienced musicians, you'll find yourself in competition with other bandleaders for their services. This makes booking a band more stressful than it already is. For instance, if one of your musicians works in two bands, you may find yourself in a situation where you're not able to confirm your performance dates in time to compete with the earlier confirmation dates of a competing bandleader. As a result, you may end up with an empty chair at a confirmed gig and no time left to fill it with a suitable substitute. If you've sold your band to a client on the basis of having that person and he or she doesn't show up for the gig, the client may think you falsely represented yourself.

As a bandleader, you may also find that it can work against you to employ musicians who might have a higher marquee value than you do. An audience's attention can easily focus on the members in a band who have the biggest names, not necessarily the leader. This is a common problem—one that some bandleaders have difficulty in overcoming.

I personally experienced this syndrome. My quintet of the late 1970s had a stellar lineup. Billy Hart (and later Bobby Moses) on drums, Wayne Dockery on bass, and Mike and Randy Brecker playing horns. The Breckers were old friends of mine. I was the first to record them on my early albums, *The Guerrilla Band* and *Wild Bird* on Mainstream Records. Over the years, their reputation deservedly increased through their recordings and the success of their group, the Brecker Brothers. By the late 1970s they had achieved star status and a much higher level of marquee value than I had at the time. During the period that my quintet existed, many people thought that I was playing in Mike and Randy's band as opposed to them playing in mine—a misperception that still exists to this day.

The flip side of this syndrome can happen, too: The bandleader's marquee value and presence can be so strong in the eyes of the audience that it overshadows all of the other musical personalities in the band. One of the most humorous examples of this happened during my ten-year stint with the Phil Woods group. A promoter once introduced the rhythm section to some of his friends in the following manner: "I'd like you to meet Phil Woods's drummer, Phil Woods's bassist, and Phil Woods's pianist."

MAINTAINING BAND PERSONNEL Don't underestimate the importance of maintaining consistent personnel. Younger musicians may be more available than established, seasoned musicians, yet venues will want to know "who's with you" and repeat venues will be more inclined to purchase a product they know worked well before. When you tell a new client that "this band has been together for three years," it leaves him or her with a strong impression that you have been successful enough to maintain a continuous band for that length of time.

A practical way to establish a stable band with relatively experienced personnel is to look for talented, experienced, but undervalued musicians. There are a lot of them around. Only slightly more expensive than younger, unknown musicians, they often have some degree of marquee value that can add to your band's marketability. Also, look for musicians outside your own locale. During this modern age—in which transportation and communication are so efficient—it's not necessary to look for band members only in your own backyard. It could be worthwhile to make a trade-off between adding expenses and overcoming the logistical inconveniences involved with this choice, so your musical presentation can be at the highest possible level.

Maintaining consistent band personnel keeps your expenses down for press kits, brochures, and band pictures as well. It's an absolute no-no to misrepresent your band's makeup to clients by mailing out-of-date press kits and pictures and then showing up with a different band. If your personnel has changed, mention it. If you don't have new band pictures, send them one of yourself (you should have a solo leader's picture anyway) along with your new personnel information.

Arrange for alternate backups for your personnel. When I had my quintet, I had backups for my backups. Don't get caught short of personnel because of illness or because, at the last minute, someone was offered another gig that they couldn't refuse.

One of the downsides of maintaining consistent personnel is that bandleaders sometimes become possessive about their personnel, especially if they love their playing. Avoid expressing this sentiment by using phrases like "our band" or "our drummer," rather than "my band" or "my drummer."

COMMITMENT OF PERSONNEL Another factor to consider when choosing your band members is each individual's level of commitment. When you're "courting" your personnel, make sure that you clarify your own musical and professional goals as well as your commitment to work hard for the benefit of the band. Detail what you feel will be your fair responsibilities to each other in terms of salaries, timely commitment dates, itineraries, quality of life on the road, and keeping each other informed of potential work conflicts. Give each musician a target date for starting your first tour and work out your first year's payroll. Estimate each person's commitment to what you're trying to accomplish and highlight any risks that that commitment may entail. Your interest in developing your fellow band members' careers can only help make your band more attractive to them.

Another critical factor to consider is loyalty. Avoid using musicians who see themselves as musicians-for-hire and who are loyal only from gig to gig. Commitment to a common goal is rare in the jazz world. The reverse is true in the world of rock and roll, where bands traditionally work well together and willingly make sacrifices to achieve their goals.

One rare example of a jazz band that had a high level of loyalty and achieved success was Pat Metheny's quartet. They got together when they were students at the Berklee College of Music in Boston, loved playing together, and realized they had something special and powerful to offer. Before making their first album, they went on the road for a year—working cheap, sleeping on friends' floors, developing their music, and earning their audience. By the time they made their first album, they'd earned enough of an audience to make their album sell well. They impressed their record company, and they went on to achieve uncommon success.

Administrative Details

Once you've finalized your personnel, you'll have quite a few administrative details to do before you will be ready to start the booking process. Make a to-do list of personnel information that you need and try to gather this material from all of your band members simultaneously—perhaps when you get together to rehearse. You may even find that it is easiest to make simple forms for the band members to fill out.

Each band member will need to give you the following:

- his or her name, address, and contact information;
- his or her passport and Social Security numbers;
- a biography, discography, and individual photo;
- a list of his or her instruments, including any identifying characteristics for each instrument—such as brand name, serial number, color, size, and weight (you'll need this information for border crossings into other countries).

(A slightly expanded version of the previous list appears on page 77 in chapter six.) All of the personnel information mentioned will need to be organized and filed for future reference. Once you've received this material, you will need to do the following:

- set up a schedule for band meetings and rehearsals;
- copy and mail musical parts and tapes to each of the band members;
- arrange to have a band photo taken;
- develop the group's press kit.

Once you have organized the material mentioned, you will be ready to start focusing on the music.

DEVELOPING YOUR MUSICAL PRESENTATION

Having a finely tuned musical presentation can give your band the edge it needs to compete in the music marketplace. Most audiences have had their fill of pickup bands that don't have an organized presentation, and just get together and jam tunes. Your goal as the bandleader will be to stimulate the group to create a musical identity for your band that listeners will be able to recognize.

In addition to recognizing a band's unique "sound," audiences also have a deep appreciation for the quality of a band's musical interaction. They'll be watching as well as listening. Your band's bandstand demeanor can heighten an audience's appreciation of your music. This aspect of being a professional performer was first brought to my attention when I was touring with Cannonball Adderley. He knew that the body language of the band members could help guide the audience's response to our music. When there was a solo, Cannonball advised those who were not soloing at that moment to look at the soloist. This would subtly help to focus the audience's attention on each soloist in turn. "Soloing or not," he used to say in caution, "if you're on the bandstand, you're still working."

Creating Your Band's Musical Identity

How you go about creating a musical identity for your band will be based on two major factors: the musical characteristics of each member and whether or not you and/or your band members can compose and arrange. Any band's sound is dependent on the sum of each band member's individual style of playing. Change one person in a band and the band sound changes as well. If you, the bandleader, don't compose and arrange, it is smart to hire at least one band member who can. Or, like many other bandleaders who don't have composing chops, you can hire someone outside of the band to write for you. Look for someone who needs exposure, and who is willing to write for the band for either credit or a share of recording and royalty fees.

Organizing and Rehearsing Sets

Organize and rehearse at least three one-hour sets of music. Plan sets of different lengths for different situations (i.e., 45-, 60-, 75-, and 120-minute sets). Each set will involve different pacing and tunes. The number of tunes you'll need will depend on the size of the group, and the average length of each member's solos. A trio will need more tunes per set than a quintet. Experiment with tune pacing and choice until you've found a natural and dramatic set structure. Prepare more music than you think you'll use. Some tunes may or may not work out well on the bandstand, or you just may not need to use all of them in a regular set. However, it is always a good idea to have a few extra tunes prepared—in case you need to present an encore or two.

College big bands are always looking for good, fun arrangements to play. Having a one-hour set of big-band arrangements that are based on your band's music will enhance your opportunities in the educational area. If you can't afford to invest in having big-band arrangements of your music written for you, keep your ears open when playing concerts opposite big bands. Some band directors—or their arranging students—will have written excellent charts for their bands that might work for your group. If you find an interesting arrangement, ask the band director if you can have a copy of the score. He or she will be pleased that you asked and will appreciate the possibility of their reputation being enhanced by having you play and announce his or her music at other venues. The expense of having someone write out parts from a score is less than having custom charts created for you.

When getting your new music together, you'll save time and avoid frustration by ensuring that each of the band members has his or her parts to the music well in advance of rehearsals. It is also helpful if you tape and make copies of the rehearsals— so the band can study the music at home. Parts should be easy to read, learn, and memorize. If you have personnel changes, you don't want to spend inordinate amounts of your band's time introducing a new member to your music.

When preparing for a tour, ask each of the band members to bring his or her music. But, as a precautionary measure, make two back-up copies of your music to take on the road with you. Don't put both copies in your suitcase when traveling—especially when you're traveling by plane. Baggage can easily get lost. Carry one of the extra sets with you in your briefcase.

PRODUCING AN EDUCATIONAL COMPONENT

These days a band can't survive solely on the income it receives from playing in clubs. Most likely, clubs will actually be your lowest paying (per day) venues, and there really aren't enough of them around to keep a band working. Luckily, there are more than 2,500 college and university jazz departments in the United States alone. Jazz education is big business and can be quite lucrative. In fact, fees for educational work are much higher than clubs' fees. (Festivals are the only gigs that regularly pay more than jazz education components.) These higher fees will be needed to subsidize your group's appearances in clubs.

Clubs generally hire a group to perform for one to four nights at a time. The majority of these performances will be scheduled for weekends. You'll need to work at the educational institutions in order to fill in your weeks' off days, otherwise you won't be able to afford your hotel expenses for those days you're not working. Educational components generally fall into two categories: demonstration-apprentice format and lecture-demonstration format. These formats can be utilized separately or in combination.

Many musicians are not involved in music education because they mistakenly believe that verbal abilities are a basic requirement for being an effective teacher. While this may be true for the lecture-demonstration format, it is not true for the demonstration-apprenticeship format. I had the good fortune of apprenticing with some of the greatest musicians in jazz. They were my best teachers, yet none of them could talk about the music. I learned from them by playing with them.

Demonstration-Apprenticeship Format

An educational program that is based on a demonstration-apprenticeship format can be as effective as the lecture-demonstration format—sometimes perhaps even more so. Lecture-demonstrations tend to separate the student from both the teacher and the music because the lecturer is mostly talking at the students, and the students, therefore, take a passive role. The demonstration-apprenticeship format, however, is more organic. It is sometimes called "the master-student style of teaching" because it is based upon an active involvement of both teacher and student. This approach to musical education is common in Eastern and African schools.

I was once privileged to observe an illuminating example of the master-student relationship at work. I'd been a regular faculty member at Jamey Aebersold's jazz camps for more than a decade and had seen many styles of teaching. Drummer Adam Neussbaum came to teach at one of Jamey's camps one year. As this was the first jazz camp he'd ever taught, Adam was a little nervous about his abilities as an educator. I assured him that he'd find his own way of doing things and would be just fine.

The camp's daily schedule was quite full and as the week passed I didn't have time to ask Adam how things were going. But one afternoon I was walking by a classroom and I happened to notice Adam and a student working together on something at the drum set. The student was having trouble executing a figure that involved coordination between various parts of the set. Out of frustration or instinct, Adam asked the student to get off the set. He played the figure over and over and at the end told him: "Here, man, make it sound like this." The student returned to the drum set and played the figure remarkably well. I walked away from the experience somewhat humbled. The phrase "make it sound like this" and the resulting effect on the student had a profound effect upon me, and made me completely reappraise my educational techniques.

Lecture-Demonstration Format

The lecture-demonstration format can be constructed around any special performance-oriented subjects in which the band may have expertise—either as a group or as individuals. This educational format requires some verbal abilities, as the educator will need to be able to discuss or explain the featured subjects as well as to demonstrate them.

Performance-oriented subjects can cover a wide range of topics, including how to rehearse, group interaction techniques, and the history of jazz demonstrations. Use your imagination. Have a band meeting and brainstorm and make a list of subjects that your band members are excited about and that might be useful to students. Put the subject headings in order, but leave their content open for development on the spot. Interacting with students spontaneously makes your lectures less boring and more creative. When you're in the classroom each band member should speak when he or she feels ready to make a valuable contribution to the subject. Students appreciate it when you include interesting and humorous examples from your personal experiences that illuminate the points you're making.

When I was a teenager I took a lot of dance classes. Of all of the methods that the dance instructors used, I remember especially enjoying when they demonstrated the mistakes we, the students, made. With that in mind, bassist Todd Coolman, drummer Ed Soph, guitarist Steve Erquiga, and I developed a lecture-demonstration that we presented regularly at Jamey Aebersold's summer jazz camps. During these sessions the four of us demonstrated some of the common mistakes that student-musicians made while they were playing. It always brought the house down, while at the same time educated the students.

Tape your lectures and have the band listen to them after the fact so everyone can make suggestions on how to improve them. Over time, you can develop a lecture-demonstration format that is effective, entertaining, and informative.

Additional Materials and Possibilities

Students find it helpful when you supplement your clinics with handouts. These can be photocopies of your material or articles that you, or your band members, have written. Handouts give the students something that they can take with them as a reminder of the subjects that you discussed, and the goals you've set for them.

You might also consider creating an educational press kit that you can add to your regular press kit when you're making contacts and submitting proposals to educational venues. This kit should include a list of the subjects that the band teaches—both as a group and as individuals. Survey your band members for their talents in this area.

When you're scheduling a clinic with a school, you might want to offer to audio- or videotape the clinic for the school's archives. If they take you up on your offer, make sure that you request a copy of the tape so that you and your band members can review and analyze it to improve your presentation at future clinics. And after you've finished a successful clinic, remember to ask your contact if he or she would be willing to write you a recommendation. And the next time you need to send out an educational press kit make sure to include a copy of it—or selected quotes from it.

In addition to your educational skills in the classroom, you may have undiscovered and undeveloped talents as an author. Articles and books about various musical and educational subjects are great promotion and enhance your image as an educator. Music industry magazines are in constant need of interesting educational articles. If you have published any articles, be sure to include copies of them in your educational press kit.

With a little planning and trial-and-error experience, you can develop a teaching program that will make your band attractive to educational venues.

ESTABLISHING YOUR PAY SCHEDULE

When you're making your initial agreements with your band members about forming a band, you'll want to discuss with them—right up front—how you, as the bandleader, will be organizing the finances of the band. If your band members are not already familiar with them, explain the pros and cons of the type of payment schedule that you intend to use. Since you have to keep your eye on the bottom line, try to offer salaries that are realistic in terms of what you estimate the band can earn. Stress the fact that you're offering an estimate and that band members' salaries may be adjusted once the band's earning power has been established. Your band members will appreciate your openness.

Types of Payment Schedules

The most common pay schedule options that are available are fixed-salary agreements and even-split agreements. Either of these agreements may be in effect for the life of the band or they may change from tour to tour. Elements of each agreement may be tailored to fit each situation. Some tours will earn less than that tour's overall expenses—and some tours may earn extraordinary amounts more. In the latter case, even with bonuses, you may have enough of a tour balance left over to offset some of your nontour expenses, such as start-up costs and office expenses. In each case, be sure to inform your band which agreement is in force for each tour and what each of the band member's salaries will be.

FIXED-SALARY AGREEMENTS Establishing fixed-salary agreements can make it easy for you to negotiate a fee for a gig because you have a clear idea of your bottom line. Fixed salaries are derived from a compromise between what fees each member will accept and what you believe the band's earning potential will be. (For examples of this type of arrangement, see the sample salary schedules on pages 64–65.)

Remember, when starting a new band, you may not be making a leader's fee on most tours because you'll be doing a lot of extra work booking the band and you'll have expenses that the other members of the band won't have. Any extra income that a tour earns should go to you as a leader to offset those extra expenses. Of course, you can always sweeten the pot and give bonuses to your band members when a budget allows you to do so. Another option is to offer your band members a salary arrangement that has characteristics of both the even-split as well as the fixed-salary agreements: a fixed salary that includes a bonus if a particular tour has a higher than average budget.

EVEN-SPLIT AGREEMENTS In an even-split agreement, the net profit of each tour is divided among the members of the band. Salary amounts are derived by dividing the tour balance (the amount left after the tour expenses have been deducted from the tour income) by the number of musicians plus one (a leader's fee).

Here's an example of how an even-split agreement works for the band members of a quintet whose tour has grossed $20,000: Deduct 30 percent ($6,000) from the total ($20,000) for expenses. (This is a ballpark estimate of what your tour expenses will be.) That leaves you with a tour balance of $14,000. Divided by five, this comes to $2,800 per person, with the leader making $5,600. This figure gives you a good idea of what your salaries will be. If it appears that your tour is in the red, you'll have $2,800 of flexibility to reduce the leader's fee to bring the tour into the black.

Although the even-split agreement is the fairest division of income for the sidemen, it eliminates the possibility for you to recoup your operating expenses (i.e., the expenses involved with doing business, such as your telephone bills, printing costs, postage fees, etc.). Consequently, it is best to use this type of agreement when a tour's income is below normal.

THREE SAMPLE SALARY SCHEDULES Create a pay schedule that applies to every possible contingency. Until you have it memorized, have it readily available when you make your initial contact with a client. This schedule will be one of your guides to how much you can ask for when negotiating a price for the band. These samples assume that the band members will have equal levels of experience and equal salaries.

Performances and clinics are paid on a six-day basis per a seven-day week. An extra day's performance is prorated. All payments are "on the books" and, as independent contractors, members of the band are responsible for their own taxes and Social Security payments. The leader will be responsible for issuing 1099s at the end of the year. You'll need to consult with your accountant or check the IRS's rules that govern your particular business type to determine whether or not your employees qualify for independent-contractor status. (Refer to the "Choosing Your Business Type" section of chapter three for basic information about the various business types.)

Make sure that each of the band members is aware of the following:

- All hotels will be paid out of tour income.
- Transportation (except to and from home airports), including equipment, will be paid out of tour income.
- Parking fees at home airports will be the responsibility of each individual band member.
- You will enforce a one-bag limit for each band member. Overweight charges for extra luggage are each individual's responsibility.
- Members who accept extra band duties will be given extra compensation. Extra band duties include driving, checking in luggage and equipment at airports, collecting band fees, disbursing payroll checks (or cash), and bookkeeping.

U.S. TOURS:

Performance: $200 per day. Add $100 if there is a clinic on the same day as the performance.
Clinic only: $150 per day.
Performance with radio broadcast: Same as performances.
Radio broadcast only: Income will be divided equally.
Studio recording: $750 per recording.
Extra day off: $100 (depending on the tour's budget).

FOREIGN TOURS:

Performance: $250 per day. Add $100 if there is a clinic on the same day as the performance.
Clinic only: $200 per day.
Performance with radio broadcast: Same as performances.
Radio broadcast only: Income will be divided equally.
Studio recording: $1,000 per recording.
Extra day off: $150 (depending on the tour's budget).

You might want to consider a seniority program wherein a new member's salary, in his or her first year with the group, will start at the first year's salary rate. This will create an added incentive to keep your personnel stable.

SECOND-YEAR TOURS:

Performance and clinic: (both in the United States and in Europe) Add $50 per day to the base salary mentioned in the previous schedules, with the exception of performances with clinics on the same day (which remain the same).

Performance with radio broadcast: Same as performances.

Radio broadcasts only: Income will be divided equally.

Studio recording: $1,500 per recording.

Extra day off: $150 (depending on the tour's budget).

It's important to remind your personnel that budgets and itineraries are proprietary information and that they should not be disseminated outside the band. Also, from time to time, certain performances will pay extraordinary fees. The leader reserves the right to keep balances from these performances to write off past losses and the operating expenses of running the band.

Managing Your Time and Information

Seventy-five percent of the time and energy that you put into booking your band will be spent producing, collecting, and updating information. Managing this information is an ongoing process that, at times, can feel overwhelming. However, if you spend a little bit of time up front and set up your data-management systems in a way that is comfortable and logical for you, you'll find that this part of the business is less daunting than you might have originally thought.

No matter how hard you work, you're bound to feel like you don't have enough time and energy in the day to complete all your tasks. As I've mentioned before, it's important not to waste your personal energy—because, as a performer, it is your most valuable resource. Inefficient data management can be the biggest drain of your time. It can waste time that you should use finding work for your band. As you will see, it's not possible to manage all this information successfully without using the correct tools and developing your own work methodology. The tips and tactics that follow should help you develop a system that will work for you.

ORGANIZING YOUR TIME

How you prioritize your tasks has a direct bearing on how efficiently you manage your time and utilize your personal energy. Taking hold of the reigns of your career is going to necessitate making some changes in your existing relationships and time patterns. The work-to-time ratios that will be most frustrating to change will be the relationships between your business and your music, and your business and your family. Managing the work-family ratio dilemma is a personal thing and depends on many variables— such as the number of members in your family and their attitudes toward your work. Suggestions on resolving this dilemma can be found in the many books on the subject in regular and on-line bookstores. It is also a topic that is frequently discussed in chat rooms such as the Small-Business Channel Web site at http://www.ideacafe.com, where people with home offices exchange helpful tips and information on this subject.

If you are a midcareer artist, it's assumed that you're an accomplished musician who doesn't need to dedicate as much time to learning your art as a younger musician would. By taking on the responsibility of booking your own gigs, you'll have less time to devote to your music than you're accustomed to having. You'll have to limit your musical tasks to daily maintenance and those musical efforts that have a direct bearing on your business—particularly tune research and arrangement, composition and transcription, and rehearsals. Young musicians who are still working at developing their art will have to divide their time between study and booking the band. They will have to allocate their time differently, scheduling a different work-to-music ratio than the midcareer artist.

Workday styles vary from musician to musician. However, I've found that it is best, when I'm at home, to reserve my musical tasks for the evening, after I've completed the day's business. I live on the East Coast, so this system works well for me, especially since I can't make business calls after business hours anyway, except for telephone calls to the West Coast or the Far East, or calls to contacts at their home numbers.

In general, touring leaves little time for practicing on the road and very little free time for business other than tour management, performing, traveling, and resting. However, many tours have at least a few location gigs interspersed throughout the schedule; these are consecutive gigs (often at the same venue) that allow you to stay in one location for a few days at a time. Take advantage of non-travel days to write out arrangements you've been working on at home. If you're on a location gig for more than two days, have a non-travel day off, or can arrange for an open day on location at the beginning of a tour, save the expense of renting a rehearsal studio by rehearsing at the venue. Look at your itinerary in advance and plan for this. Tell your fellow band members when a time has been allocated for rehearsing so they won't make plans for that day.

Feeling out of control creates stress. Knowing how to use your time well allows you to establish control over your work habits—as opposed to your work habits controlling you. The following personal experience is a good example of how things can get out of your control. Around 1:00 P.M. one Friday, my fax machine ran out of paper in the middle of an important incoming fax from Europe. I only received a part of the fax—but, thankfully, it was just enough to know who had sent it to me. I was on the computer, working on a contract, and I stopped what I was doing to install a new roll of fax paper. I then shut down the computer program I was working in and accessed my fax writing program so I could compose, print, and send a fax to the sender, notifying him that I didn't get his fax. Aware that it was after normal work hours in Europe, I hoped that the ill-received fax wasn't the sender's last transaction of the day. It was.

The sender's office was closed for the weekend and I had to wait until Monday for a response. However, that Monday was the beginning of a European holiday and the sender was off for a five-day vacation. He had no idea that his fax didn't come through, and left no forwarding number. Ten days later, while I was on the phone confirming a gig with a new client, my call-waiting beeped—it was my European contact resending his original fax. To receive the fax, I had to get off the line with the client, apologizing for the interruption and promising to call him back shortly. It took about twenty minutes to exit the client-contact program I was in, and to compose, print, and fax a response. Then I called the new client back, but he'd left for lunch.

I left a message that I had called and requested a callback, but I didn't hear anything from my new client for the next two hours. I called the client again and his secretary said, "He's on another line." Later I called and was told, "He's in a meeting now and doesn't know when it will end." Aware that some clients are sensitive and don't like being cut off during a call, I wondered if I'd just gotten a "long no." It took me a week to find out that everything was okay.

If a situation like that doesn't make you apoplectic, you're made of steel!

One way to avoid this kind of scenario, is to keep your primary telephone line free for incoming and outgoing calls. If you install a second, dedicated phone line for your on-line computer tasks, then you can log onto the Internet or receive or send a fax *while* you're talking on the phone. Although it costs a little more to have a second phone line, this can really save you time—and can save your clients from the frustration they might feel if they call you and your line is busy.

Reserve the daytime for contacting potential clients. Invariably, however, there are tasks that can only be executed during business hours and that will take away time from making important phone calls. These daytime tasks include:

- making trips to printers and photo labs;
- copying and collating press kits;
- designing and printing business cards;
- buying stationery, envelopes, stamps, fax and computer paper, and CD mailers;
- buying and installing fax paper and print cartridges;
- maintaining office equipment, including telephone/fax/answering machines, computers, and printers.

Some tasks don't need to be completed during business hours. Reserve the evening hours for:

- collecting and updating promotional information;
- designing and printing press kits, brochures, and photos;
- assembling itineraries and tour budgets;
- manipulating and printing contracts and calendars.

Unless you have a multi-tasking computer, you won't be able to access your contact files *and* use your printer simultaneously. Since you will need to access your contact files when you're contacting potential clients (which is mostly during business hours), you'll want to print your contracts and calendars outside of regular business hours—and leave your computer free midday for other organizational tasks.

There are lots of things that can be done outside of regular business hours. Use your time on the weekends or in the early mornings to research venues as well as to organize your contacts for upcoming phone calls. Arrange tour transportation and hotels in the evenings. Most of the services that you will need to arrange travel and accommodations are available twenty-four hours a day via toll-free lines or on the Internet. There are benefits to doing these tasks off-hours, too. During peak calling hours, airlines and car-rental agencies can easily keep you on hold for five minutes or more. If you have to make these arrangements during peak hours and do get caught on hold, you'll find that your speakerphone is a handy tool that keeps you free to do other tasks while waiting in a phone queue.

It's my belief that the only good artist is a compulsive artist, and, as such, one risks becoming a compulsive businessperson. Striking a balance between work and play as well as managing time and stress will be your two greatest challenges.

MANAGING YOUR INFORMATION

When you're first setting up your business, you'll need to establish your own systems for organizing the volumes of information that you'll need to have on hand once you start the booking process. There is a direct connection between how well you organize this material and how smoothly the booking process will go. Information management covers a wide spectrum of tasks, the most predominant being:

- organizing your files;
- creating, filing, and updating worksheets and checklists;
- creating tour budgets and itineraries;
- writing agreements and cover letters.

To efficiently manage this information you'll need a computer that has several basic software applications: a contact manager with a calendar, a word processor, and a spreadsheet program.

Contact managers organize client information and create preformatted letters and contracts that automatically merge names and addresses. Make sure that the software for your contact manager program includes a calendar function that displays more than four weeks at a time and that the calendar can be integrated with the contact manager. This integration function allows you to easily schedule when you will do the things on your to-do lists, write memos, and make callbacks. Some contact manager programs automatically dial telephone and fax numbers, which eliminates the possibility of wrong numbers. This feature also saves time because you won't have to write a fax, print it, put it in the fax machine, dial the number and wait for it to finish transmitting. Some contact manager programs also record the time and date of when a call was made or a letter was sent and store this information for future reference.

You can use the calendar function of your computer to create a visual overview of a tour-in-progress. You can manipulate the dates and experiment with different routing possibilities by moving dates around, using your computer's drag-and-drop functions. You can also use the calendar function to send yourself timely reminders to ensure that you don't forget to make key callbacks.

You'll use a word processor to write letters, agreements, itineraries, worksheets, checklists, and larger documents such as fax brochures and academic articles. And you'll use the spreadsheet program to manipulate your financial information, such as tour budgets. (Tips on using spreadsheet programs are discussed in chapter nine.)

Organizing Your Files

You'll need to experiment with different ways to organize your files before you come up with an information management style that suits your needs. One of the key challenges in developing this system is maintaining a balance between the number of files and their sizes. If you have too many separate files, you'll have to wait for them to load when you're switching between them. However, if your files are too big, you might find that working within them is unwieldy.

RAW VERSUS RELEVANT DATA As you're collecting your venue data, divide it into two categories: raw data and relevant data. Raw data is venue information that is incomplete or remains untested for accuracy. You will retrieve raw-data files only when you're researching new contacts. Relevant data is venue information that has been tested for accuracy. It may be information that you've gathered from one or more phone calls to a prospective venue; relevant data may even include potential performance dates that you've discussed with that venue. Relevant data is *relevant* because it's something you will be using immediately.

Avoid information overload by storing raw-data leads in a folder of paper files for future reference. When you have time, you can enter this data onto a computer disk. Or you might consider hiring someone to enter the raw data for you. Secretarial rates average about $7 per hour. It's a choice between spending hours logging data you may not use for a year or two (after which it may no longer be accurate) or using that time to make phone calls that could result in a few thousand dollars of income for your band.

Enter raw-data information into a relevant tour file *only after* you've made telephone contact with a potential client and have received positive feedback for a current or future tour. Even if you don't get the gig the first time out, you've made your presence known and established a relationship with a client that could eventually lead to a future date. Relevant data can be stored in one of the seven potential categories listed in the sample filing system below. However, the majority of your relevant data will belong in the "contact file."

A SAMPLE FILING SYSTEM

Most contact-manager programs can be customized. How you use keywords and your own personal codes is up to you. It may take you a while to create a system that is simple and efficient to work with. And you may find that, as your contact files grow larger and more detailed, you need to change your system for organizing your information more than once. The following is a system for organizing contact files that I've found useful.

Contact File: This file should contain relevant contact information only (i.e., current tour contacts, repeat venues, or clients who couldn't commit but are interested for future tours). When you're inputting this information, be sure to specify fields for location, date, and venue type; establishing these search criteria will make it easier to retrieve these files—as explained below.

I've found it convenient to list the state abbreviations (instead of spelling out the state name) in the addresses field for all of my contact leads. That way, if I'm working on a Midwest tour, I can search for all of my contacts in Ohio (OH), Indiana (IN), Illinois (IL), etc. (See page 154 for a region-by-region breakdown of the states in the United States, along with their two-letter abbreviations.)

Festivals usually have fixed dates. When you're entering information for festivals into your contact file, add a keyword for the month that that festival is generally held. This will allow you to search by month, and pull up all of the festivals that are happening during any given time of year.

Make sure to specify the venue type for each of your contacts. The following eight categories will cover most kinds of venues: clubs/U.S., clubs/foreign, arts presenters, schools/U.S., schools/foreign, festivals/U.S., festivals/foreign, and jazz societies.

Using keywords, you can create lists within a contact file for different tours you're working on such as: 1999 Fall Tour, April Eurotour, etc. You can also create separate files for agents, clients, media and press contacts, fan lists, personnel lists, etc. When you have the document open you can type in any one of your keywords into a search box and the search function will bring you to that point in the document. Most contact programs also have a checkmark feature that highlights the venues that have requested return engagements. You'll probably also want to create a separate field or fields for information about how you were treated, favorite restaurants, hotel, and local contact info.

Agent-Promoter File: This file should contain information about agent-promoters that you've worked with in the past—or that have been recommended to you from other musicians. Even though you're doing your own booking, some gigs—especially festivals and foreign gigs—are best arranged by agents or promoters.

General Business File: This file should contain all information related to travel, including contact information for airlines, car-rental agencies, train and bus companies, and travel agents. This file should also contain all general business contact information, including printing companies, credit-card companies, computer technical support organizations, bank, lawyer, and accountant.

Personal File: This file should contain all personal contacts, including musicians. Create fields for instruments—and other keywords—for easy searching.

Mailing-List File: This file should contain fan information that was obtained from the mailing-list cards that fans filled out at past gigs. You'll use this list to send out pretour notices as well as newsletters. So, you'll want to customize the fields of this file so that it can be searched by location (again, I find the two-letter state code to be most efficient), tour date, and recordings that have been purchased (either on-site or by mail order).

Promotion File: This file should contain all print, radio, and television contacts.

Record-Company File: This file should contain a list of record companies that have recorded you or your band members in the past or might be of use in the future.

Raw-Data File: This file should contain your uncontacted and untested venue leads.

Developing Worksheets and Checklists

The process involved with booking a tour requires attention to detail. Because of the nature of tight schedules, differences in time zones, and constantly changing information, an incorrect number or an overlooked detail can be disastrous.

During one of my European tours, for example, I mistakenly typed, on our itinerary, two digits incorrectly for the telephone number of the hotel where we were staying while the band was doing a residency in a small town in Germany. The bane of most traveling musicians' lives, a family crisis occurred and because of the typing error my family wasn't able to reach me. We were busy teaching and performing day and night for three days. I usually go over the itinerary with my family and set up a schedule for phone calls before I leave, but this time I was so busy before the tour that I hadn't done that. I didn't call home until after we arrived at our next location and at that point I learned about the crisis. Everyone, including me, was upset. That's the last thing you need when you're thousands of miles away from home. When I'm doing European tours, I now include the name, telephone, and fax number of the agent or promoter on my itinerary—just in case another typing glitch occurs again.

In another instance, I was booking a tour in the Northwest that included traveling back and forth across the United States–Canada border by ferry. The client mentioned the ferry and its departure times. I entered the data on the itineraries—as it was given to me by the venues. While studying the itinerary a couple of days before we were to leave, a little voice reminded me that I hadn't spoken to the ferry companies myself and perhaps I should, just to be sure. It turned out that three different ferry companies were involved with the crossings. After spending six hours on the phone, I unearthed the fact that ferry admittance was granted on a first-come, first-serve basis, and that all overwater travel times were longer than what the venue had told me. Also, because of long lines on certain days and delays in customs, we would have to leave for the ferry an hour and one-half earlier than we had originally planned. And in at least two instances, take an earlier ferry. Had I not listened to that little voice, we would have missed some gigs.

The most foolproof way to avoid the glitches mentioned in the previous scenarios, is to use client and venue worksheets and checklists to keep track of all touring information. Fill one out worksheet for each gig *at the time that the engagement is confirmed.* Frequent callbacks to a client for information waste time and create an unprofessional appearance. Be considerate of your client's time. Ask if he or she has a few

A SAMPLE CLIENT AND VENUE WORKSHEET

Tour dates from _____ to _____

Event date(s)_____

Venue_____

Confirmation date_____

Total income_____

Performance type: concert [ ] solo clinic [ ] group clinic [ ]

Mr. [ ] Mrs. [ ] Ms. [ ] first name _____ last name _____

Telephone numbers (work) _____ (home) _____

Fax number _____ E-mail address _____

Venue street address_____

City _____ State _____ Zip code _____ Country_____

Mailing street address _____

City _____ State _____ Zip code _____ Country_____

Who calls back? They do [ ] I do [ ] Call back on _____

Sent press kit? Yes [ ] No [ ] With CD? Yes [ ] No [ ] Mailed on _____

Concert venue _____ fee _____

Number and length of sets _____ from _____ to _____

Sound check? Yes [ ] No [ ] at _____ Intermission: _____ minutes

Clinic venue _____ fee _____ from _____ to _____

Currency: U.S. [ ] foreign [ ] Exchange equivalent _____

minutes to go over the worksheet with you. The worksheet (shown below) will help you later on when you're working on transportation and accommodation checklists (shown on the following pages) as well as on your itinerary.

Gigs can be from one to seven days in length. The former are called one-nighters, the latter, location gigs. You'll make a client and venue worksheet for each gig, not each day of a tour. If you're on a location gig where some days have different events (an afternoon clinic, rehearsal, etc.) or different set times, make a notation in your notes section of the client and venue worksheet and enter the specific information onto your calendar when you're making your itinerary.

Checklists are extremely helpful. Depending on the level of sophistication of your software programs and your level of expertise, you can save the time it takes to manipulate information in your various checklists by merging that information with your itinerary—and then manipulating it directly in the spreadsheet documents.

(Sample Client and Venue Worksheet Continued)

Deposit _____ Received on _____ Balance due _____

Paid by: Cash [ ] Check [ ] By mail [ ] Before performance [ ] After performance [ ]

Meals included? Yes [ ] No [ ] Per diem? Yes [ ] No [ ] Amount _____

Radio broadcast? Yes [ ] No [ ]

Station and contact name _____ Telephone number (work) _____

Fee? Yes [ ] No [ ] Amount _____

Paid by: Cash [ ] Check [ ] By mail [ ] At performance [ ]

Who owns tape? They do [ ] Band [ ] Exploitation rights? Yes [ ] No [ ]

When will we receive a copy of the tape? By mail [ ] End of broadcast [ ]

Preceding event date and location _____

Travel time from previous location _____

Time zone change? Yes [ ] No [ ] Time zone _____

Following event date and location _____

Travel time to following location _____

Time zone change? Yes [ ] No [ ] Time zone _____

Notes _____

Agent fee? Yes [ ] No [ ] Percentage _____ Amount _____

Name _____

Telephone numbers (work) _____ (home) _____

Fax number _____ E-mail address _____

A SAMPLE AGREEMENT CHECKLIST

Contract [   ]   Letter of intent [   ]   Verbal [   ]   They send [   ]   I send [   ]

Sent on _____ Received on _____ Returned on _____

Rider included [   ]   Arrangements for CD sales?   Yes [   ]   No [   ]

Grant applications: They send [   ]   I send [   ]

Mailed _____ Returned _____

Work papers [   ]   Visas [   ]   Tax papers [   ]   They send [   ]   I send [   ]

Mailed _____ Returned _____

Radio broadcast exploitation agreement signed and received [   ]

A SAMPLE ACCOMMODATION CHECKLIST

Venue reserves hotel [   ]   Band reserves hotel [   ]

Hotel info received [   ]   Number of days _____

Venue pays hotel [   ]   Band pays hotel [   ]

Extra days?   Yes [   ]   No [   ]   Before event [   ]   After event [   ]   Number of days _____

Extra days paid by: Venue [   ]   Band [   ]   Cost per day _____

Hotel name _____

Street address _____

City _____ State _____ Zip code _____ Country _____

Telephone number _____ Fax number _____

Confirmation number _____

Early check in [   ]   Late check in [   ]

Smoking rooms [   ]   How many? _____ Nonsmoking rooms   [   ] How many? _____

Are first-floor rooms available (for motels only)? Yes [   ] No [   ]

Restaurant in hotel?   Yes [   ]   No [   ]   Hours of operation _____

Restaurant near hotel?   Yes [   ]   No [   ]

Laundry facilities in hotel?   Yes [   ]   No [   ]

Travel time from hotel to venue _____

A SAMPLE EQUIPMENT CHECKLIST

Piano type and size _____ Condition?   Fine [   ]   Good [   ]   Poor [   ]

Tuned before performance?   Yes [   ]   No [   ]

Seating capacity _____

Acoustics?   Fine [   ]   Good [   ]   Poor [   ]   Outside [   ]   Inside [   ]

Play venue: Acoustic [   ]   Amplified [   ]

Sound equipment provided (see rider)?   Yes [   ]   No [   ]   Drum set [   ]   Bass amp [   ]

Stage diagram sent?   Yes [   ]   No [   ]

A SAMPLE PROMOTION CHECKLIST

Sent to venue: Press kit [   ]   CDs [   ] How many? _____ Photos [   ] How many? _____

Sent CDs to radio station? [   ]   To press? [   ]

Sent press releases to local press? [   ]

Interview: On-site [   ]   Telephone [   ] Date and time _____

Contact name _____

Telephone number (work) _____

Location _____

A SAMPLE TRANSPORTATION CHECKLIST

Travel by: Airplane [   ]   Train [   ]   Van [   ]   Ferry [   ]   Other _____

Transportation paid by: Venue [   ]   Band [   ]

Transportation reimbursed by venue? Yes [   ]   No [   ]   If yes, amount _____

Transportation arranged by: Venue [   ]   Band [   ]

Tickets received? Yes [   ]   No [   ]

Pick up and return by: Venue [   ]   Band [   ]

Venue notified of arrival and departure times? Yes [   ]   No [   ]

Travel information is entered into an airline checklist when someone in the group is flying to a gig. Band members may or may not live in the same area. If they don't live in the same area, they may or may not travel to and from the first and last gigs of the tour on the same day. However, regardless of whether the band members travel separately or together, you will only fill out *one* transportation checklist for the initial date of travel.

When your tour involves international travel, be sure to keep an eye on the time zones. When you're flying from the United States to Europe, your arrival date might be on the day *after* your departure date. And when you're flying from the United States to Japan, because you pass over the international dateline, you'll arrive the day *before* you left!

My trio once went from the United States to Hong Kong for a festival and I forgot about the international dateline. My itinerary was completely out of synch—gig dates and itinerary days were mismatched for the whole tour. You can imagine the confusion it caused.

The first and last travel dates of a tour are called the bracket travel dates. Travel days inside the bracket dates are internal travel dates. Except in a situation where band members are in different locations before the first gig of a tour, bracket travel info and internal tour info will be the same for all band personnel. If band members are traveling from different locations to get to the first gig, then the bracket travel dates may have multiple airline entries. Internal travel dates will have single entries—as in the sample airline checklist on the following page. Baggage and overweight fees won't be entered on the airline checklist—as you won't know those figures until you take that flight.

Major European airports have trains that will take you to the central train station. If you have to use this service, jot down the schedules of these trains in your calendar and notes section.

A SAMPLE AIRLINE CHECKLIST

Travel date _____

Person _____

Airline _____ Flight number _____

Departs from _____ at _____

Arrives in _____ at _____

Fare _____

A SAMPLE VAN-RENTAL CHECKLIST

Rental date(s) from _____ to _____

Company _____

Telephone number _____

Confirmation number _____

Pick up time _____ Return time _____

Grace period?   Yes [ ]   No [ ]   Overtime charge: _____ per hour

Rate: _____ per day [ ]   per week [ ]   (tax included)

Rate for extra day(s): _____ (tax included)

Mileage charge: _____

Van paid by: Venue [ ]   Band [ ]

Van reimbursed by venue?   Yes [ ]   No [ ]   If yes, amount _____

A SAMPLE TRAIN CHECKLIST

Travel date _____

First train: Train number _____ Car number _____

Seat numbers _____

Reservation numbers _____

Departs from _____ at _____

Arrives in _____ at _____

Second train: Train number _____ Car number _____

Seat numbers _____

Reservation numbers _____

Departs from _____ at _____

Arrives in _____ at _____

Transportation paid by: Venue [ ]   Band [ ]

Transportation reimbursed by venue?   Yes [ ]   No [ ]   If yes, amount _____

Pick up and return by: Venue [ ]   Band [ ]

Venue notified of arrival and departure times?   Yes [ ]   No [ ]

European travel often involves trains. Taking between one and four trains per day to get to and from a location is not unusual. (For an example of a portion of a European itinerary that involves extensive train travel, refer to Thursday, October 29 in the Completed Sample Leader's Itinerary (Foreign) on pages 81–82.) By now you should be getting the idea how checklists are constructed. Checklists for ferries and other unusual modes of transportation can be added as needed.

A SAMPLE PERSONNEL FILE

First name _____

Middle name _____

Last name _____

Instrument _____

Serial number _____

Street address _____

City _____ State _____ Zip code _____ Country _____

Telephone (work) _____ (home) _____

Fax number _____ E-mail address _____

Social Security number _____

Passport number _____ Expiration date _____

Issued at _____

Date of birth _____ City _____ State _____ Country _____

U.S. resident?   Yes [ ]   No [ ]

Visa number _____

Union card number _____

Seat preference: Aisle [ ]   Center [ ]   Window [ ]

Carrier and frequent-flyer numbers _____

A personnel file should contain all the information you'll need for passports, visas, and work permits. As the bandleader, you should carry completed sample personnel files for all of your band members with you when you travel. Having this information will expedite the process of filling out the paperwork that needs to be processed during your travels.

Your contact-manager program will have a letterhead feature that automatically saves documents and checklists in a letter archive for each client when you print. You can use this function to create a merge document for these checklists. When you check a box or fill in an item and print the checklist, it is saved in the letter archive for future reference.

Drafting Tour Budgets

Creating budgets can be a particularly cumbersome, time-consuming, and complicated process. However, a spreadsheet program can help you customize your tour budget, as well as compute your taxes and other financial matters. It can also help you successfully keep track of your tour income and expenses, eliminating costly mistakes. Every tour is a different entity. Accordingly, you'll want to create a new spreadsheet for each subsequent tour budget. (As tour budgets and routing are dependent upon each other, I've included examples of tour budgets—which are linked to the actual routing of a tour—in chapter nine.)

Although most software applications can be customized, I have yet to find one that has all the necessary information management functions that make up the booking process. Therefore, you'll find that you will have to switch back and forth among many applications to manage this information. Macros automate computer tasks by using keystroke shortcuts. A convenient program for the Mac that automates most computer functions and facilitates the process of switching between applications is Tempo-EZ by Affinity Microsystems. This can also be ordered on the Web at http://office.software-directory.com/cdprod1/swhrec/020/761.shtml. This program is user-friendly and a real time saver.

Preparing Tour Itineraries

A complete and thorough itinerary serves many useful functions. It frees the band-leader from having to answer constant—and distracting—questions about what's going to happen next. It helps spouses, family members, record companies, and other venues on your tour keep in touch with you while you're on the road. If, while on tour, a band member misses a plane or train or otherwise gets separated from the group, an itinerary will allow him or her to resolve the problem. If an airline sends your baggage to the wrong destination, an itinerary can help the lost-baggage service ensure that your bags will eventually end up in the same place you are (which is especially tricky if you are doing a series of one-nighters). But one of the most important functions of an itinerary is that it will help you address one of the biggest concerns of road travel: figuring out when you're going to have time to do your laundry.

Knowing when you can get your laundry or dry cleaning done will determine how you pack for a tour, and how much weight you carry. Before you pack, scrutinize your itinerary for the places and lengths of the location gigs (days where you spend more than one day in a town) throughout your tour. If your tour has only one or two loca-tion gigs that are interspersed among a series of one-nighters, you'll have to pack very differently than if your tour has a number of location gigs.

An itinerary should contain the following information:

- dates (both for the duration of the tour as well as for the individual day that is featured on any particular page of the itinerary);
- travel information;
- schedule information;
- accommodation information, including the name and address of the hotel, as well as the telephone, fax, and reservation numbers;
- contact information, including agent's and/or client's work and home numbers;
- a tour calendar, which gives a quick overview of the tour, should be stapled to the first page of the itinerary;
- income and salary information (on bandleader's version *only*).

The travel information section will be the most comprehensive section of the itinerary. Most often the band will travel together. If this is the case, make sure to mark "all" in the travel section. If you're traveling separately, list the specific travel arrangements for individual personnel on the same itinerary. The travel section should also include the airline, flight number, departure point and time, plane changes, and destination and arrival time. If you're renting a vehicle and driving to a final destination, include the reservation numbers, the credit card that you used to make the reservation, and the driving time. Driving time from the hotel to the venue should be on the leader's itinerary. If you're sharing driving duties, you may also want to include maps from the airport to the hotel and from the hotel to the gig on the itinerary; these maps can be obtained from a map software program or any of the Internet mapping programs. If the venue is arranging your travel to and from the airport, include a note to that effect. When you're traveling by train, include the departure time (with station name), arrival time (with station name), train name and number, car number, and seat numbers for reserved seats. Many large European cities have multiple train stations, and for that reason it is important to note the station name for all travel details. If you arrive in a city by train, don't assume that you will leave from the same station—even if you are returning to your original destination.

In the schedule section of your itinerary, you'll want to note whether it's a workday, an off day, or an off travel day. If it is a workday, list the name, address, telephone and fax numbers of the venue, as well as your contact's name. Also note the sound-check time, set times, number of sets, intermission length, and the type of gig (concert, clinic, rehearsal, etc.).

A SAMPLE ITINERARY FORM

Tour dates _____

Date _____

Travel information _____

Venue _____

Schedule _____

Accommodations _____

Contact person(s) _____

Notes _____

To begin to set up an itinerary, first copy the form above and save it in your computer's word-processing program. Then select the text and copy it to your clipboard. Open a new, blank page in your word-processing program and copy the form into your new itinerary file. Add the start and end dates of your tour at the top of the form, then copy it the same number of times as days you have in the tour, minus one. If the tour is fifteen days long, you'll copy the form fourteen times—for a total of fifteen itinerary formats. Add the day and date to each consecutive itinerary form. Now you're ready to start filling in the details.

The following are partial examples of what itineraries can look like.

AN EXCERPT FROM A COMPLETED SAMPLE ITINERARY (U.S.)

Tour Dates: March 12 to April 6
Date: Thursday, March 12
Travel Information: (All) Take Delta flight #1870. Depart from Newark at 5:10 P.M. Arrive in Seattle at 7:19 P.M. Pick up rental van at National. (confirmation #1511955609) Airport Plaza Hotel, 10000 Pacific Highway South, Seattle, Washington. Telephone number: (1-206) 555-1212. (Quest Card, confirmation #410477)

Tour Dates: March 12 to April 6
Date: Friday, March 13
Travel Information: Drive to ferry (trip takes approximately three hours). Ferry leaves on every odd hour; trip takes one and one-half hours. Drive to Victoria (trip takes approximately half an hour).
Venue: The Bebop Jazz Club, 1000 Ajax Street, Victoria, British Columbia, Canada
Schedule: Two 60-minute sets, starting at 9:00 P.M.
Accommodations: Quality Inn Harbor View, 500 Jones Street, Victoria, British Columbia, Canada. Telephone number: (1-250) 555-1212.
Contact Person(s): Al Fresco (1-250) 555-1212

Tour Dates: March 12 to April 6
Date: Saturday, March 14
Schedule: Off day.
Accommodations: See above.

Tour Dates: March 12 to April 6
Date: Sunday, March 15
Travel Information: Take ferry. Drive to Vancouver.
Venue: The Golden Club, 1000 Victor Street, Vancouver, British Columbia, Canada
Schedule: Two 75-minute sets: 8:00–9:15 P.M. and 9:45–11:00 P.M.
Accommodations: Ajax Hotel, 1000 North Street, Vancouver, British Columbia, Canada. Telephone number: (1-604) 555-1212. (Quest Card, confirmed by Paul) The hotel is ten minutes from the club.
Contact Person(s): Billy (1-604) 555-1212 (work)

Tour Dates: March 12 to April 6
Date: Monday, March 16
Travel Information: After clinic, drive from Vancouver to Portland (trip takes approximately five hours).
Venue: Vancouver College, Tree Building, Room 113, Vancouver, British Columbia, Canada
Schedule: Quartet clinic from 10:30 A.M. to 12:30 P.M.
Accommodations: Sleep Inn, 500 Front Street, Portland, Oregon. Telephone number: (1-503) 555-1212. (Quest Card, confirmation #820837)
Contact Person(s): Bob McBop (1-604) 555-1212, ext. 2172 (work) or (1-604) 555-1212 (home); Mary McJones (1-604) 555-1212, ext. 2305 (work)

AN EXCERPT FROM A COMPLETED SAMPLE LEADER'S ITINERARY (FOREIGN)

Tour Dates: October 24 to November 22
Date: Saturday, October 24
Travel Information: (All) Take KLM flight #6058. Depart from Newark at 6:35 P.M.

Tour Dates: October 24 to November 22
Date: Sunday, October 25
Travel Information: Arrive in Amsterdam at 6:50 A.M. Connect with Maersk Air flight #272. Depart from Amsterdam at 9:45 A.M. Arrive in Billund at 10:45 A.M.
Venue: Musikkonservatorium, Fuglesangs Alle 26, Århus, Denmark. Telephone number: (011-45-86) 555 121.
Schedule: Individual and quartet clinics from 12:00 to 6:00 P.M.
Accommodations: Ritz Hotel Banegårdsgade 12, Århus, Denmark. Telephone number: (011-45-86) 555 12 12.
Contact Person(s): Lars Christian (011-45-86) 555 121 (work)
Notes: Pick up at airport, check into hotel, and go immediately to school.
Fee: $1,500, plus CDs at 100 krone apiece.

Tour Dates: October 24 to November 22
Date: Monday, October 26
Schedule: Off day.
Accommodations: See above.

Tour Dates: October 24 to November 22
Date: Tuesday, October 27
Travel Information: (All) Take Intercity train #40. Depart from Århus at 1:40 P.M. Arrive in Copenhagen at 4:27 P.M. Club will pick us up at the station.
Venue: Denmark Jazz Club, Niels Hemmingsens Gade 10, Copenhagen, Denmark
Schedule: Sound check: 5:00 P.M. Two 50-minute sets: 8:30–9:20 P.M. and 9:50–10:40 P.M.
Accommodations: Ibsen Hotel, Vendersgade 23, Copenhagen, Denmark. Telephone number: (011-45-44) 55 12 12. Breakfast is included, as is a hot meal before the concert.
Contact Person(s): Jens Millborg (011-45-33) 55 12 12 (work)
Fee: $1,500, plus hot meal before gig.

Tour Dates: October 24 to November 22
Date: Wednesday, October 28
Travel Information: School will drive us to the train station. (All) Take Intercity train #23. Depart from Copenhagen at 7:51 A.M. Arrive in Odense at 9:08 A.M.
Venue: Musikkonservatorium, Islandsgade 2, Odense, Denmark. Telephone number: (011-45-66) 55 12 12. Jazzhus Bird, Vindegade 65, Odense, Denmark.
Schedule: Trio clinic: 10:00 A.M. to 4:00 P.M. Trio concert: begins at 8:00 P.M. (approximate)
Accommodations: Hotel Mulchburg, Østerstationsvej 32, Odense, Denmark. Telephone number: (011-45-551) 55 12 12.
Contact Person(s): Jurgen Elph (011-45-551) 55 12 12 (school) or (011-45-551) 55 12 12 (school/mobile phone); Poul Falck (011-45-551) 55 12 12 (club)
Fee: $2,500

Tour Dates: October 24 to November 22
Date: Thursday, October 29
Travel Information: (All travel to Berlin.) Take DSB Intercity train #125 (heading to Esbjerg). Depart from Odense at 9:31 A.M. Arrive in Frederica at 10:05 A.M. Take DSB Interreagionaltog train #2183 (heading to Hannover). Depart from Frederica at 10:15 A.M. Arrive in Hamburg at 1:27 P.M. Take Eurocity train #179 (heading to Prague). Depart from Hamburg at 2:02 P.M. Arrive in Berlin (Ostbahnhof) at 4:42 P.M.
Venue: Jazz City, Pestalozzistraße 105, Berlin, Germany
Schedule: Sound check: 6:00 P.M. Trio concert: 10:00 P.M. Two sets.
Accommodations: Hotel Berliner, Altmoabit 99, Berlin, Germany. Telephone number: (011-49-30) 55 12 12.
Contact Person(s): Hans Meuller (011-49-30) 55 12 12 (work)
Notes: 1,000 deutsche Marks per night, plus 75 percent of money received from door and the cost of the hotel. Leave agent's fee with client. CDs will be sold at twenty-five deutsche Marks apiece.

Tour Dates: October 24 to November 22
Date: Friday, October 30
Venue: See above.
Schedule: See above.
Accommodations: See above.
Contact Person(s): See above.

Although the preceding examples contain the minimum amount of necessary information, some itineraries, depending on the size of the band and the complexity of the tour, can be as large as a book. This happened to me once when I had booked a three-week tour for two bands, my trio and the TanaReid quintet. Because of the tour's logistical complexity, I enlisted an agent-friend to handle the contact, contract, transportation, and housing details. Before we left, each leader received two loose-leaf folders with every possible piece of information included. It was very professional, but too much to carry on the road. I removed the covers and culled what I thought was nonessential, until the folder became manageable.

Whenever possible, mail the itineraries to your band members in advance. If some band members have partners who need the contact information as well, send those members two copies. Include a cover letter with the itinerary that clarifies any potential points of confusion and that states what their salary will be for the tour.

You may have to teach your spouse how to read and understand an itinerary. It's well worth the effort. The more he or she knows about what you're doing on the road, the easier it will be for him or her to cope with being separated. As I mentioned earlier, you may also want to schedule phone calls with family members *before* you leave for the tour. After a hard day of traveling, you don't want to get a call in the middle of a much-needed nap before a gig. Make sure that all of the band members understand that the itinerary is proprietary information that belongs only to the band members and their families.

By the time you're leaving for a tour, most of the itinerary information will be set. However, from time to time, an additional gig will confirm or cancel while you're on the road, or you won't know a particular hotel for a particular day. You can always give the information to the band members when it comes in, and they can call home to update their families.

When you're on the road, your itinerary will be a handy place for you to make notes about each gig as you progress through a tour. As you go along, you'll want to note:

- how you were treated by venue personnel;
- venue pick up and return problems;
- hotel problems;
- venue equipment problems (piano, drum set, sound system, etc.);
- important contacts you met at the venue;
- good restaurants;
- the exchange rate on the day that you converted currency;
- how well you drew at the gig;
- if the venue requested return engagements.

Your itinerary is also a good place to schedule personal errands, such as when you:

- can cash checks (i.e., arrange for a ride to and from a bank);
- might be able to do laundry;
- will call home;
- when you can make advance calls to upcoming venues.

Communication mistakes or language problems can lead to contractual misunderstandings. Having copies of your contract on hand while you're traveling will go a long way toward resolving these differences. After the tour is over, save your itinerary in a manila file folder for quick reference. And while they are still fresh in your mind, copy important notes you've made about each gig into each venue's contact file.

Creating Venue Agreements

Venue agreements are usually in the form of a contract (yours or theirs), a letter of intent, or a verbal agreement. A contract is only as good as the people who sign it. Unless you are performing for large sums of money, it will not be worthwhile for you to seek legal remedy for a broken contract. Matters of this nature often take years to settle and cost more in legal fees than the contract is worth. The best insurance you have against broken contracts is the reputations of your clients.

Educational institutions, arts presenters, jazz societies, and cultural institutions rarely break contracts, except in the case of acts of God (i.e., any kind of natural disaster). Always check to see if your contract has an act-of-God stipulation in it. If you're traveling to an area that just suffered from a natural disaster, better call ahead. If you don't, you might show up for a venue that no longer exists.

The most common people in the music business to break contracts with performers are club owners, tour promoters, and agents. However, because word of mouth travels so rapidly in this business, most clients have a vested interest in maintaining a reputation for reliability. If you're not sure about a client's reliability, call someone who has worked the venue. With proper research, you can minimize your chances of having contracts broken.

Client-performer agreements vary widely in both form and content. Either party to the agreement can issue a contract. The contract can be formal or informal—as simple as a handshake, or as long as ten pages. The form and content of an agreement depend on many factors, but most often the agreement will take the form of a performer's contract, client's contract, union contract, letter of intent, or verbal agreement. Foreign contracts will be discussed later in this chapter.

When finalizing any type of agreement, make sure you have your venue worksheet in hand. This will help to ensure that you and the client have mutually agreed upon all of the details of a gig. Repeated callbacks to a client waste valuable time, annoy the client, and give him or her the impression that you are incompetent. Using the worksheet also circumvents the need for any "but I thought you said this" type of conversation at a later date.

CLIENT CONTRACTS Educational and cultural institutions, festivals, and arts societies generally prefer to issue their own contracts. The most pragmatic way to generate a contract is to have the venue do it. It saves you time, and you'll be sure that the information is correct. When you agree to take a gig, ask your contact how long it generally takes for him or her to generate the contract. Then, in your client and venue worksheet, make a note of the approximate date when it will be mailed. Likewise, note on the worksheet when you receive the contract, and when you return it. Generally, there will be two original copies of each agreement—one for you and one for the client. If the contracts arrive unsigned by the venue, sign them, make a copy of one for your files, and send the originals back to the client. The client will eventually send you one fully signed contract. But until the contract is returned, having a copy of the partially signed contract can be useful if you need to refer to it.

Verify that your Tax Identification number or Social Security number is correct. If you're not set up as a corporation and you need to cash a venue's check while on the road, specify in the contract that the check should be made out in your name, not your band's name. Out-of-state banks will not cash business checks. You will have to wait until you return home and deposit these checks in your own business account. If you are set up as a corporation and the contract is written in your band's name (The Joe Johnson Quartet) as opposed to your name (Joe Johnson), the check will be made out to the band and you will not be able to cash it on the road.

Verify that your contract states that you will be paid at the end of the concert, especially if you're dealing with an educational institution. Otherwise, your check may arrive months after the gig. Colleges and universities are noted for having cumbersome administrative procedures.

Your band may have particular requirements—such as a sound system or other equipment. You may also want to make arrangements for the venue to handle on-site product sales. The venue may stipulate these requirements in the contract, or a verbal agreement may suffice. If these details are not specified in the contract, make sure you have discussed them with the client and have sent a follow-up letter of confirmation. When the venue is supplying accommodations for the band, make sure that the dates and number of rooms for the accommodations are stipulated in the contract.

When you address *any* mailing, you should avoid handwriting the address labels. This is especially true with contracts. Instead, use your computer's timesaving automatic addressing program to create your mailing labels. This will ensure that you don't make any addressing mistakes that would delay the arrival of a contract.

PERFORMER CONTRACTS Some venues never issue their own contracts. Instead, they will ask you to submit your own. Create a generic contract form on the computer, with open spaces for contact, venue, fee, and rider information. You can streamline the process of generating the contract if you write down your contact information in your venue contact list when you first contact the client, and then if you fill out a client and venue worksheet when you're confirming the engagement. Most likely, all of the information that you need for a particular venue will not be in the contract, so you'll want to fill out the client and venue worksheet for yourself anyway.

The information from your client contact list can be merged into the contract. The client and venue worksheet also ensures that you and the client have discussed all of the logistics of the engagement. Most computer contact-manager programs allow you to automatically merge the information from these lists into the worksheet and contract, so you don't have to enter the information again when writing out the contract. Generate two copies of the agreement, sign both and send them to the client. The client will countersign both agreements and then send one fully signed copy back to you.

The following example shows a sample format for a generic contract.

A SAMPLE ARTIST/PURCHASER AGREEMENT

This agreement for services of performing artist(s) for the engagement described below is made between the undersigned purchaser of talent (hereinafter called "Purchaser") and the undersigned performing artist(s) (hereinafter individually or collectively called "Artist").

I. Engagement:
- A. Purchaser:
- B. Name and address of engagement:
- C. Artist:
- D. Number of artists:
- E. Date(s) of engagement:
- F. Time(s) of engagement:
- G. Type of engagement:
- H. Special provisions:
- I. Promotion shall be as follows:

II. Purchaser Provisions:
- A. Compensation:
- B. Method of compensation:

III. Artist Provisions:
- A. Artist shall at all times have complete supervision, direction, and control over the services of his/her personnel and reserves the right to control the manner, means, and details of the performance.

(Sample Artist/Purchaser Agreement Continued)

    B. Artist guarantees the number of performers listed

    C. Recording, reproduction, or transmission of Artist's performance is prohibited absent written consent of the Artist.

    D. Responsibility for payroll taxes and charges will be assumed by Artist (an independent contractor).

IV. Additional Terms and Conditions:

    A. The individuals signing this Agreement, either personally or in a representative capacity, acknowledge their authority to do so.

    B. Signing of this Agreement shall be deemed acceptance by the Parties of all the terms contained herein.

V. Parties to the Agreement:

    Purchaser's name: _____

    Address: _____

    Telephone and fax number(s): _____

    Signature: _____ Date: _____

    Artist's name: _____

    Address: _____

    Telephone and fax number(s): _____

    Signature: _____ Date: _____

    Social Security number: _____

Please sign both copies of this agreement and return one to me at the above address.

UNION CONTRACTS Although the American Federation of Musicians would prefer that every performer and every client use a union contract for every gig, most of the time this is not an absolute requirement. Only certain U.S. club gigs or show gigs require union contracts. The advantages of using a union contract is that it adds a modicum of security to an agreement, it can come in handy if something goes wrong with a gig on the road, and it allows for a payment to be made to each musicians' union pension account. The disadvantage to using a union contract is that you will have to pay work dues for each gig in each area in which you sign a union contract. These dues are nominal and can vary from one union jurisdiction to another. They are based on a small percentage (from 1 to 3 percent) of the performance fee, and the number of musicians in the band. You will be billed for these dues, by mail, after the performance. For more information, you can call 1-800-ROAD-GIG or check out their Web site at http://www.afm.org. The American Federation of Musicians can often help out with legal and financial advice and/or support.

Union contracts are often not as detailed as the contracts that are generated by either clients or bandleaders. Therefore, they sometimes require a separate rider or an additional and more detailed contract that incorporates the information from the union contract in it. If you would rather use union contracts than your own contracts for engagements, contact your local chapter of the musicians' union. They will supply you with contract forms and educate you about how to use them.

Union contracts are a prerequisite for most gigs in Canada—no matter the type. If you don't have a Canadian promoter or agent handling your contracts for you, you will have to work under the auspices of the Canadian musicians' union to get your work papers and your NR-16, Non-Resident Tax Waiver Certificates. These certificates guarantee that you won't pay double income taxes—both in the United States and Canada. Pay particular attention to the tax certificate deadlines. Contact your local musicians' union office for information about working in Canada. (For more information about the special requirements for Canadian gigs, see page 142.)

LETTERS OF INTENT Letters of intent, which are less formal than a contract, are not necessarily legally binding and are generally used for informational purposes by educational institutions prior to the drafting of the contract. Private educational institutions may require the letter of intent to be submitted by either the client or bandleader, as a precursor to a formal contract. The letter of intent will spell out the general terms of the contract, including the venue name and address; date, time, and type of engagement; fee; bandleader's Tax Identification or Social Security number; and contact information. Two copies of the letter should be made. Both copies should be fully signed by the parties involved—the client (or the client's responsible representative) and the bandleader. The institution should keep one signed copy and you should keep the other. The purpose of the letter of intent is to ensure that the institution fills out the forthcoming formal contract accurately. State colleges and universities have very formal contracts because they have to adhere to state laws that require strict reporting and contractual stipulations, most of which have less to do with the performers' concerns than the client's.

The following is a sample of a generic letter of intent:

A SAMPLE LETTER OF INTENT

(Your logo or band name and address, telephone and fax numbers, and E-mail and Web site addresses)

(Date)

(Client and venue name and address)

Dear Client,

It was a pleasure talking with you today. As per our conversation, this letter of intent shall serve as a legally binding agreement in full between (venue name) and the Joe Johnson Band. The Joe Johnson Band agrees to perform at the (venue name) on (xx/xx/xx) for a fee of ($xxxx.xx). (The venue) further agrees to supply four hotel rooms for one night. The performance begins at 10:00 P.M. and will include two 80-minute sets with an intermission. Payment is to be made in cash at the conclusion of the performance. (The client/venue) agrees to supply a drum set, bass amp, and sound system as well as to arrange hotel accommodations. All media promotion will include the names of all band members. I'll contact you as the performance date approaches for details about accommodations and the sound check. Contact me for any further assistance at any time. Please sign both copies and return one copy to me.

(Client's name) _____ Joe Johnson _____

A letter of intent is almost always required when either you or the client is applying for a performance support grant from a foundation or government agency. Letters of intent that are created for this purpose contain the information that is listed above, as well as any additional information that may be required by the granting agency. The letter verifies to the grantor that you and the client have negotiated a mutual agreement.

VERBAL AGREEMENTS Some venues never issue contracts and only use verbal agreements. A verbal agreement is not legally binding on either party, but it is secure if you have worked the venue before, or you have done some background research on the venue and determined that its reputation is impeccable. However, to avoid any misunderstandings, after the agreement is finalized, send a letter of confirmation that outlines the terms of agreement. A client's signature is not required. Keep a copy of the letter on file. Below is an example of a letter of confirmation.

A SAMPLE LETTER OF CONFIRMATION

(Your logo or band name and address, telephone and fax numbers, and E-mail and Web site addresses)
(Date)

(Client and venue name and address)

Dear Client,

It was a pleasure talking with you today. As per our conversation, this letter of confirmation shall serve as confirmation of the details we discussed. The Joe Johnson Band agrees to perform at (the venue name) on (xx/xx/xx) for a fee of ($xxxx.xx). (The venue) further agrees to supply four hotel rooms for one night. The performance begins at 10:00 P.M. and will include two 80-minute sets with an intermission. Payment is to be made in cash at the conclusion of the performance. (The client/venue) agrees to supply a drum set, bass amp, and sound system as well as to arrange hotel accommodations. All media promotion will include the names of all band members. I'll contact you as the performance date approaches for details about accommodations and the sound check. Contact me for any further assistance at any time. Please inform me within thirty days of receipt of this letter if any of the terms herein are not as mutually agreed.

Warmest regards,
Joe Johnson

RIDERS Riders are stipulations that spell out the specific needs of your band; these riders are added to the end of the contract. As mentioned above, riders could pertain to equipment, hotel, transportation, or on-site sales arrangements as well as promotional stipulations. If your needs are minimal, discuss them over the phone with the client. If your band's requirements don't change from gig to gig, include the riders in your generic contract form when you're sending your own contracts. For the most part, small groups don't require elaborate riders, if any. Avoid asking for extraordinary requests that will needlessly add to the venue's expenses. Only the larger or very popular bands usually have extensive rider requirements.

I heard one story about a well-known pianist who required that his hotel room be blue. Another high-profile fusion band had a rider so thick that every venue refused to sign it because they would have gone broke catering to its stipulations.

FOREIGN CONTRACTS Most foreign contracts will be generated by the venue or agent-promoter. When a contract is in a foreign language, go over it line by line with the venue or agent to be sure that it's correct and you understand its stipulations. Except for educational institutions, most foreign venues pay in cash. If you are being paid by check, make sure that the client will make it out to you individually (and not the band) and that you will have enough time to get to a local bank to cash it. Cashing foreign checks in the United States can be time consuming and expensive.

Whether your performance fees will be paid in U.S. or foreign currency will be a subject for negotiation. Many European venues prefer to pay in their local currency. Whether you accept this condition will depend on whether you are willing to speculate on the exchange rate of the dollar on a particular date. One way to protect yourself is to have the contract stipulate the fee in local currency, with an added clause that specifies what the fee will equal in U.S. dollars. This clause should specify that, if there is a discrepancy in the conversion rate on the day of the performance that is not in your favor, then the venue will compensate the band for the difference. Otherwise, stipulate in the contract that the performance fees should be paid in U.S. dollars, wherever possible. (Financial concerns will be discussed in greater detail in chapter twelve.)

PART II:

Booking Your Tour

Chapter 7

Researching Your Venue Contacts

In chapter one we asked the question: Is there enough work out there? In the United States alone, the American Federation of Musicians estimates that there are 100,000 performance venues. However, the majority of these venues are tallied because they are union gigs—commercial, club-date, and classical venues in particular. In other words, this figure represents *only* the number of gigs for which union contracts have been filed. Since many gigs don't involve union contracts, this estimate is much lower than the number of venues that are actually out there.

Your ultimate goals in acquiring venue contacts should be twofold. First, you should try to increase your contact base by an average of 10 percent a year. To accomplish this goal you'll have to network, keep your eyes and ears open, and ask questions. Second, you'll hope to secure as many repeat venues as possible from gigs you have played.

INCREASING YOUR VENUE LEADS

In chapter six you learned how to organize your information. So, now you're ready to start the ongoing process of collecting and researching your venue contacts. Your client base will expand over the years as you tour and collect new sources of information. Although leads can come from almost anywhere, this section deals with the most common resources for acquiring potential clients.

Having viable contact information is only the *beginning* of the booking process. You also need to know what each venue's lead time is—in other words how much time in advance of a gig you need to call a venue to set up the gig. And you need to learn how to balance your time on the road versus your time at home booking your next tour. Coordinating lead times and balancing the booking/touring equation requires patience—and is a complicated art to master. But after reading through this section, you'll be more prepared to tackle the process.

Information Sources

Begin collecting your leads for gigs from sources that are most convenient for you. The obvious place to start is with your friends who are musicians. Subscriptions to national and regional music industry magazines, and jazz society and arts presenters' newsletters will also be valuable resources for venue contacts. If you have access to the Internet, you might browse the Web for additional leads.

To maximize your efforts, every time you talk to someone about venue leads you should also ask if he or she can think of anyone else who can help you out. Think in terms of networking: Each contact can give you two contacts who can then give you four more contacts who can then give you eight more contacts, etc. This data is the lifeblood of your business and should be carefully nurtured. Some of the relationships you build from the contacts that you make in the initial stages of starting your business will provide the basis of your work for many years to come.

Personal Contacts: If you've been a professional sideman, you have, over the years, probably made a number of useful contacts. Personal phone books are a source of venue leads and musician friends will also have numbers that can help you expand your contact base rather quickly.

Itineraries: Review old tour itineraries for venue contact information as well as for the names of helpful or knowledgeable people who you met during the tour. Then research and update these contacts so that you have the most current information. Contact information changes from time to time. Regular updating will become part of your routine. Also check other artists' Web sites for their itineraries. They often list contact information; and even if they don't, a phone call or two can easily get you in touch with the right person at a particular venue.

Recommendations from Clients: Each client you interact with can potentially expand your contact base. Always ask clients for recommendations. Networking is a common practice, so most people will be happy to give you a suggestion or two—especially if they're happy with your work. Asking for a recommendation can also boost the client's ego. (You must think he or she is important, otherwise you wouldn't be asking.) But don't dig for information and come off as pushy. Calling a referral is easier than cold-calling a potential client. The ice is broken when you truthfully say "So-and-so recommended that I call...." Like all businesses, jazz is made of networks and over the years you will build up your own extensive network of clients and contacts worldwide. Plus, after you've established a reputation, your clients will recommend you to other contacts on their own.

Trading: There's a growing international grassroots movement of independent musicians who, like you, are looking to expand their client base. Get in touch with them and ask if they'd like to trade contacts. E-mail is the perfect medium for sharing information. You can easily reach out to, and stay in touch with, people from all over the planet, without investing hundreds of dollars in mailings and phone calls. Networking with other musicians can double your number of leads, simply by trading your leads one for one. Avoid information overload by limiting your requests to relevant leads for the area in which you're booking a tour.

Magazine and Newsletter Subscriptions: Subscribe to every jazz support organization's newsletter and every jazz magazine. These publications often have a "What's Happening" column that lists performance venues and performers; often these columns include contact numbers. If a venue's telephone number is not listed in one of these columns, you can get it from Directory Assistance/411 or on the Web at GTE SuperPages at http://superpages.com. Once you have the telephone number, call the venue and ask who handles the artist roster.

JazzTimes prints a yearly list of venues, festivals, record companies, and college jazz departments. You can determine the likelihood that a venue would be interested in hiring your band by evaluating the marquee value of the artists they've booked. Many venues hire only the biggest attractions. Don't waste valuable time trying to book gigs you have no chance of getting. Conversely, don't bother calling venues that only book local bands. Newsletters and magazines can also be valuable promotional outlets for information about your band's activities (for more information about this, see the "Free Advertising" section in chapter thirteen).

For subscriptions, contact:

- *Down Beat*, 102 North Haven Road, Elmhurst, Illinois 60126. Telephone: 1-800-535-7496; Fax: (1-630) 941-3210; Web site: http://downbeatjazz.tunes.com.
- *JazzTimes*, 8737 Colesville Road, Fifth Floor, Silver Springs, Maryland 20910-4898. Telephone: (1-301) 588-4114; Fax: (1-301) 588-5531.
- Marge Hofacre's *No Name Jazz N.E.W.S.*, P.O. Box 2441, Idylwild, California 92549.
- *The International Musician*, which is published by the American Federation of Musicians, 1501 Broadway, Suite 600, New York, New York 10036. Telephone: (1-212) 869-1330. *The International Musician* contains Burt Korall's column, the "Pop & Jazz Scene."
- *Jazz Now*, P.O. Box 19266, Oakland, California 94619-0266. Telephone: (1-510) 531-2839; Fax (1-510) 531-8875; E-mail: Jazzinfo@jazznow.com; Web site: http://www.jazznow.com.
- *The Jazz Report*, 592 Markham Street, Suite 7, Toronto, Ontario M6G 2L8, Canada. Telephone: (1-416) 533-2813; Fax: (1-416) 533-0973; Web site: http://www.jazzreport.com.
- *Cadence Magazine*, The Cadence Building, Redwood, New York 13679. Telephone: (1-315) 287-2852; Fax: (1-315) 287-2860; E-mail: cadence@cadencebuilding.com; Web site: http://www.cadencebuilding.com.
- *Jazz Educators Journal*, P.O. Box 724, Manhattan, Kansas 66502. Telephone: (1-785) 776-8744; Fax: (1-785) 776-6190; Web site: http://www.jazzcentralstation. com/iaje/splome.asp.

There are approximately 100 jazz societies in the United States, which altogether boast memberships of more than 100,000 people. Many of these societies publish newsletters. For information contact the American Federation of Jazz Societies, 2787 Del Monte Street, West Sacramento, California 95691. Telephone: (1-916) 372-5277; Fax (1-916) 372-3479; Web site: worldmall.com/wmcc/afjs.

Foreign jazz magazines are another source of venue data and information lists. One of the best European English-language jazz magazines, which is produced by one of the world's oldest jazz societies, is *Jazz Forum*. For more information, contact Pawel Brodowski, Nowogrodzka 49, PL-00-695 Warsaw, Poland. Telephone: (011-48-22) 21 9451, (011-48-22) 42 6439.

Jazz Databases: National and international databases print and market jazz information listings. One of the drawbacks of purchasing a database is that the information contained in it may not be tailored to meet your needs. For instance, not all of the jazz clubs listed in a database may be booking national and international groups, or may be booking groups that have marquee values that are equal to your own. Prices for these listings vary.

- *Tele Jazz+*, Jazz Time Verlag, CH-5425 Schneisingen, Switzerland. Jazz Time Verlag prints complete northern European jazz information lists.
- *Agenda*, Ofa Orell Fussli Werbe, Holbeinstrasse 30, Kurt Linski, 4022 Zurich, Switzerland. Ofa Orell Fussli Werbe prints complete northern European jazz information lists.
- *The Directory of Jazz Festivals*, The International Jazz Federation, The Danish Jazz Center, Borupvej 66B, DK-4683 Ronnade, Denmark. Telephone: (011-45-53) 71 13 27 or (011-45-53) 71 13 81; Fax: (011-45-53) 71 17 49. The Danish Jazz Center prints an international directory of jazz festivals.
- *The Jazz World Database*, P.O. Box 777, Times Square Station, New York, New York 10108-0777. Telephone: (1-212) 581-7188; Fax: (1-212) 253-4160; E-mail: jwd@village.ios.com; Web site: http://www.jazzsociety.com. The Jazz World Database is a constantly updated global network of thousands of individuals, companies, organizations, events, and products.
- *The Euro Jazz Book*, IRMA, 21 bis rue de Paradis, F-75010 Paris, France. Telephone: (011-33-1) 44 83 10 30; Fax: (011-33-1) 44 83 10 40; E-mail: info@irma.asso.fe; Web site: http://www.irma.assoc.fr. This book offers 8,000 contacts in thirty countries in Europe, including festivals, clubs and venues, booking agents, managers, record companies, distributors, press, radio and TV organizations, schools, and more. It costs $50.
- *European Music*, rue de la Science, 10, 1000 Brussels, Belgium. Telephone: (011-32-2) 280 43 95; Fax: (011-32-2) 280 43 98; E-mail: emo@euromusic.com; Web site: http://euromusic.com. With 20,000 contacts in more than thirty-three countries, Eurobase is one of the most comprehensive European music industry databases on the Internet.
- *The International Association of Schools of Jazz*, Juliana van Stolberglaan 1, 2595 CA The Hague, Holland. Telephone: (011-31-70) 381-4251; Fax: (011-31-70) 385-3941. The International Association of Schools of Jazz is an international educational data resource. An individual membership fee is currently $50.

The Internet: The Internet is a fount of worldwide jazz contacts that are too numerous to list here. Start browsing and you'll find more leads than you'll have time to contact. Venues are listed by country or genre. Also, almost every music Web site has links to other information sites. If you don't know where to start, check out the Bookmarks Page on my Web site at http://www.upbeat.com/galper. Another good starting point for Internet leads is Euromusic at http://www.euromusic.com.

Jazz Service Organizations: Jazz service organizations not only have newsletters that contain valuable venue info, they also offer support services (mailing lists, advice, discount publications, etc.) that are not available elsewhere. Join as many of them as your budget can afford.

- *Inside Arts*, The Association of Performing Arts Presenters, 1112 Sixteenth Street, NW, Suite 400, Washington, DC 20036. Telephone: (1-202) 833-2787; Fax: (1-202) 833-1543; E-mail: artspres@artspresenters.org; Web site: http://www.artspresenters.org.

- Arts Midwest, 528 Hennepin Avenue, Suite 310, Minneapolis, Minnesota 55403-1899. Telephone: (1-612) 341-0755; Fax: (1-612) 341-0902; E-mail: info@artsmidwest.org; Web site: http://www.artsmidwest.org.
- Mid-America Arts Alliance, 912 Baltimore Avenue, Suite 700, Kansas City, Missouri 64105. Telephone: (1-816) 421-1388; Fax: (1-816) 421-3918, E-mail: info@maaa.org; Web site: http://www.maaa.org.
- Mid-Atlantic Arts Foundation, 22 Light Street, Suite 300, Baltimore, Maryland 21202. Telephone: (1-410) 539-6656 (ext. 105); Fax: (1-410) 837-5517; E-mail: maaf@midarts.usa.com; Web site: http://www.charm.net/~midarts.
- New England Foundation for the Arts, 330 Congress Street, Sixth Floor, Boston, Massachusetts 02210-1216. Telephone: (1-617) 951-0010; Fax: (1-617) 951-0016; E-mail: info@nefa.org; Web site: http://www.nefa.org.
- Southern Arts Federation, 1401 Peachtree Street, Suite 460, Atlanta, Georgia 30309-7603. Telephone: (1-404) 874-7244; Fax: (1-404) 873-2148; E-mail: saf@southarts.org; Web site: http://www.southarts.org.
- Western States Arts Federation (WESTAF), 1543 Champa Street, Suite 220, Denver, Colorado 80202. Telephone: (1-303) 629-1166; Fax: (1-303) 629-9717; E-mail: staff@westaf.org; Web site: http://www.westaf.org.

Record Company Distributor Listings: If you're associated with a record company that has touring bands on its artist roster, check to see if the company posts touring itineraries on its company Web site and sends itineraries to local distributors. If the company does this, ask to be included on that mailing list.

Disk Jockeys: There are at least eighty-five major radio stations and more than 500 small college and independent radio stations in the United States that play some type of jazz—and there are even more worldwide. Put together a database of jazz radio stations and their on-air staff as well as music and programming directors. Your record company will have jazz radio and disc jockey listings. You can also get them from Northwestern University's Web site, the JazzWeb at http://homepage.interaccess.com/~chassaxe/jazzweb.

Contact the jazz disc jockeys and music directors in each city on your tour. They know what's going on locally and will be glad to talk with you. Making personal contact with a disc jockey will also result in your music being played more on the radio, and more on-air mentions of your local appearances. Local radio stations often work in conjunction with clubs, nonprofit organizations, and educational institutions to present jazz concerts.

It should be apparent by now that there are more possibilities for work out there than you could have imagined. If you want to know where the gigs are, you now know where to look.

Lead Times and Commitment Dates

The farther in advance you book a gig, the better off you are. As you compile your venue research, one of the most crucial pieces of information will be how far in advance you need to call to book a gig. Each venue has its own lead time, which can vary from one month to two years in advance of a gig. Make a call-back note on your calendar for each gig you've contacted for a current or future tour. Set it for between two weeks and a month before the time the person asked you to call back. It will sometimes take that long to get through to your contact. If you call too late, you'll miss an opportunity to include that venue as part of your tour.

Don't assume that you've got the gig just because a venue told you to call back on a certain date. Situations change. It's better to call back too soon than too late. Venues are often considering more than one band for each date they're booking. By calling a client back before the agreed-upon date, you may learn key information.

It doesn't hurt to confirm that you're still on a client's short list for a date. You might just find out that they've booked another band that was going to be in their area at the same time as yours. Even though the venue may have other dates open that you could use to fill in your itinerary, the client may have assumed that you have no alternative dates other than the one you discussed and crossed you off his or her list. A phone call far enough in advance may allow you to adjust the dates of some other gigs to fit that venue into your tour. (This will be discussed further in chapter nine.) Lead times tend to fall into certain patterns, depending on the venue type. They will be discussed as we analyze venue types later in this chapter.

Commitment dates (i.e., the time at which a venue can commit to an engagement) vary as much as lead times. Every tour you're booking will be composed of a variety of venues whose lead times and commitment dates are different. Coordinating them requires patience and nerves of steel, as many tour dates are dependent on other tour date commitments. Lose one gig and three others could go down the drain.

As your tour starts to come together, you will be looking at some open, unconfirmed dates in your tour calendar, wondering if they are going to commit or not. Because open dates are costly and can easily affect the financial viability of a tour, they start to look like big holes in your itinerary and take on added significance as the tour approaches. A venue can only commit when it says it can, or, in most cases, later than its original estimated commitment date. You'll have to resist the temptation to repeatedly call the client back in the hopes of getting an early commitment. If you don't have a back-up gig for this date, the only solution to this hurdle is patience.

Foreign venues have different speeds at which they book and confirm engagements. Venues in northern European countries (Netherlands, Germany, Switzerland, etc.) tend to book and commit six months to a year in advance, whereas southern European venues (Italy, Spain, Portugal, etc.) tend to book and commit one to three months in advance. This can become problematic when you're combining northern and southern European venues within the same tour. Accordingly, it is advisable to book your first tour dates in the northern countries. Avoid booking the southern countries in either the first or the middle segment of the tour. Instead, book venues in southern countries at the end of a tour. This will allow you to confidently purchase your tickets to Europe as well as minimize the risk that a hole will occur in the middle of a tour. Outgoing flights for prepurchased round-trip airline tickets cannot be changed. Excessive days off on any tour will devour a tour's budgetary resources. If southern gigs end up not committing and you have scheduled them for the later part of your tour, you can change your return flights for a small surcharge. (For more information about this, see chapter ten.)

Booking and Touring Patterns

There is a limit to how much time you can spend touring per year. While traveling, your duties as a bandleader won't leave you with much free time for booking other tours. Instead, you'll need to be home for a certain amount of time each year to book your band for the future. For example, if you've managed to book a full year's worth of work for your first year, you won't be home enough to work on tours for the following year and your band will be out of work.

Your busiest times of the year will be fall and spring. Because weather conditions during the winter can make touring unpredictable and potentially costly, you won't be touring much in the winter, unless you travel to places with warm climates. Conversely, touring in the summer is possible, but there are fewer available gigs. Most of the gigs that are available are festivals—the most difficult gigs of all to get—and filling in open dates is problematic. For example, educational institutions are closed during the summer and can't be counted upon to fill off days during this period.

There will always be a conflict between the amount of time you need to tour with your band and the amount of time you need to be home to book it. Even if you have a laptop computer with a modem and travel with all of your contact files, the most you could do while you're on the road would be to find a moment here and there to book a gig or two. If you're on the road at the time you need to be home booking gigs for a particular time period, you might find that you have passed certain venues' lead times. Striking a balance between touring and booking will be a constant source of frustration. You'll have to accept the reality that the more you work in one year, the less you may work in the next.

In terms of giving you at-home time to book your next tour, shorter tours can be more advantageous than longer ones. Though you might think that longer tours create more income, the reverse may often be true. Both financially and for future bookings, a series of two- to three-week tours—with breaks of varying lengths in between—could be more practical than one, long two-month tour.

UNDERSTANDING DIFFERENT VENUE TYPES

Gigs can show up in the most surprising places: private parties, country clubs, business conventions, government functions, public events—even people's homes. The variety is endless. Likewise, it is important for you to remain open to the range of possibilities. Invariably, your tours will have a mix of every type of gig. Because of space limitations, this analysis is confined to the most common types of venues: festivals, educational institutions, cultural institutions, nonprofit arts presenters, jazz societies, and jazz clubs.

Festivals

 Lead Time: From eight months to a year.
 Fee Range: From nothing to the highest.
 Accommodations: Paid by venue. Extra days paid if dictated by travel restrictions.
 Transportation: None, partial (i.e., from previous gig and to next gig), or full transportation paid by venue.
 Periodicity: Once a year.
 Frequency of Return: Festivals rarely feature the same musician or band twice.

Festivals number in the thousands and occur worldwide. Except for college festivals (which run during the academic year), festivals are most frequently held during the summer months. Festivals generally run for as few as two days or as many as ten days. They can also be spread out over a long time frame—as a series of weekly or monthly performances. Short-term festivals often feature many bands, which perform at the same time, as opposed to long-term festivals, which may have only one to three artists per concert.

Festivals pay high fees and offer the greatest degree of audience exposure of any of the venue types. Consequently, emerging artists, agents, and record companies compete fiercely for festival performance spots. Festivals are particularly beneficial for emerging artists, because each individual artist or group doesn't shoulder the full responsibility of drawing the audience. Most festival tickets are presold, therefore, audiences for particular performances within a festival are built-in. Additionally, the draw is increased because more than one band perform on any particular day. Festivals are the best vehicle for expanding a band's fan base.

Individual festivals are produced and controlled by one organization or promoter. Agents who represent the biggest names in the music industry make a point of developing personal relationships with festival promoters. As a result, the agents' requests for festival spots often take precedence over independent artists' requests. Agents make their biggest commissions from booking festivals. And, unfortunately, festival promoters have a vested interest in booking bigger names, even when their fees are excessive, because their names draw big crowds, which helps to offset a festival's extraordinarily high overhead. This is not to say that all festivals only feature the biggest names. Many festival promoters mix their name levels and take pride in offering emerging artists a chance for exposure.

Many festivals offer concerts that are free to the public. These are prime venues for emerging artists, but they pay very little, if at all. In addition, these gigs can be difficult for the independent band to acquire because major record labels often buy performance slots at free festivals for their emerging artists. The major labels have determined that it is worthwhile to offer their artists' services for free, paying the bands' salaries and travel expenses, because festival appearances increase a band's audience exposure and create promotional opportunities. This has become common practice in the music industry. Free music is an offer no festival promoter can afford to refuse. However, as a bandleader of an independent band, if you're diligent about promoting your activities (i.e., making sure your tour information appears in all of the jazz publications) and recording, eventually you'll become attractive to festival producers.

Although festivals may not be on exactly the same dates each year, they tend to be approximately around the same time period. Some jazz festivals have a particular musical focus, such as freestyle, experimental, blues, Dixieland, bebop, or contemporary. Other festivals have different themes from year to year. For example, one year a particular festival might focus on a tribute to Bird, and the next year a tribute to Duke.

If you are asked to participate in a foreign festival, you should consider applying for a travel grant through Arts International's Fund for U.S. Artists program. Established for U.S. artists who are touring abroad, this organization offers grants of up to 100 percent of your round-trip airfares for transportation expenses. Contact them to find out their application guidelines and deadlines. Arts International, 809 United Nations Plaza, Eighth Floor, New York, New York 10017; Telephone: (1-212) 984-5370; Fax: (1-212)

984-5574; E-mail: artsinternational@iie.org; Web site: http://www.iie.org/ai. Mentioning that you have access to this funding source can often spur a festival to commit to booking your band. This in turn helps you get the grant, as you'll need a signed contract for the gig by the application deadline in order to apply for one of these grants.

Educational Institutions

Lead Time: From one to two years. It's best to contact the institution near the end of the school year (around April or May), before it has used up its budget for the following school year.

Fee Range: From $200 (for a solo clinic) to $1,500 per day or more (for a concert and residency).

Accommodations: Paid by venue. Sometimes the venue also pays for an extra day, if you have to get there a day early to make a morning clinic.

Transportation: None, partial, or full transportation paid by venue (varies according to budget).

Periodicity: Once a year (festivals); varies according to school budgets (clinics/concerts).

Frequency of Return: Every five to ten years (concerts); every one to three years (clinics).

Private and state colleges and universities, high schools, music schools, summer jazz camps, and school-band festivals offer many opportunities for employment. Budgets vary greatly from one department to the next. Some are limited to hiring only single soloists to perform with school or faculty bands and/or to present solo clinics. Others can afford to hire groups for festival concerts, clinics, adjudications, and/or residencies of up to one week in length. Many college and university jazz departments reserve small amounts of their budgets for a solo clinic or concert on short notice, just in case an artist is touring in the area.

A music department's budget is dictated by the financial conditions of the school and the whims of the administration. Each department's funds are spent at the discretion of the department head. Educational institutions are either state or privately funded. Private institutions usually have more money than their state-funded counterparts. At the time of this writing, almost every state is cutting funding to its educational institutions. Consequently, music departments at state-run institutions have less funding available to them than the music departments at private institutions. Keep this in mind when you're negotiating; you may have to negotiate a lesser fee for a gig at a state institution.

Academic clients may be inexperienced in seeking outside funding. It helps if you can direct them toward funding possibilities that they may not have considered, such as piggybacking department funds with those of a local organization that might partially support an engagement. For example, the community might have a local public radio station that would be willing to contribute some of its funds in exchange for being able to broadcast the event. A call to the local jazz disc jockey will determine what the needs of the broadcast area are and might spur on an interesting partnership.

Educational institutions can raise funds in many ways. I had an eye-opening experience the first time that I performed at a high school in Portage, Indiana. The music department head of the high school was innovative and aggressive. He encouraged his students to go door-to-door in the community, selling prepackaged pizzas to finance our concert and solo clinic. And now each time we tour that area, we contact the department head and his students collect enough money to pay for our fee and hotel rooms. I also once talked with a high school department head whose students earned $10,000 per year in extra funds to support concerts and clinics by selling candy and pizza.

Stay up-to-date on the funding possibilities that are available from local, regional, and national arts support organizations. You might be able help a school find some or all of the money it needs to bring you to its venue. (For information about researching funding sources, refer to pages 45–47.)

The situation is improving, but generally academic clients are not as savvy or business wise as operators of other types of venues. Some understand the realities of the touring business, but many times I have run into incredible ignorance. One department head, who wanted my trio for an off-day clinic for only $600, asked: "Gee, how can you guys afford to come all the way out here for just this clinic?" Be patient. Explain the realities of touring to them.

Some educational institutions host jazz festivals, which are often run by student committees. I shudder in fear whenever I hear the term "student committee" because these groups are the most frustrating and least competent of all venue operators. Even though your contact may be the supervisor of student affairs, you'll need to remember that he or she is just an overseer and has little influence upon the student committee's decisions. Because their personnel changes yearly, these committees are inconsistent. If you didn't get a gig one year, you'll probably have to start all over again the next time you approach them for a gig; quite often the CDs and press kits you send disappear. Committee members are young and have little business experience and, because of class schedules, they are often difficult to reach and poor at returning calls. Most often student committees decide to get the biggest name they're familiar with and blow their year's budget on one act. I contact student committees from time to time, in the faint hope of getting a gig, but for the most part I avoid them.

Those festivals that are coordinated and run by one person (usually the head of the jazz department) are generally more approachable for emerging and midcareer artists. The people running these festivals will be interested in conserving their budgets by not spending the money all at once on an expensive well-known artist and will be interested in assessing the quality of your music as well as your teaching abilities.

Nonprofit Arts Presenters

Lead Time: Up to a year. In some cases two years. You'll have to research each individual presenter for its booking periods.

Fee Range: From $1,000 and upward.

Accommodations: Paid by venue. Sometimes the venue also pays for an extra day, if you have to get there a day early.

Transportation: None, partial, or full transportation paid (varies according to budget).

Periodicity: From once to twelve times a year (varies according to budget).

Frequency of Return: Arts presenters rarely feature the same musician or band twice, but it happens from time to time.

Funded by contributions from foundations, government agencies, as well as private and corporate organizations, arts presenters are primarily concerned with supporting the arts, educating the public, and presenting artistic events not normally offered. Because they're not subject to the same commercial pressures as for-profit presenters, the personnel at arts presenters are easy to work with and salaried professionals. Unlike the gigs coordinated by jazz festival organizers, college jazz departments, and jazz clubs, jazz presentations may be only a part of the yearly schedule of mixed genres that any one arts presenter may be organizing.

The existence of nonprofit arts presenters is a relatively recent phenomenon. Individual presenters are usually part of larger regional and/or national arts presenter organizations. Although oriented to supporting artists in their region, most arts presenters book national artists as part of their yearly calendar. Like other venues, some are partial to booking big names, but many are open to presenting new and unknown groups as well. Subscribe to arts presenters' regional newsletters for information about application guidelines and deadlines.

A partial listing of venues that are coordinated by arts presenters includes: museums, galleries, exhibitions, conventions, fairs, arts centers, arts councils, unions/professional associations, schools (elementary to college level), libraries, historical societies, humanities councils/agencies, foundations, corporations/businesses, community service organizations, correctional and health care facilities, religious organizations, parks and recreation departments, government organizations (executive, judicial, legislative), media organizations (press and radio), cultural series organizations, and jazz societies.

Arts presenters often cooperate with other regional venues that can assist them in finding support work to add to a tour in their region; this process is called "block booking." For a small fee, regional presenters will send you mailing lists for other area gigs. Always ask if an organization is involved in block booking.

Jazz Societies

Lead Time: From six months to a year or more in advance.
Fee Range: From $300 to $1,500 for solo artists; higher for groups.
Accommodations: Paid by venue. Sometimes the venue also pays for an extra day, if you have to get there a day early.
Transportation: Occasionally paid by venue.
Periodicity: From once to twelve times per year.
Frequency of Return: Every five years, or more.

Jazz societies exist almost everywhere. Usually set up as nonprofit organizations, they depend on government funding, private and corporate sponsors, membership fees, and in-kind contributions for support. Jazz societies tend not to be as name conscious as other venue types and will hire lesser-known groups. Jazz societies may not be as well funded as arts presenters, however, they are usually staffed with volunteers who are real jazz lovers and, as a result, it is often easy to work with them.

The audiences for jazz societies are generally older. The jazz societies in Florida, for example, are almost exclusively oriented toward Dixieland and tend to prefer a more historical genre of music. However, many jazz societies have an appreciation for more modern sounds as well. The people who attend jazz societies' performances represent the segment of the jazz audience that supported the early jazz record labels and jazz clubs. They're true fans—and are sometimes our greatest audiences.

Jazz societies tend to book Sundays or Mondays, although their schedules may be flexible and they may be willing to book off days. They also may be able to connect you with an educational gig to make it more financially attractive for you to visit their area. Many better-funded societies are involved with festival productions as well.

Jazz Clubs

Lead Time: From three months to more than a year, depending on the size of the city. Small-city clubs have shorter lead times and big-city clubs have longer lead times.

Fee Range: Depends on the level of the club and the kind of agreements they make. (See chapter eight for more information.)

Accommodations: Negotiable. Some savvy club owners have their own properties that they use to house bands.

Transportation: Almost never paid by venue.

Periodicity: Varies from club to club.

Frequency of Return: Every nine months to two years.

Although jazz clubs may only account for 5 to 10 percent of your gigs, they can come in handy when you're trying to fill in those hard-to-book weekends. Because they have such high overheads, jazz clubs offer the lowest fees. However, even if you play a jazz club for a fee that is lower than your base salary, that gig will help keep your budget on track if your agreement includes hotels. It is better to work for less money and have your hotels paid for, than to pay for hotels on your days off. You can usually make up the shortfall from your better-paying gigs.

Summer is one of the most difficult times (especially in Europe) to find club and educational gigs. Music fans are on vacation. If they live in comfortable suburban areas, they're less likely to come into the city during the summer months. Clubs in vacation areas are the exception to this rule. However, if you're a midcareer or an emerging artist, this fact can work to your advantage. During the summer, clubs may not want to spend big fees for name artists when they expect audience attendance to be at a seasonal low. They can't afford to close, but they have to keep music in their venue and their overhead low. At times like these, clubs are more open to booking less expensive bands with lesser-known names.

There are clubs that book for a full week (six nights), however, they're only in the biggest cities. Most clubs now only book national bands on weekends, allocating from one to three days per band. This second category of clubs has three-night weekends that go either from Thursday to Saturday or from Friday to Sunday. Some clubs, to broaden their audience base, follow the European example and book different bands, genres of music, and kinds of entertainment each night of the week. When you're booking, you may only be able to acquire one night at those kinds of venues. If Tuesday is Blues Night at a particular club, you won't be able to use that venue to fill an open Tuesday in your itinerary. Some clubs reserve off nights for traveling bands specifically so they can take advantage of bands that are touring in their area.

Chapter 8

Contacting Venues and Negotiating Gigs

Now we've come to the heart of the matter: contacting venues and negotiating gigs. These are the key responsibilities of any bandleader. Your success in these arenas directly affects the success of your band—because if you are able to secure a nice amount of well-paying gigs, then your band's exposure will be increased, which will in turn help you get more gigs (that may even pay more money). It is a natural cycle that has the potential of going up (and becoming easier) as you establish your reputation in the industry.

Solidifying gigs for your band is a multistep process. In chapter seven you learned about the different kinds of gigs that are available. Once you've done your research, you have to contact these potential employers and then convince them not only to hire your band but to pay you a fee that will cover your band members' salaries as well as a portion of the expenses that you will incur by taking your band on the road. The success of this process hinges on being a good negotiator.

Some bandleaders become unnerved by the prospect of having to enter into a negotiation with a potential client. Negotiating is a skill. Some people are naturally inclined toward negotiation, others aren't. However, each of us can develop and improve this skill with time and practice. If you feel intimidated by the prospect of negotiating, you are not alone. This chapter should help you to address the fundamental issues that are involved with negotiating. If, after reading through this section, you're still not convinced that you want to take on this aspect of the business yourself, you might try to hire an agent to assist you with this process.

HIRING AN AGENT

In chapter seven you learned about the many resources that you can use to scout your own venue leads. Agents are another useful resource for gig contacts—and they can also help musicians with a wide range of business tasks that are associated with the booking and touring processes. Although this volume is intended to teach you how to book your own band, odds are that you'll work with an agent from time to time. You may eventually become so successful that a recognized agent will seek to represent you. Having realistic expectations about what agents can and cannot do for you will put you ahead of the game.

As an independent bandleader who is booking his or her own tour, you may find that agents can work against your interests. Agents—especially those who have high-profile artist rosters—will often make arrangements with festival organizers to buy three or four of an agent's acts. This agreement may be contingent on the fact that the festival can book no bands other than those on that agent's artist roster. This can be a problem for the independent artist. Because of their exclusive agreement with the agent, the festival organizers can't book you for their gig, even if they want to. You'll be effectively "locked out."

The Pros and Cons of Having an Agent

The dilemma of whether an independent artist should engage the services of an agent is best expressed by two old (and mutually exclusive) adages: "It's worth it to give up some money in order to get some" and "No one cares about your business as much as you do."

There is a long-standing disagreement among musicians about whether it's better to represent yourself or to have someone represent you. Some believe that you get more respect from venues by having representation. Others feel that personal contact between an artist and a venue increases the likelihood of getting a gig. The three deciding factors involved are: the personality of the artist, the personality of the venue contact, and the type of venue.

If you are not accomplished in the verbal arts, it may be best to try to arrange for representation. However, there are many books and courses that teach people how to improve their verbal skills. Professional communication is a skill that anyone can learn. Some clients appreciate personal contact more than others. You'll actually find that some clients will *only* talk to artists directly. Still others will not talk to artists and prefer to deal with a middleman.

Clients often suffer from the popular misconception that musicians are standoffish and difficult. However, as you know, generalizations like that are untrue—the temperaments of musicians vary as much as those of people working in any other profession. Once a client finds out that an artist is a human being no different from him- or herself, the client enjoys talking with the artist. Establishing good artist-client rapport with your contacts can help you instill confidence in your client that you will be an easy and responsible artist with which to work.

There are so many bands looking for representation that good, well-established agents often have more clients than they can handle. As much as you might like to be represented by an agent of this stature, working with an agent who has too many clients could mean that you won't get the individual attention your band needs to keep working. Agents can certainly help your career—but sometimes they can hinder it as well.

PROS An agent with a good reputation can add to your band's credibility. If a client hasn't heard of you before or if he or she is familiar with your name but doesn't know your music and your ability to draw a crowd, having a reputable agent might help give you the edge that you need to secure a gig. The client might think: *If this agent believes in that band enough to represent it, it must have something to offer that can help me as well.* In addition, an agent can offer you the power that goes along with having a strong roster. A venue will be less likely to cause trouble for your group if it knows that by doing so it jeopardizes its future access to the other acts that your agent represents. Agents can also book an "in-demand" act at a venue, contingent upon that venue agreeing to hire your group at that time or a later date.

A good agent, especially one who has been in the business for a long time, will not just see you as a commission, but as an artist whose survival depends upon his or her ability to get work for you. Good agents have long lists of contacts with whom they've worked and have developed long-term relationships with promoters and venues. It takes decades to achieve the number and level of contacts that a good agent has. However, agents deliberately nurture these relationships because they directly increase their booking potential. Agents attend booking conferences where they network with promoters. Because of lack of time, interest, or money, musicians rarely attend these conferences. In addition, agents also network with other agents; occasionally, to fill a hole in an artist's or band's itinerary, an agent will work with another agent and the two of them will split the fees.

A good agent will:

- negotiate higher fees for your group than you might;
- be considerate in planning a healthy tour schedule;
- arrange a band's transportation and accommodations, including airport and train pickups and returns, local transportation, and van rentals;
- oversee the drafting of contracts and riders;
- request that venues provide down payments, which add extra security to a tour and which are helpful when unforeseen events (i.e., nonpayment of fees, payments by check instead of cash, missed flights, transportation strikes, etc.) occur;
- offer protection from a venue treating you poorly, especially if his or her talent roster includes other bands that are much in demand;
- mail or publish his or her talent roster, which provides free promotion for your group;
- make life easier for you so you'll have more time to work on your music;
- believe in your music as well as communicate that belief to his or her clients in a manner that will positively affect the band's image.

Agent's commissions range from 10 to 20 percent of performance fees. It's a commission well spent if an agent can negotiate performance fees that are from 10 to 20 percent higher than the fee you would have normally quoted.

CONS When you put your career in the hands of an agent, you put yourself in a passive state, which is a strategically weak position. The welfare of your band—and the families of each of your band members—will be out of your control. You won't know what's going on with your own business. Because agents don't have time to inform the musicians on their roster of every little detail of a negotiation, if you hire an agent, you won't know how you are being represented and sold to venues.

Some agents see their talent only in terms of dollar signs. And they sometimes engage in sketchy business practices in order to maximize their own profit. One such practice is called "buying and selling." This is how it works: The agent works out an agreement to give a band X amount of dollars per performance or per tour (i.e., "buying") and, without the knowledge of the band members, he or she offers the group to a venue or promoter for a higher fee (i.e., "selling"). You see only the contract you signed with the agent, not the contract between agent and venue.

A bad agent may:

- overprice you and you'll wonder why you're not getting any gigs;
- have an abrasive manner;
- not be attentive to a client's commitment date or financial needs;
- engage in the unethical practice of "buying and selling";
- "buy" a band for a set fee, rent a venue, collect the door charges, and make more money than the band did;
- book a tour and then expect a percentage of any extra gigs or record dates that you may have booked on that tour (the rationale being: "Any gigs you arranged because I booked the tour and paid for the tickets are mine.");
- route physically demanding tours with too many hours of traveling between venues.

Some agents have no consideration for the health of a band and will orchestrate physically demanding tours. Not only does this practice negatively affect the health of the band members, but it affects the music as well. A minimum number of hard travel days can be expected on any tour, but in order for the band to get some rest a good agent will try to synchronize them with off days or arrange an off day after a hard day of traveling.

Exclusive and Nonexclusive Artist-Agent Agreements

An exclusive agreement between an artist and an agent can be based solely on a handshake. In this situation, both parties act as though they had a signed an exclusive agreement. The artist refers all work queries to the agent. Likewise, the agent lists the artist on his or her roster as "an exclusive" and collects a fee for all referrals. Although not legally binding, exclusive artist-agent agreements are preferred by many established artists because the agent acts as a buffer between the venue and the artist. The artist's contracts are protected by the agent. Under an exclusive arrangement, the artist works with no other agents, and if he or she is queried by one, the artist refers that person to his or her agent.

If you are an emerging artist and you attract an exclusive offer from an agent, it's best to have a signed contract with him or her. Hire a music lawyer to oversee the contract process. Again, it should be stressed that by signing an exclusive contract, you put the sole responsibility for the livelihood of your band in the agent's hands. The contract is legally binding and the agent must guarantee a specified amount of yearly income to the artist.

The most common kind of arrangement between an artist and an agent is the nonexclusive verbal agreement. Based on mutual faith, it's not legally binding but has advantages for both parties. The success of this kind of agreement depends upon the performance of both the agent and the artist. Both parties are motivated to perform well because each person's economic survival depends on it. The artist has the right to book himself, can supply leads to the agent, and, generally, takes a more active part in the booking process. The agent is not under pressure to meet economic goals that would be stipulated in a written agreement. The artist retains his or her "right of refusal" (i.e., the right to reject a gig that has been arranged by the agent).

The weakness of a nonexclusive verbal agreement is that either party can cancel the agreement without notice. When an agent agrees to book a certain time period for a band, the artists leave it open and make no attempt to book anything in that period. If anything happens to jeopardize that part of the tour, the artists could end up with a costly hole in the middle of their tour and risk having the tour canceled.

For example, when I was the pianist with a well-known quintet, this type of situation arose. A lengthy European tour was being worked on between the band's agent and a well-established and powerful European promoter. The fees involved tallied to more than $60,000. A month before we were supposed to leave, signed contracts still had not arrived from Europe. A dispute over a small sum of $1,000 per week arose between the agent and the promoter. A week before the tour, the dispute had still not been resolved and the tour was canceled by the European promoter. The promoter lost little because he had many other bands on tour at the time. The agent lost little because he had many other bands on tour at the time. The quintet lost more than $60,000 of income and was suddenly out of work. An international lawsuit was instituted to redress the issue, without success.

Lawsuits are difficult and expensive to litigate, especially international lawsuits. Unless thousands of dollars are at stake, lawsuits are not worth the time and effort they require to bring to court. Most promoters, agents, and record companies are aware that disputes of small sums of money are not worth litigating and hold this advantage over musicians who cannot afford the expense of litigation. A verbal agreement does have a certain amount of legal validity (depending on the jurisdiction of the agreement). However, it is a truism that "a contract is only as good as the people who sign it." And the final words in any contract dispute are often: "Sue me!"

Because of language problems, booking gigs in foreign countries can be problematic. You can solve this problem by hiring regional agents in each country that might have an interest in booking your band.

It's unethical for an artist to bypass an agent for a return engagement at a venue that the agent had booked on a previous tour. It's common practice to use the original agent (even if he or she no longer represents you) to negotiate a return engagement, otherwise you'd be perceived as beating the agent out of his or her commission. Establishing and maintaining good client relationships is the way agents earn their living. You risk your credibility by putting yourself in a bad light with both the agent and the client and may jeopardize future work opportunities from that agent, that venue, or even from another agent. There's a grapevine among agents, musicians, and venue operators that can either enhance or ruin a career.

New Agents

New agents, people who are just starting out in the business, can be valuable assets, especially if they come highly recommended. Although hiring a new agent doesn't offer the same protection that comes with having a well-established agent with a stable of artists, you may consider beginning a relationship with a new agent who is looking for artists to book. New agents have to come from somewhere, and one of the benefits of hiring a new agent is that he or she will need you as much as you need him or her. Only a free flow of information between the agent and the artist will make this relationship successful. If you decide to hire a new agent, negotiate an agreement that protects each of your contact leads. The term of this agreement should be no more than two years in length, including mutual, renewable options of one year each. Include a clause that specifies that cancellation of the options will require six months notice from either party. This gives both parties time to make adjustments.

I know of one new European agent who—just to meet the owners and promoters and check out the hotels—drove throughout Europe to personally visit all of the venues she had on her venue list. She also traveled with the band. This kind of hands-on treatment can be terrific. However, it also has the potential of creating problems. For instance, if your agent runs a one-person operation and he or she is on the road with another band at the same time that you're on the road, then you will be inconvenienced if you have a transportation problem or an artist-client dispute that needs your agent's input in order to be resolved.

An agent represents you to the world. Likewise, you must be aware that your band's image can be affected by your agent's actions. It's in your best interests to know how your band is being presented to clients. If you decide to hire a new agent, you can assess how well he or she negotiates on your behalf by giving him or her some solid work leads that you know will bear fruit. Before you do this, however, you should ask your agent to promise that he or she will not use any of your leads to book any other artists until you have worked these venues first.

Because the agenting process is so labor intensive, an agent working without any support staff can successfully handle no more than five artists. If an agent books $75,000 worth of work for you a year and receives a 15 percent commission, he or she will make $11,250 from your band. Assuming that each of the five artists on your agent's roster earns a similar amount, the agent would gross a total of $56,250 that year. The agent has to deduct his or her operating expenses from that figure—the biggest of which will be the phone bill. At a rate of $4,000 worth of phone calls per artist, per year, the phone bill will cost your agent $20,000. Excluding any other operating expenses, your agent will receive a net of $36,250 per year. Your agent will be booking at least a year in advance and will not see any income from his or her efforts until those gigs have happened. Consequently, most beginning agents can't afford such an outlay of funds.

Since you'd be spending $4,000 a year on the phone bills to book your own gigs anyway, you may consider paying for the calls the agent makes on your behalf. If your agent wants to make this kind of arrangement, negotiate the commission down from 15 to 10 percent. This way, if the agent books $75,000 worth of work for you that year (as above), the agent will net $7,500 for his or her efforts and you can take the tax deduction for the phone calls. This way, the agent booking five artists earns more for him- or herself and shoulders less of the financial burden. If you enter this kind of arrangement, ask the agent to keep phone logs of the calls he or she made on your behalf and list the clients contacted and their telephone numbers. A copy of the agent's phone bill will confirm that these calls were actually made. This is also a good way to track your agent's activities.

Creating Your Own Agent

One alternative to using a new agent is to create and train one yourself. This is a good option for midcareer musicians, especially those who have done some of the booking process themselves. If you've spent years booking your own band, you have expertise that you could pass on to someone who would like to begin a career as an agent. If you decide to take this route, start by giving your agent-to-be a copy of this book. Then sign a mutual contract for a three-year minimum arrangement, during which time you will advise and instruct him or her on how to do the job. Setting the minimum commitment time protects you as well as the information that you've gathered over the years of being in this business. You don't want someone to take your expertise and leave to go on their own until you have received a return on the investment of your time and energy. Include a clause in the contract that outlines how your leads will be protected (i.e., that any venue leads you supply your agent cannot be used for another artist until you have been booked at that venue first) and another that outlines the penalties for breaking the contract. Make the same arrangement as described in the section on new agents about offsetting phone expenses in return for a reduced commission. (For more information about this, see pages 109–110.)

Agreeing to pay your agent's phone expenses in exchange for paying him or her a reduced commission is a good example of a successful negotiation. Negotiating is something we do every day and it's something we can all learn to improve. Top-notch negotiation skills help you more than with just getting what you want. They also help you give others what they want, too. After a successful negotiation, everyone comes away feeling good about the deal. If you polish your negotiating skills, you'll come across as fair, flexible, and tough when you need to be. Understanding the negotiation process and techniques as well as developing a negotiation plan can only enhance your chances of obtaining a successful result. (This will be discussed further on pages 129–142.)

MAXIMIZING YOUR COMMUNICATIONS

The success of your business will be determined, in part, by how well you handle the negotiations that occur during the process of booking your band. Negotiations rarely occur face-to-face and are generally facilitated by the use of communication devices. Learning how to use these devices is the first step that you can take to ensure the success of your negotiations.

Your lifelines to the world are your telephone, fax machine, modem, and the post office. Along with your computer, these four items are the basic tools of your job and they demand the most of your time, patience, and energy. Some days they're your best friend, and some your worst enemy. Most of the time they work for you, but you can easily become a slave to them. Having the right communications equipment and knowing how to use it will make your job, and your life, much easier.

Enhancing Workspace Ergonomics

Creating a comfortable and healthy working environment is an essential element in the negotiation process. If you're not physically comfortable at your desk, the wear and tear on your lower back, neck, and wrists cannot only make you a regular visitor to a chiropractor, but can also reduce the level of confidence and enthusiasm that you communicate to your potential clients. You also can't concentrate very well if you're distracted by pain. All of these factors cumulatively reduce your effectiveness as a businessperson. When you're developing your office space, try to create a comfortable environment, one in which you want to spend a lot of time and one that makes you feel good.

Your desk and chair should be at ergonomically correct heights. Your chair should provide back support so that you are not leaning over your desk for extreme periods of time. Your chair should also be on rollers so that you can easily move to an out-of-reach filing cabinet without getting out of your chair. Everything that you need to make or respond to a phone call or fax should be within easy reach.

To keep their hands free for taking notes while on the telephone, many people use a headset with an attached microphone. I don't have this kind of setup because I like to have my local twenty-four-hour jazz radio station on while I'm working. The music helps me work better and I couldn't hear it if I was wearing a headset. Some telephones have a speaker-phone feature so you can move around while you're talking. These phones are handy for off-hook dialing and for waiting for customer service representatives to pick up your call, but most have hollow sound effects that can make your voice seem cold. Don't use a speakerphone when you're negotiating a gig, especially if you're not really tight with the venue operator and if the effectiveness of your negotiation depends upon the personal quality of your interaction. A shoulder-neck holder that sticks onto the back of a telephone handle is an inexpensive and comfortable way to keep your hands free while you're on the telephone.

Use a communications system that has telephone, answering machine, and fax capabilities in one unit. It saves desk space and is convenient. An off-hook dialing feature is advantageous as well. It can save you from having to keep picking up and putting down the phone, especially when you're getting busy signals and making repeated phone calls. Automatic redialing is also a useful time- and effort-saving feature. And finally, ask your phone company to install call-waiting as part of your telephone service so you won't miss important calls on those days when the phone is jumping off the hook.

Developing Good Telephone Techniques

Well-developed telephone techniques are crucial to the success of the client contact process. Potential clients can sense when you don't feel confident speaking with them. Developing strong verbal skills is a large subject unto itself and is beyond the scope of this book. However, many books have been written on the subject. So, if you lack confidence or are shy, you might consider learning about how you can strengthen your telephone selling techniques by reading one of these books. They are available in bookstores and on the Internet at http://www.amazon.com and at http://www.barnesandnoble.com. If you decided to browse for these books on the Net, go to one of the bookstore's sites, then find the subject section and do a search using the words "telephone selling." This should generate a thorough listing of the relevant books that are readily available.

Some musicians don't think it is respectable to call a client themselves. They believe that clients have less respect for musicians who represent themselves than for musicians who are represented by agents. Therefore, they want to have an agent who will call the client on their behalf. However, it is common knowledge that television advertisements where the owner of a business promotes his or her own product are rated higher and more effective than commercials that don't have the owner present. Based on this information, it is logical to deduce that potential clients might be more convinced of your merits as a musician if they talk with you directly—rather than with an agent. As discussed earlier, one of the other benefits of representing yourself is that you know how you are being presented to a potential client.

Telephone calls are an inexpensive form of self-promotion. Every call you make promotes you and your music. If your phone technique is good, potential clients will remember you when you call again. For example, I was attending a panel for arts presenters at the 1996 International Association of Jazz Educators' convention in Atlanta. A number of actual and potential clients I had contacted at one time or other were present and my name must have come up during the panel discussion at least fifteen times. At one point, much to everyone's amusement, the moderator asked, "Is there anyone here who has *not* received a phone call from Hal Galper?" Only one person raised his hand and said, "I haven't." I asked him if we could talk later. Work on developing a good phone rap.

Preparing for the Call

There will never be enough time in the day for all of the calls you need to make. As they say, life interrupts the best of plans. No matter how organized you are, you will never get all of your calls done within the time you've set aside to make them. Phone calls may be longer than expected. You may get a busy signal or not reach a person on the day that you had hoped you would. Taking notes, returning calls, adding to to-do lists, writing letters, sending faxes, preparing press kits to be mailed, as well as doing your normal, daily domestic tasks will consume the time available for making calls. You will always feel behind in your business, but this is an illusion. Don't let it overwhelm you. You can only do so much work in any given period of time.

Booking a band is high-stress work. Learn when to stop working and say "enough is enough." If you're tired, don't make any phone calls. Fatigue will show in your voice, and it may come across to a client as a lack of concern. If you've had a good day and have managed to confirm three important tour gigs, take the rest of the day off to do something distracting and relaxing. If you have had a bad day—as you will from time to time—and haven't been able to pull any gigs in and you're feeling discouraged, stop calling. You don't want to talk to clients with that kind of attitude.

At this point, you are probably wondering: *How many phone calls a day will I be making and when should I make them?*

Let's assume that you are booking a four-week tour. That's twenty-eight days with a minimum of one day off per week, which means you've got to find twenty-four days of work. Because of hotel expenses, you can't afford too many off days on the road, so you're going to need a lot of contact leads, in case a number of gigs don't confirm. Ideally, you should have three possibilities for gigs for each working day. This means that for twenty-four days of work you're going to need at least seventy-two leads. If as your booking your tour you find that you've exhausted your leads but you still have too many days off, you'll have to do more research. Maybe call one of the "possibles" back for a new lead recommendation, or call someone else for new leads. After making a few phone calls, you may not have any luck finding other gigs. However, after staring at your calendar for an hour, you might realize that by readjusting your routing, you can minimize your days off. You'll then have to call some of the "possibles" back to see if you can change their dates. Most venues are familiar with routing problems and understand if you have to change a date. If they can, they will.

The best days for calling are Tuesday through Thursday. Mondays and Fridays are the worst days to try and reach anyone. On Mondays, most people are just coming off of their weekends, reorienting themselves for work, catching up on the work they left undone on the Friday before and organizing their work week. Most people have meetings and do errands on Mondays. On Fridays most folks are impatient about getting out of the office for the weekend and are preparing for an early departure. They're trying to finish their work so they won't have to play catch-up on the following Monday. That means you only have three business days a week to make calls, so you have to make the most of those days.

Shotgunning Your Leads

Before you start dialing the phone to book a tour, make sure you have all the calls you're going to make that day lined up in your database. This is the first step you need to take to utilize a technique called "shotgunning." Shotgunning means you are going to try to call twenty to thirty contacts in as short a time as possible—the idea being that in the majority of instances your contacts aren't going to be available to talk to you at the time that you call and you'll need to leave a message, explaining the purpose of your call and asking your contact to call you back when it is convenient for him or her. So, if you leave twenty to thirty messages during a short period of time, you can sit back and wait for those people to call you back.

There are two principal benefits of shotgunning your leads. First, by leaving detailed messages for a lot of people all at once you break the ice. This way, when your contacts call you back you can get right down to business. Second, shotgunning your leads allows you to put the ball into the courts of a whole bunch of people all at once. This increases your chances of being able to maximize your time after you've shotgunned your leads. If all goes well, you will make a steady stream of calls in a relatively short period of time, which is obviously more efficient than making just a few calls and waiting around for a small handful of people to call you back.

Here are some tips about how to set up your database in preparation for shotgunning your leads. In your computer's contact-manager program, create a file called "current calls" (or you might name the file by the dates of the tour). Organize and collect from your contact files all of the leads that you think might work for a tour's geographical area. Before you start calling, have a notepad and pen ready. If you're a two-fingered typist, the information from your initial calls will be coming in too fast for you to accurately type in your notes from the conversations. Instead you'll want to write your notes down on the pad during each conversation and then enter them into your computer file after you have made as many of your calls as you can during your calling period. If you get a busy signal or leave a message once you start calling, it is easy enough to note this information into the computer directly without any mistakes. My contact file is customized so that I can hit a button and it automatically notes the call date and time as well as "busy," "message," or "call back."

Leaving Messages

Sometimes it's preferable to leave a message than to make an immediate first contact with a client. As we discussed in the section on shotgunning your leads, you can make more contact calls in a short period of time if you leave messages for a large number of the people rather than if you speak with all of them directly. Also, leaving a message gives your potential clients time to think about your call. That way, when they call you back or when you call them back for the second time, they are ready to talk with you and start negotiations for the gig.

It is a common experience among independent musicians that most of your first calls will not be returned and you will need to follow up with two to three more calls before you actually speak with a potential client person-to-person. How many messages should you leave? As a general rule, leave no more than three messages per client without a call-back. Try to be patient and give the client a chance to return your call. Don't leave more than one message per day, and allow a week between messages. After three messages, I usually retire the contact to a dead file for recontacting at another time, or I keep it for trading. Another musician may have better luck with that particular lead than I did.

Not returning a call is a sign of bad manners and I have to admit that I get a little perverse about this sometimes. If I've left three messages and haven't received a return call from a client, I might leave five more messages—once a week for five weeks—just to bug them. I mean, they're not going give me a gig anyway, so what do I have to lose? It also keeps my name in front of their faces, so that in whatever context it comes up again, they are less likely to forget it.

Many clients have good reasons for not returning your calls that have nothing to do with you. If you haven't received a call back from someone, do a little extra research. The number could be wrong or the person whom you're trying to reach may no longer be working there. If you are calling a client who is associated with a college or university in March or April, he or she could be on spring break. The person may be on vacation or at a booking conference. Or, if you've called a working musician, he or she may be on the road. After a while, you will develop an instinct about these things and can sense whether you should call back later or not. Also, try to have your contacts' home numbers on file. Many times I'll leave messages on both business and home answering machines, saying that I have done so. By calling a person's home number, you might reach a client's family member and learn why you haven't been able to reach that person and when he or she will be available.

When one client recommends another, always ask if he or she has that person's home phone number. Club owners rarely give out their home numbers until a gig has been confirmed, if then. Some schools, high schools in particular, prohibit giving home phone numbers of their faculty members to callers. In this case, ask the secretary to please call the client's home for you, and relay the message that you've called. In any case, as soon as you've connected with a client who expresses interest in booking your band, be sure to ask for his or her home number, if he or she wouldn't mind giving it to you.

Sometimes you'll get a secretary instead if an answering machine. There are good secretaries, and bad ones as well. Some act as gatekeepers and protect their bosses from unwanted calls. If the secretary doesn't know your name, or if your name isn't on the boss's client list, he or she will never forward the message. Instead you'll be told that the boss is in a meeting, or on the phone, or at lunch, and to call back at another time. Or the secretary will take your name and number and will tell you that his or her boss will call you back. After the third message, with the same answer, you'll know you're getting a "long no." File it!

I happen to have a name that is difficult to catch over the phone. It's phonetically amorphous. To compensate for this, when I'm being introduced to someone or when I'm mentioning my name over the phone, I usually overenunciate it. Ninety-nine percent of the time people don't get it and I have to spell it out, and even then they have a hard time pronouncing it. However, I've managed to turn that in my favor when dealing with secretaries. If a secretary takes my number but doesn't ask me how to spell my name, I can usually assume that I won't get a callback. If he or she doesn't ask for a number and doesn't ask how to spell my name, I know he or she is not going to pass my message on to the client and I'm not going to be calling him or her back either. A professional secretary will ask for your number—even if you mention that the boss already has it—and will repeat it back to you. If you don't have a name like mine, it can be a good test to mumble yours a little to see if the secretary asks you to repeat it.

If you don't get a callback after your first message and you are ready to leave a second message, rephrase your rap a little so it won't sound like you are on autopilot. You already left enough information on your first call anyway. There's no need for you to repeat yourself.

If, several days after your second message, you *still* haven't received a callback, be patient. It is advisable to wait a week after your second message before you make the third call. This gives the client time to respond, and, most importantly, it protects you from making a nuisance of yourself. You don't want to be perceived as too pushy. Again, don't forget, always note the results of every call.

Keeping track of your negotiations and updating your information into your contact-manager program is a major component of the booking process, so it is absolutely essential to make good notes. Set the calendar in your computer so that it creates a call-back alarm that will remind you when a client is going to call you, or vice versa. Make sure that you note if you sent press material and a CD and the date. You should also note if and when you received a contract and the date you returned it. Most importantly, note the date by which the venue intends to give you its confirmation. This information is absolutely necessary to have when you're juggling tour dates and routing problems.

On the third callback, leave the same message as on your first call, but abbreviate it slightly. Finish your rap with the phrase: "I'd appreciate the courtesy of a return call." This gently reminds the client that he or she is being rude. Many a client has finally returned my call after I've said that.

Using Fax and E-mail

Generally it is not advisable to establish your initial contact by fax. It is too impersonal and you risk turning a potential client off. Only in certain situations is it advisable to make your initial contact by fax. The most commonly accepted situation in which to use a fax machine for making an initial contact is when you're contacting potential clients in a foreign country. Foreign contacts understand that time zones and telephone costs are factors in international communications. And they know you're going to follow up an international fax with a phone call anyway. You should have a fax version of your band's brochure, which you can send before or after your call. At the end of your introductory fax always include the statement: "A press kit and CD will be sent upon request." (This will be discussed further in chapter thirteen.) Wait a couple of days after you send the introductory fax and then make your first follow-up call.

I never send a fax to a contact at a school or an arts presenter unless he or she is expecting it. Some of these venues have only general office faxes and they are rarely found in individual's offices. In this situation a fax can easily get lost or ignored and never reach your client.

Of course, using a fax machine is proper and practical in situations other than making initial contact with foreign venues. It is especially useful in follow-up communications. A client's work schedule may differ from yours and vital information that you or your client needs is often best sent via fax. Faxing is also handy if you've got a full day of calls and a client's phone line is busy, or if your client is not in the office at the time you're free to contact him or her.

Letters of intent and contracts can often be sent by fax, but you'll want to check with the client first to make sure that this is acceptable. My contact-manager program has generic letters of intent and contracts in which the information from my contact file is automatically merged into a client and venue worksheet that will contain all the pertinent data for the gig on that date. After all the gig information is entered into the worksheet, information needed for contracts or letters of intent can be merged into them from the worksheet. Once the contract information has been entered into the contract, all I have to do is hit the print button and the contract is printed out in finished form. Only in rare situations, where the circumstances of a gig are unusual, do I have to create an individual letter of intent or contract. Automated generic letters and contracts can save you a lot of valuable time.

For some reason, contacting your potential client via E-mail, especially if that client is an educator, doesn't come off as cold as a sending a fax. There's another key benefit to using E-mail: attachments. For instance, you can attach the text from your brochure or press kit as a word-processing file or your band photo as a j-peg, tiff, or gif. And if a client has E-mail, he or she usually has Internet access as well, so you can direct him or her to your Web site, if you have one (and you should).

Determining Mailing Strategies

Shotgunning press kits is a common technique utilized by musicians who feel insecure about not being well known. To compensate for their lack of confidence or for their lack of knowledge about the industry, these musicians often mail out hundreds of press kits and CDs at a time. In the mailing-list business these kind of mailings are called "cold" mailings. The rule of thumb for cold mailings is that they yield, at the most, from 1 to 3 percent. If you mail 100 packages, you might get from one to three expressions of interest, and maybe one of them will eventually confirm. A good press kit—if you include the cost of paper, printing, photos, CDs, and mailing—can cost between five and seven dollars. Therefore, a cold mailing of 100 press kits can run between $500 and $700. If you only get one $1,500 gig out of the mailing, this approach is not very cost effective.

Shotgunning press kits may be good promotion in the long run, but it is an expensive and time consuming way to get gigs. It takes a lot of time to get the kits ready for mailing. Even if you use a form letter and mail merge, you still have to write and print a letter for each kit, assemble them, address the envelopes, and take them to the post office. And this doesn't include the time you have to spend researching your contact information to make sure you have the right person and contact address and phone number. There is no point in sending a kit to someone who no longer works at a particular venue.

Sending a press kit cold has a bit of a desperate feeling associated with it. This sort of initial contact can easily be construed by potential clients as overkill. Look at it from their point of view. They might wonder why a perfect stranger, whom they've never talked to, sent them such an expensive mailing. As experienced professionals, they'll assume that since they didn't receive any introductory call from you, it was a cold, mass mailing. It will appear that you're thinking of them as number forty-two of a mailing of one hundred. That's very impersonal, a little insulting, and doesn't make the client feel like you believe he or she is very important. It's not a very good way to begin a relationship. In fact, it could work in reverse and turn a client off. Establishing a personal relationship with a client is the key to successful marketing. You'll get more respect if you call first and then offer to send the client a kit as a follow-up to your discussion.

I don't send a press kit out until after I've made telephone contact and received an expression of interest. Even at that point I might just send a brochure. When a client is really interested, I follow up the brochure later with a press kit and CD. Most people are bombarded with information and don't have the time or the attention span to evaluate a comprehensive kit and listen to your CD.

If you feel the need to do a cold mailing, use a brochure. (For more about press kits and brochures, see chapter thirteen.) Even though you'll have to spend time writing a letter and labeling the envelopes, it's more cost effective to send brochures than to mail press kits.

One of the side benefits of doing a mailing is that it gives you a reason to call a contact: You want to confirm that he or she received the package. You've spent time and money mailing the material and it's perfectly reasonable to ascertain whether or not it arrived safely. You can then use the opportunity to feel the client out for a reaction. If the contact tells you that he or she can't use your band at that time, but that he or she will "keep your kit on file" for future reference, don't count on it. You'll probably have to send another one next year. Venue operators and administrations change and old files get thrown out. CDs mysteriously disappear and end up at home on people's CD racks.

ANTICIPATING THE ISSUES BEFORE YOU BEGIN NEGOTIATING

Although it may seem intimidating at first, anyone can learn the art of negotiation. The more you negotiate, the easier it becomes. Clients appreciate negotiating with a professional. Your ability to grasp the issues involved and the attitude you present will affect the outcome of your negotiation efforts. It takes time and experience to become comfortable in your new role as bandleader and come up with reasonable fee quotes. Initially, it's easy to either over- or underprice your group. Be patient. Don't expect to be right on the mark from the very beginning. It may take a year or two for you to find the right balance between what you are worth and what you can earn. With research, study, and experience, you'll eventually develop negotiation chops. Although touched upon here, the shelves of your local bookstore are filled with books on the subject of negotiation. If you don't find one that suits your needs, contact the Fisher Creative Group at (1-630) 378-4109 or on the Web at http://www.mcs.net/~fishercg/moneymusic. html and request a copy of the company's catalog of music-business books.

The Eight Rules for Booking a Band

Many bandleaders become discouraged the first time they begin booking their band. The majority of these frustrations stem from the fact that the bandleader is not familiar with the realities of the booking process. It is a slow process that takes a fair amount of time and dedication. It takes practice to learn how to speak confidently and convincingly about your band's merits without feeling as though you're being pushy or egotistical. It also takes time to become comfortable with the financial aspects of booking a band. Although there are no guarantees, keeping certain basic realities in mind will keep the odds of success in your favor.

The eight rules that will ensure that you have a realistic framework that guides your booking policies are:

- Keep your band on the road.
- Be flexible with your leader's fees.
- Never work for assholes.
- Price your band realistically.
- Know your bottom line.
- Book anchor, secondary anchor, and support gigs.
- Avoid conflicts of interest.
- Avoid double-booking and cancellations.

As you begin the booking process, try to remember each of these eight rules in turn. If you find yourself in a booking quandary, chances are that you have veered into a danger zone from one of these rules. If this happens, don't get discouraged. Simply take a minute to reevaluate the thinking process that led you to that quandary. It is okay to make mistakes; it is a sign that you're pushing yourself to try—and potentially succeed at—new things. But you should also try to learn from your mistakes. If you take the time to analyze how you made them, chances are that you'll be less likely to make the same mistake again.

KEEP YOUR BAND ON THE ROAD Experienced bandleaders realize this basic truth: Nothing can happen for your band if you don't keep it on the road. Performances are your most effective and least expensive form of self-promotion. Gigs lead to other gigs. However, each tour's budget is different. Just because the budget for a previous tour was high doesn't mean you shouldn't tour if you can't make the same income on a following tour. This also applies to your budget from gig to gig. One gig may earn $5,000 and another may earn only $500. If you need to fill in an open day, you can't afford to refuse the $500 gig. Besides, you never know what might happen on a gig.

I was once booking a tour in the Midwest that ended on a Thursday. The tour's budget was cool and I didn't need to book any more gigs to make the tour financially successful. Through a recommendation, I learned of a restaurant in a small town that featured jazz on weekends. The venue paid $300 less than our base salary for the two weekend nights, but the owner had an arrangement with a local hotel so the rooms were free. The owner was also a gourmet chef and the food was free. Because my two primary concerns for the band are creating maximum exposure and playing as much music as possible, I took the gig.

The second night of the gig, the director of a local arts presenter organization came in to hear the trio. His organization just happened to be a network site for the Lila Wallace–Reader's Digest Foundation. If you played a network site, you became eligible for funding from the Foundation's Satellite Tour Support program. The director loved the band and invited us to play a concert for the organization's concert series the next year. The concert paid five times what the restaurant gig had paid (plus expenses), earned us thousands of dollars of satellite tour support, and became an anchor gig for another three-week tour. That tour would have never happened if I hadn't taken the restaurant gig. You can't afford to get an attitude just because one gig doesn't pay as much as another.

Even the biggest names adjust their fees to fit the situation. Art Blakey's band would come back from a tour in Japan and take a week-long gig in San Francisco for a third of the price they got for the Japanese tour—simply because the band was on its way back to New York and the gig fit into the travel itinerary.

This point is also illustrated by a promoter's story. He got a call from an agent who was booking one of the biggest names in jazz. It was a quintet that traveled with a road manager and a roadie—that's seven people who needed to be paid, transported, and housed for each day on the road. Because of the band's high overhead, they couldn't afford too many days off. They had a Thursday night open that the agent was trying to fill. He offered the band for $12,000. The promoter had that night open and wanted to book the band, but declined. He knew his local audience couldn't support such a high fee. The agent called back a week later and offered the band for $8,000. Again, the promoter had to decline. A week later the agent called back again and made an offer for $4,000, with the promoter paying hotel expenses. The promoter knew that a concert for that fee would work, so he accepted.

BE FLEXIBLE WITH YOUR LEADER'S FEES As a new bandleader you'll have to accept the fact that from time to time you won't make as much money as the musicians in your band, let alone a leader's fee. This is not exactly an unknown phenomenon and is a subject of much wry humor among bandleaders. A top-named ex–Miles Davis sideman left Miles's band to begin his own career as a bandleader. His sextet reportedly lost $10,000 the first year it was on the road. Fortunately, he was using the income from a hit tune he'd written to support the start of his own band.

Don't expect your sidemen to block out a period of time for your tour and then, at the last minute, cancel the tour because you are not making enough money for yourself. They held that time open for you and will suffer economic hardship because they've refused work with other bands. This type of situation can seriously affect your band's stability and your credibility as an employer. Be as committed to your band members as they are to you. If you cancel a tour, you'll also appear undependable to those clients who booked your band, and could end up losing gigs at those venues for future tours. You will also have wasted all of the work that you did on the tour up to that point. There are strategies that I'll discuss later on in this chapter that you can use to put the odds in your favor and keep this kind of situation to a minimum, but it happens to many bandleaders, established or not.

Strange as it may seem, the length of a tour can affect a leader's take-home pay. Longer tours can often result in less take-home money than shorter ones. Sometimes, even though you've added more income to a tour, the added expenses of transportation and housing for open dates can reduce a tour's overall balance. A tour balance is the amount, plus salary, that a leader takes home after all the expenses of a tour have been paid.

NEVER WORK FOR ASSHOLES Trying to achieve your long-term goals is going to be hard enough without working for unreliable people who cause you added stress, trouble, and expense. One of the most basic policies I established when I began to book my trio was: "Never work for assholes." If you're on the phone with a client and your asshole detector starts going off, forget the gig, get off the phone, and don't bother calling again. Even if you get the gig, it won't be worth the trouble it will cause you.

Here's a story about the only time I ever had any trouble with a gig in all of the years I've been booking my own band. I once booked a gig at a club in Detroit. As contracted, and advertised on the club's marquee, we were supposed to play the club for three nights—from Friday through Sunday. It was a percentage deal with a guaranteed minimum, and the venue was paying the hotel rooms. The owner did virtually no promotion for the gig. Accordingly, Friday night's business was pretty skimpy. Because of word of mouth, Saturday night's crowd was about 50 percent better, but the owner was starting to look at us funny, and I was getting a bad vibe from him.

At ten o'clock on Sunday morning my phone rang. It was the club owner telling us not to come in that night. I tried, to no avail, to convince him that the word of mouth was growing and that we would do well that night. I bitched that if this happened, I would be losing money on the gig—as I had to pay the other guys anyway. In compensation, he offered to absorb the cost of the third night's hotel rooms, which I accepted. Later that day I called an old friend who had been at the gig every night and told him what happened. He mentioned that he'd been driving by the club that afternoon and had seen the owner up on a ladder knocking our names off the marquee with a broomstick. I called the club later that day pretending to be a customer wanting to make a reservation. They told me that my band had only been booked for two nights. From that time on I instituted my "no assholes" policy.

PRICE YOUR BAND REALISTICALLY The two elements that go into successful pricing are your bottom line and what the market will bear. Your fees are *not* based upon what you feel you are worth. No matter how much you feel your music is worth, without setting realistic economic goals, you'll never get a gig. Coming to a realistic self-evaluation of your marquee value can be very difficult. It depends on the length of your career to date, your media exposure, your recording career, and how much you have traveled with other bands. Some musicians have name value and underestimate it, others have no name value and overestimate it. Research this issue with other bandleaders of similar name value to see what their fees are for the same venues you play. Opinions may vary as to your band's value. Each bandleader has to find out for him- or herself, through experimentation and experience, the practical fee range for his or her band.

One of my early mentors, Jaki Byard, was playing intermission solo piano opposite a big band in a Boston club. He had just finished a set and swung so hard that he received a standing ovation. Not exactly happy with the club's pay scale, he was standing outside the club after the concert yelling, somewhat tongue in cheek, "I should be getting paid $100 a note for this music!" As much as you'd like to be paid $100 a note, in a market economy your value is dictated by the realities of the marketplace, which includes your client's perception of your ability to provide an exceptional service for a reasonable fee, your marquee value, your contribution to the venue's image, and your client's profit motive.

A new band can't command the same fees that a well-established band can. Unless you have an expensive band of all-stars, you have a distinct advantage over most well-established bands. You can offer good music at a lower price than they can. Don't get greedy just because you think the venue has a humongous budget. In the beginning, you should be figuring your fee in terms of what you can afford to work for in relation to what you think the market will bear for a new band. If your band eventually gets hot, you can adjust your fees accordingly.

Whenever possible, do extra research on a venue by calling someone whom you know has already played at the venue. Try to find out what they were paid, how they were treated, and any other relevant information about the client and venue. This information will help you determine your financial and logistical parameters as you negotiate with the client.

Don't price yourself out of the market and get so locked into a price range that real opportunities get away from you. Be willing to adjust your bottom line according to such factors as the relationship you are trying to establish with the client, the significance of a particular gig, and whether you are filling a weekday or a weekend slot. Always regard the price you are offering as the starting point of the negotiation. Your starting point should not be so extreme that you turn off the client and have to backtrack to a much lower fee position in order to get the gig. You'll look like you're greedy or unrealistic and don't know what you're doing. Clients are constantly in contact with musicians who are poor businesspeople. They appreciate it when they run into a good one. You'll stand out and you may even get a gig on that basis alone. Ask the client what his or her budget considerations are. Most clients have a good idea of how much money is available or how big their audience is for your kind of music.

If the client says that he or she has to check the budget and get back to you, or balks at your first offer, mention that there may be some flexibility in your fee, depending on the amount of support work in the area. This is an especially valid strategy when negotiating with colleges and universities. Also if a few other gigs in the area have not yet committed, mention it, saying that you will have a better idea of how your tour budget stands at a later date. This extends the negotiating time without either party making a decision and leaves you open to lowering your price later on.

KNOW YOUR BOTTOM LINE When pricing your band you'll have to consider two things: what the market will bear for each venue (this varies according to each venue type) and your bottom line. Three factors go into estimating your bottom line: your total tour income, your total base salaries, and an estimate of your total tour expenses. Your total tour income is derived from adding up the income from each gig. Your total base salary figure is derived from the total amount of your band's salaries, including yours (without a leader's fee). Tour expenses, such as hotels and transportation, usually average between 20 and 30 percent of a tour's total budget. With exceptions, each gig should pay more than your base salary for the day of the gig. This overage can range from $50 to $1,000 or more per gig.

Your base salary figure also depends on how much work you'll be doing for a client and can vary from venue to venue, depending on its type. Club gigs are usually limited to two or three sets. Salaries for club gigs usually don't vary that much because of this factor. However, college gigs (where you're doing solo and group clinics), big-band rehearsals, and concerts will have more complex base salaries.

Suppose you have a quartet that operates with a base salary of $200 per musician, per gig. That comes to a base salary figure of $800 per working day. Let's also assume that your tour expenses will add an additional 25 percent to each working-day's expenses. That's an additional $200 per gig for tour expenses. Your average basic income requirement will then be $1,000 per gig. To keep abreast of how well the finances of a tour are going, divide the total tour income by the number of working days. If the figure you get is more than $1,000 per day, your tour is looking pretty good.

Another quick way to get a ballpark figure of the financial status of your tour at any particular moment is by deducting from your total tour income your total base salaries (without deducting your tour expenses). That shouldn't be too difficult because your tour income and your salaries are the first, and most fixed, figures you'll enter into your budget. Your transportation and hotel costs are usually variable, and are the last figures to be entered into your budget. If, after deducting your total salaries from your total tour income, your tour balance is between 25 and 30 percent or more, your tour is in good financial shape. With this kind of estimate at your fingertips, you can judge how flexible you can be from gig to gig.

BOOK ANCHOR, SECONDARY ANCHOR, AND SUPPORT GIGS Although one of the goals of any tour is to make it financially profitable, it is sometimes the bandleader's lot to make less than his or her employees. That is an inescapable reality that every leader will have to accept from time to time. However, there are certain strategies that you can employ when booking a tour that can increase your tour's income, thereby keeping the tour's budget in the black—and in turn increasing your own income from the tour.

Tour gigs fall into one of the three categories, which are defined by the range of their fees. Listed from the highest to the lowest fees, these categories are: anchor gigs, secondary anchor gigs, and support gigs. Each of these three categories is discussed in the pages that follow.

Anchor Gigs: Anchor gigs are your best-paying and most important gigs in a tour. They are also the foundation upon which a tour is built and are the first gigs to look for when you're booking a tour. Anchor gigs put the odds in your favor that you'll have enough money in the budget to pay your band and make your expenses. These better-paying gigs are usually festivals, college festivals, concerts or residencies associated with educational institutions, and gigs that are sponsored by cultural or non-profit arts presenters.

Anchor gigs set the geographical region of your tour, and determine where you'll be looking for secondary anchor and support gigs. Anchor gigs are the gigs that you book the farthest in advance. Some musicians don't like to book a year or more in advance, but it's very practical to do so. For instance, while booking a current tour, you may find that one of the venues you've contacted is already booked for the time period on which you're working. However, if you have an anchor gig confirmed in the same geographical area a year or more later, you're in a good position to ask your client if he or she would be interested in having your band perform during that later period. This is the advantage of booking anchor gigs as far in advance as possible.

Ask your contacts at your potential anchor gigs what their lead times are. Make a note in your calendar to call them a month before those times. This separates those venues that have genuine interest from those that don't, because some clients won't directly say "we don't want you" (which I prefer), but will instead give you a "long no" by giving you a call-back date that is too late. If you call a venue for which you've confirmed the lead time and the client says, "Sorry, we're already booked. We'll keep your press kit and CD on file and call you next year, if we need you," reverse the situation before the client gets in his or her "sorrys" by saying, "Thanks for taking the time to consider us. I'll keep your name on file and call you sometime in the future when we're coming back your way." This response puts the shoe on the other foot, and leaves the client with the impression that you have self-respect and expect to be a touring band for a long time to come. Keep the contact info on file.

Securing a couple of gigs in some clubs doesn't ensure that you have enough work upon which to base a tour. You need at least one anchor gig to make a tour work. In addition, having more than one anchor gig in neighboring regions can extend the length of your tour.

An anchor gig may pay for part or all of your transportation from your home to the venue, and back again. This financial commitment on the part of the anchor gig venue significantly lowers your transportation expenses for the entire tour. An anchor gig with full or partial transportation support has made many a tour possible that otherwise would have been difficult to finance. Even though you may have other gigs on your tour, figure this expense as a home-to-venue-to-home round-trip fare. Have your travel agent send you a copy of the estimated fares and submit it to the venue. The venue can pay your transportation expenses in one of two ways: They can pay it in advance, after the contract is signed, *or* they can reimburse you at the time of the performance.

Whenever possible, discourage the venue from making your travel arrangements for you. As an anchor gig will be one of the first gigs you will book for a tour, you won't know your tour routing at the time that you book the anchor gig. For this reason, the responsibility for travel arrangements is safer in your hands. Occasionally you may find that your client is resistant to letting you make your travel arrangements yourself. One of the main points of resistance is that some clients may be under the impression that you will use their transportation money to help finance your tour (and not just their gig).

If this is the case, the client will sometimes suggest that other venues on the tour should share some of your band's transportation expenses. This argument is best countered by making the client understand that it is not financially viable for your band to come to their venue for just one gig. Explain to your client that you have a responsibility to your band members to keep them working, that your band members may have offers for work that they will be missing or interrupting by going on this tour, and that you need to offer your band members a decent inducement to come on the road.

The fee range for anchor gigs should be between three and four times your base salary. For instance, if your base salary (for a quartet) is $200 per musician, per gig, that means your fee for an anchor gig should be between $2,400 and $3,200. Of course, you'll have to be flexible within your client's budget, but this is a practical way to estimate a beginning asking price.

Secondary Anchor Gigs: Secondary anchor gigs fall into the mid-range of performance fees. The fee range for secondary anchor gigs should be between double or triple your base salary, or (assuming the same base salaries as in the example above) between $1,600 and $2,400 per gig. Sometimes, if you haven't been able to secure an anchor gig for a tour, you can make a tour financially viable by booking three or more secondary anchor gigs. The combined income from these secondary anchor gigs may even be higher than that of one anchor gig.

Once you have confirmed your anchor gig, you can begin looking for secondary anchor gigs to add additional income to the tour budget. Although not always possible, you should try to book and confirm the higher-paying gigs of a tour first. Remember, when shotgunning your calls, you'll be contacting venues in every range. The higher-paying gigs may not commit before some of the lower-paying gigs.

Support Gigs: Support gigs are your tour's lowest paying gigs. Jazz clubs are the main venues that will fall into this category. Fees will vary according to the gig and the contractual agreement. As mentioned above, you will want to try to book your higher-paying gigs before you book your support gigs. However, this is not always possible.

One of the functions of support gigs is to fill in open dates in your tour's schedule. Sometimes it will be necessary for you to accept a gig that pays a fee that is lower than your base salary. The rationale behind this is that it is better to have some money coming in—to offset travel and accommodation expenses—than to have open, unpaid days in your tour itinerary. Hotel and van-rental fees for open days can eat up a tour balance. However, as long as you have an anchor gig or two in place, your tour balance should come out okay. For instance, if you have two anchor gigs that are paying $2,500 each, you'll have $5,000 of tour income. Deduct your base salary of $1,600 from those two gigs (i.e., $800 per gig), and you'll have $3,400 of income left over. This "extra" money can be used to cover tour expenses and the shortfall from lower-paying gigs on your tour. Add to that balance any income from secondary anchor gigs and you have quite a bit of flexibility in accepting fees that don't meet your base salary.

Because their overhead is usually so high, clubs are highly competitive and have to be cautious about who they hire. Most club owners are tough negotiators. With some exceptions, clubs usually hire out-of-town bands only on weekends, their strongest nights. Weeknights are usually reserved for local musicians. Clubs attract a certain kind of audience that other venues don't. If building an audience base is one of your long-term goals, you'll need to play them—even if they don't pay as well as other gigs on your tour.

Clubs usually can't afford to hire a new band or a midcareer artist who hasn't developed a large audience base. Similarly, because of the low pay scale at clubs, your band probably can't afford to play them exclusively. As a result, club work for emerging or midcareer musicians who don't have a large following is usually subsidized work. You can only afford to play these clubs *if* other better-paying gigs in a tour can make up for the salary shortfall. Because of these factors, club gigs are usually a shared experience between a club owner and a band. When negotiating with a particularly hard-nosed club owner, you might want to gently and respectfully remind him or her of this fact.

I spent the first twenty years of my career playing in jazz clubs. Funky as they sometimes were, clubs still generate a special fondness for me, especially because playing in them is such an intimate experience. However, now that I am booking and touring my own band, I focus my booking efforts in what is called the "fine arts sector" of the music business: cultural presenters, jazz societies, educational institutions (high schools, colleges, and universities), and other nonprofit presenters. When I was coming up in the jazz world, there were more clubs that hired bands for five to seven nights a week than there are now and you could fill a whole tour playing them. In this day and age there just aren't enough jazz clubs like that in existence to work them exclusively. Looking over my booking history, I would estimate that jazz clubs account for only 5 to 20 percent of our bookings. They still come in handy for filling in weekend dates and sometimes off nights, and I still love to play in them.

Before proposing your fee to a club owner, ask how many seats the club has, how many sets you will play, and if the club plans to turn the house over after each set. You should also ask what the owner would expect to charge at the door for your appearance and whether he or she charges different prices for first and second sets. If it's a 100-seat club and they charge $10 per person, then you know the *most* you can ask for is $1,000—maybe less if the venue is going to pay for your hotel. If you're not sure how well you can draw at a club, estimate your fee at half of the house seating (i.e., from the previous example, $500) plus hotels, if possible.

Avoid negotiating a fee that you can't earn. If you are talking to a client about playing a club for the first time and you want a return performance at a later date, set your fee reasonably. If you don't earn your fee from the cost of admissions, there is a good chance that you'll never get asked back to that club again. One way to avoid not being asked back to a venue is to accept a low fee for the first appearance. However, if you decide to do this, frame your agreement as a "first-time" fee. That way, if you do well during that appearance, you can raise your fee for return engagements based upon your draw for the first gig, assuming that your audience base for that venue will increase for subsequent engagements. If you don't draw well the first time but also haven't charged an excessive fee, you may still be able to return to the club for your original fee.

An alternative to a low, fixed fee is a percentage agreement. This kind of agreement generally gives you a minimum, guaranteed fee and a percentage of the cover charge. With percentage agreements both you and the venue share the risk. There are many different kinds of percentage agreements. One kind of percentage agreement is the "minimum guarantee plus." Under this kind of agreement, the minimum, guaranteed fee is generally 50 percent of what the house would make if it was a sold-out show. In other words, if the club has 100 seats and the owner is charging $10 per person, then your guaranteed fee would be $500. Plus, you will receive a percentage of the admission price for all of the tickets sold after the club has recouped the cost of your guarantee.

Another standard percentage agreement (one that is slightly more risky for the band) is that the band receives 100 percent of the door charge, but only *after* the club's expenses have been covered. If you enter into a percentage agreement with a club owner, make sure you know at which point the percentage kicks in. Will it start after the guarantee has been made at the door, or after the club's total expenses—like advertising, staff, and hotels—have been covered? Sometimes working for a percentage means that your band will be paid no matter what the turnout, but that your salary, as the band-leader, is at risk. This can be an acceptable risk, if you have excess funds in your tour balance and can absorb the loss if you don't make your full fee.

Even more risky than a percentage agreement is an agreement whereby you work for just the money received from admissions and the cost of your hotel. This is a very risky proposition and is only advisable if you are sure you are going to do good business, or that your tour budget can absorb the salaries of the band members—if something happens, like a torrential downpour, and you don't draw a crowd. Some big-name artists work only for the door and make incredible amounts because they draw so well.

When negotiating with a club client, I have sometimes observed that when I readily agree to a percentage arrangement, the client will quickly change his or her mind and offer me a better flat fee. I think that clients interpret my readiness to take a gamble as a sign of confidence that I will draw well. If club owners sense that a gig is going to go well, they would rather give the band a flat fee, taking the chance that they will make more profit for themselves, rather than let the band take the chance and make the profit.

The process of setting a fee can be quite creative, especially if you feel that the client is interested, but is having a hard time figuring out a way to hire your band. You may have to pay for your band's accommodations or not, depending on the club's situation. If you accept a bigger gamble on a percentage arrangement, you might be in a good negotiating position to convince a client to absorb the costs for your hotel charges. This approach can be especially beneficial if you have a gaping hole in your itinerary for a weekend.

Clubs will often ask you if you have any tour support from your record company. If you have any kind of record company tour support, mention it during your negotiations. It might make a difference whether or not a club can afford to hire your band. (For more about this, see chapter thirteen.)

AVOID CONFLICTS OF INTEREST Whenever you're planning to book gigs that are within an hour and one-half drive of one another, ask both venues if doing the other gig would be a conflict. You can really get on a client's bad side if, after signing a contract, he or she finds out you took another gig nearby. This is because two gigs in close proximity could undermine each other's success. Most of the time this isn't a problem at all, but it is always better to check.

The band of a well-known tenor player had a $5,000 anchor gig concert at a library. It was planned as the first concert of a major tour. The contract stipulated that the tenor player couldn't play any gigs within a 120-mile radius of the library within two months of the engagement (either before or after), which is a common provision. There was, in the same town, a small jazz club that hired singles to play with a local rhythm section on weekends. A month before the concert, assuming the gig was so low profile that the library wouldn't know about it, the tenor player took the $500 gig. The library *did* find out about it, and canceled his contract. Not only did he lose out, but so did his band and his agent. Because the library concert was also the anchor gig for a tour, the budget was so seriously affected that the tour had to be canceled.

If there is a conflict, you'll have to decide which gig you want to take. Your decision will be based on budget considerations, audience exposure, whether or not you are likely to return to the venue, the potential for media exposure, and the ease of routing. If one gig doesn't pay as much as another, but there's a radio broadcast involved, the higher exposure and the possibility of ending up with a potential record master might outweigh the higher fee at the alternative venue. If a conflict arises, save the rejected gig for a later date. It's always better to turn down a gig because you are too busy than have a gig refused to you.

AVOID DOUBLE-BOOKING AND CANCELLATIONS In general, it is advisable to avoid double-booking and cancellations. However, booking a tour is a complicated process, one that requires a lot of flexibility. There are some strategies that you can use to avoid these circumstances, but it is impossible to avoid scheduling conflicts all of the time. When these conflicts arise, it is crucial that you handle them professionally and respectfully.

When booking a tour, there often comes a time—and sometimes it happens more than once—when you reach a brick wall and don't know how you're going to drum up any more gigs to flesh out your tour schedule. You may have no luck finding any other gigs, but after staring at your calendar for an hour, you realize that by readjusting your routing, you can minimize your days off. If you decide to reroute your tour, you'll probably have to call some of your "possibles" (i.e., the clients with whom you have been negotiating, but with whom you haven't yet solidified a deal) to see if you can change the dates under discussion. Most venues are familiar with routing problems and understand if you have to change a date. If they can, they will.

You may think it's not fair to a venue to triple-book each day on your tour. However, be assured, you are not the only artist a venue is considering for a particular date. Most venues are at least triple-booking you—juggling three or four bands for a date they want to fill. If, by happenstance, you double-book a date, it looks much better for you to call the client back and say, "I'm sorry, we're already booked for that day," than for him or her to call you back to cancel the gig. You might even be able to book that gig for another open date.

Be careful about canceling doubled dates. If you cancel one gig before the other one comes through, the second gig may fall through and you'll be left with a hole in your itinerary. Canceling a doubled date is a judgment you can make only when you have enough information to feel that it's safe to do so. You might want to wait until you're relatively sure the date is going to happen. Although you may never be absolutely sure about a gig until you get a signed contract, for the most part you can count on clients who make verbal commitments. Don't wait for a signed contract to come in before canceling a doubled date. Canceling too late could cause a booking problem for the venue and you could come off as looking unreliable to the client, which may cause you to lose a gig at that venue in the future.

When booking a tour for a region that you've previously toured, you will undoubtedly contact many clients that you've worked for in the past. Some may not want you back for this particular tour. In this case, you might be able to use a gig you canceled last time this time around. It is important to be professional, even if a gig doesn't work out for a particular tour. If you find that you've double-booked a day, rather than call a venue and cancel a date outright, see if you can find an alternative date that works for both of you. If not, thank the client for his or her interest and ask if he or she would mind if you called the next time you're in the area. That venue could come in handy when you're filling in a hole the next time around; and you've already done the groundwork to establish the contact, so you may as well nurture it so you can use it next time.

If a potential client can't confirm a particular gig, ask him or her for suggestions of another venue to work. It is important to do this while you're still on the phone with the client. Forgetting to do this and calling the client back later wastes his or her time and makes it look like you're scuffling for work, an image you must avoid. However, sometimes—like when you have a tour just about fully booked and need to fill in a hole or two—you can call someone back for an information request. This is recommended only if you've got a lot of work booked at that time. You don't want to be telling any stories. Word can get around to presenters, which may result in a loss of credibility.

UNDERSTANDING THE FIVE STAGES OF NEGOTIATION

Some people say that "all life is politics." Since negotiation is a big part of politics, if life is politics, then negotiation is a part of life as well. We negotiate all the time, quite often without even consciously being aware of it. Each negotiation involves elements of psychology and is constructed in stages. Being aware of and in control of these elements and stages will help you become a successful negotiator.

Negotiations progress in stages. Each stage has its own separate focus. The five stages to every client negotiation are:

- making the introductory call;
- setting the date;
- negotiating your fee;
- making follow-up calls;
- getting a commitment.

The skills that it takes to become a successful sideman are very different than the skills that it takes to be a successful bandleader. And this fact is perhaps most readily detected when you, as the bandleader, take on the role of negotiator. Be patient with yourself as you begin to become comfortable wearing this new hat. It takes time to develop strong negotiation skills. Focusing on the five stages listed above should help keep you on track.

Making the Introductory Call

The focus of an introductory call should be the client, not you. The first few minutes on the phone with a potential client are the most crucial stage of a negotiation. This introduction sets the tone for each stage and carves the pathway for the negotiation. Successful negotiations rely on an intuitive process that in turn depends on understanding a client's psychology and needs. A client will send you the appropriate signals and, if you're paying attention and know what to look for, these signals will give you the clues for an appropriate response. Each stage of a negotiation follows certain general, predictable paths of call and response. The end goal of the introductory call is to receive an expression of interest from the client. To attain this goal, your personality must successfully interact with the client's personality, and you must stimulate the client's interest in hiring your band. Once you have gained an expression of interest, you can move on to the later stages of the negotiation.

HOW PERSONALITIES INTERACT The music business is 25 percent business and 75 percent personal relations. Try to establish good personal relations with every client. This will directly affect the success of your business. The tone of your voice and the attitude you project say a lot about you. Your manner should be friendly and humorous, low-keyed but upbeat, and devoid of any suggestion of high-pressure tactics. I had one client with whom I had been talking for several years, just over the phone. Finally a gig came together and I got to meet him in person. One of the first things he complimented me on was my ability to make our communications so personal, as though we were old friends. Relationships in the music business are generally informal. Use first names whenever possible. Reactions vary from client to client, but I have found that most of the people in the music business respond well to this personal touch.

The attitude you adopt before calling a client is crucial to the success of the contact. Prepare your attitude before you pick up the phone. Essentially, you're calling the client to tell him or her: "You're going to give me a gig." However, you don't want the client to know that this is what you're thinking. Your attitude should communicate that you are a friendly, well-mannered, and serious musician, and that you are offering a valuable and affordable service that no one else can provide. You don't want the client to feel that he or she is *supposed* to hire your band, or is an idiot who has no appreciation for music, or has no respect for who you are. No one *has* to hire you. The decision is up to the client. You want to make that decision as easy as possible.

When you call a potential client, you are, fundamentally, selling yourself as a person as well as an artist. If your introductory call doesn't seem to be working, try reevaluating and revising your approach and the attitude you project to see if your selling rap is turning potential clients off. Even if you're not naturally gregarious, you can develop good telephone skills over time. Be patient with yourself, it will happen. It just takes practice and regular self-evaluation.

UNDERSTANDING YOUR CLIENT'S PERSONALITY Most clients are pleased to talk with an artist, especially if they know your name and music. They also have a chance to assess your personality and business acumen as well as whether you're reliable, easy to work with, and honest. When you call a client, the psychology of "rubbing elbows with the artist" goes to work for you. The rubbing-elbows factor is an important ingredient in the music business. Jazz music departments graduate approximately 30,000 students a year. Rather than becoming working musicians themselves, the greater percentage of these graduates end up providing valuable services in the jazz music community by working as part of the vast support structure it takes to keep performing artists functioning. They are knowledgeable jazz fans and supporters who become arts presenters and administrators, recording engineers and executives, club owners, promotional people, agents, and managers, to name but a few. Most of these people started with the same goals as performing artists, love the music deeply, and like to feel that they're part of the music. For these reasons, most of the people you talk with enjoy the client-artist interaction. Even if you're a new artist, you will find that people will want to talk with you because they like to know who's coming up on the music scene and they appreciate speaking with someone who is talented and working hard to make his or her place in the world.

Clients are inundated with calls from agents, managers, and artists with attitudes. This can work in your favor. If you have good phone technique, your potential clients will enjoy talking with you. However, they are often as short on time as you are. Be considerate of this. You can tell by the tone of your contact's voice when he or she picks up the phone if you've caught him or her at a particularly busy or stressful moment. Accordingly, you won't always run into clients who are all sunshine and have hearts full of love.

The mind-set of a client comes in all colors and sizes. Sometimes clients will put up a barrier that is hard to break through. However, quite often you can employ countermeasures that will get you past the stumbling blocks. The trick is to determine what the block is and why it is there.

Some clients think you're calling just to take their money. Since this is partly true of any gig that you're booking, you should assume that this will be part of the mind-set of every client. If you sense this is happening, explain that working for the client would be a partnership between you and the venue. If the client offers you a fee that is very low, explain that, in general, you can't afford to work for a fee that low. However, if you look at your tour and determine that your budget will allow you to take this lower-paying gig, then accept the gig, adding the explanation that the higher fees of other gigs on the tour are making your appearance at their venue possible. This approach will allow you to accept the gig at the lower fee (whereby filling a costly gap in your itinerary), make the client feel that you are accommodating his or her financial needs, and hopefully break the ice so that you can work at the venue again (for a higher fee) at a later time.

Clients often think you need them more than they need you. They have an over-inflated estimation of their importance and don't realize that there are more gigs out there than you could work in a lifetime. I once buttonholed a presenter at a convention whose venue I had been trying to book for years without success. I asked him when he was going to have our trio perform. He replied, "Oh, Hal, you don't need us. You seem to be doing quite well." I agreed with him saying, "That's true. We don't need you. We're working all over the world, but *you* do need *us*." (The point being that, as a musician, you are providing a valuable service that many people enjoy and it's not a matter of what the venue can do for you, but what you can do for the venue.) Interestingly, we played that venue a year later.

Every now and then you'll encounter a client who is so "star" oriented that he or she won't talk to you if you're not a big name. These kinds of clients are intoxicated with power because they hold the purse strings to fat budgets and control the artists' roster at a high-profile venue. Be patient. Assure the client that you intend to be around for a long time, that you'll be calling again, and that you hope he or she will keep you in mind for the future. These people network all the time and the word about your music will eventually get around. Also, administrators and venue operators change all the time. The next time you call you could be speaking with someone completely different.

Many clients have preferences for particular kinds of music. If you sense that a client has a strong leaning toward a musical genre, tell him or her something about your band and its music. Describe the tunes you play. Emphasize that your band is not just a pickup group, but that it has been together some time and has a high level of rapport. Most audiences are tired of hearing pickup bands that were put together for just one gig or tour. Assure the client that your music is well appreciated by audiences of all ages, and mention similar gigs you've played. Suggest that he or she contact other venues for an evaluation. Offer to send the client a CD and brochure.

The most difficult clients are the ones who have "a clarinet in their closet." This expression is used to describe an individual who started out playing music, but failed or gave up. These kinds of people often love you because they wanted to do what you're doing, but at the same time they envy you because you're doing it and they are not. People with "a clarinet in their closet" are different from the people described earlier who went to music school. Music school graduates studied music, but at an early point in their development decided that they wanted to be involved indirectly in the industry, rather than become musicians themselves. A person "with a clarinet…" attempted to do what you're doing and didn't stick with it. The fact that he or she feels compelled to tell you about past accomplishments indicates that he or she is still carrying around a chip on his or her shoulder. Most often these people are insulting and demeaning. Avoid them like the plague.

Achieving some intuition regarding a client's psychological makeup is the first step toward creating a good personal relationship. And the key factor that will determine how well you evaluate a client's makeup is how well you listen to the client and pick up on the subtle—and sometimes not so subtle—signals that he or she sends to you. Learning to "read" a client is where the real art of negotiation begins; sometimes it is not so much what you say, but what you *hear* that can get a relationship off on solid ground. Once you've established a general rapport, then you're on your way toward gaining an expression of interest from your client.

GAINING AN EXPRESSION OF INTEREST The primary function of the first few interactions with a client during an introductory call is to stimulate a client's interest in hiring you. You've initiated the contact, so the ball is in your court and you may have to work very hard to create that interest. When calling a client for the first time, don't assume that he or she will recognize your name and know all about your career. If you sense that a client needs to know more about you, tell him or her something about yourself and offer to send a brochure. If the client expresses interest in receiving the material, say that you'll pop it in the mail immediately. Then, a week or so after you have sent it, call the client to see if he or she is still interested, and if so, say that you'll be glad to send your press kit and CD. Watch out though, you'd be surprised at how many clients act like they're interested in hiring you, but are only interested in having your CDs in their personal collections.

You'll know you've gained a genuine expression of interest when the client starts asking *you* questions—for example, if the client wants to know more about you, your band, and when you will be in their area. Getting an expression of interest doesn't mean you've got the gig, though. This is just the clincher of the first step in the five-step negotiation process. If you gain an expression of interest, it means that you've handled the introductory call successfully and you can move on to the succeeding stages of setting the date, negotiating your fees, making follow-up calls, and getting a commitment.

SAMPLE SCRIPTS

Once the client has picked up the telephone, the negotiation path that you choose to follow will be guided by your status as a musician. One path is for musicians who are just starting to build a reputation. Another is for the midcareer musician with some name value. You could also have name recognition, but if the client has not heard of you, then you may have to take a more general approach—at least at first. These initial transactions serve two purposes: They give you the opportunity to get information about the client's attitude and needs as well as generate interest in your band.

Sometimes you can sense a client's attitude by the manner and tone of voice that he or she uses when answering the phone. If the client picks up the phone and brusquely says "Yeah?" without mentioning his or her name, the client has poor manners. You might be talking to someone who has an arrogant personality and who automatically assumes that everyone knows who he or she is. This modus operandi puts you in a defensive position. Arrogant people prefer for you to ask them questions, rather than to ask the questions themselves. So when you say "Hello. Is this Joe Johnson?" and you get another "Yeah," the odds are that this individual is not going to do the normally polite thing and ask who's calling. This kind of interaction keeps you on the defensive and in the position of having to introduce yourself. Whether you have a name or not, if your conversation starts out this way, you can be pretty sure you've got a hard sell on your hands.

At this point, many callers get a little nervous because the client is not responding in a human fashion. Get off the defensive by turning the client's approach to your advantage. If he or she is using short statements, you should use short statements. Don't give the client your whole rap in the next response. Just announce yourself, declaring "This is Bill Smith calling." Don't use the phrase "My name is...." This is slightly defensive behavior. By mentioning your name, the ball is in the client's court and he or she is forced to ask you the questions.

The client's next response will be very telling. If he or she follows with another "Yeah?" then your tactic failed. Give it one last shot by saying "Sorry to bother you. It sounds like I called at a bad time. Perhaps it would be better if I called you at a later date." At this point, the conversation will go in one of two ways. If the client says, "Okay," then hang up and put the client's name in your circular file. If the client finally relents and says, "What can I do for you?" then you have gained the client's attention. The client is now asking the questions. You can proceed to the next set of transactions.

Most of your clients are not going to be as difficult as the client described in the above scenario, but it's no secret that there are some rather forbidding people in the music industry.

The next series of transactions tends to follow only a few standard variations. Without seeming to brag, when talking with a new potential client try to frame your responses in a way that gives that person the impression you're working quite a bit. If you're a young musician and just starting out, you can safely assume that the client will not be familiar with your name.

> **You:** *"Our [band, trio, quartet, quintet] will be on tour, promoting our new record release and will be in your area in March." (Make sure to mention just the time period and not any specific dates.) "I thought I'd give you a call to see if you'd be interested in having us come to [the venue's name] to play for you during that period."*

If you're a midcareer musician, the transaction could go in several different ways, depending on whether the client knows your name or not.

> **You:** *"Hi, [client's first name]! This is [your name] calling from [your state or hometown]." (Wait for the client's response. You need to know if he or she recognizes your name.)*
>
> **Client:** *"Hi, [your name]. What a pleasant surprise to hear from you!" (You can tell by this kind of response that the client is familiar with your name and you can begin your rap.)*
>
> -OR-
>
> **Client:** *"Yes?" (You sense that the client is not familiar with your name.)*
> **You:** *"Are you familiar with my name?"*
> **Client:** *"No, I can't say that I am."*
>
> -OR-
>
> **Client:** *"Well, I've heard it before, but I'm not sure where."*

Both of these responses require you to respond in the same manner.

> **You:** *"I've been working with [the biggest name, or names, you have been working with], but I have since left the band and now have my own group."*

Some venue clients are familiar only with big names. Don't go on too long about your credits. If the client sounds interested, you can always send him or her a brochure, and possibly a press kit and a CD later.

> **Client:** *"I see. How can I help you?" (The client is still not sure of your name, but is interested in at least continuing the conversation.)*
>
> -OR-
>
> **Client:** *"Oh, yeah man. I've heard you with that band on record. To what do I owe the pleasure of this call?"*

The conversation can go on from here to include a discussion of your mutual friends, when the client heard you live, or a response he or she had to an article you wrote. In any case, both reactions call for the same response from you.

You: *"Our band is going to be on tour in your area during [month and year] and I thought I'd call to see if you would be interested in having us come to [name of venue] during that period to [play and/or teach.]"*
Client: *"When will you be coming and what other venues are you working in the area?"* (*The client is checking your credibility.*)

You can answer this question in two different ways.

You: *"We have a few gigs in [place and name of venue] on [date] and we're looking for more work while we're in the area."*
-OR-

If you have no other committed gigs at this time, but are in the process of negotiating with a few potential clients, you might take this approach.

You: *"I've been talking with people at [other venues' names], and they have expressed an interest in having us come, but they are checking their budgets and available dates. Because of routing considerations, I'm waiting to see how they fall into place before I decide which date we're doing when. I'm just lining up "possibles" at this time, but can be more definite about our routing in a [month, week, etc.].*

You'll want to be prepared for the situation outlined above. Before you call a client, familiarize yourself with the contact or commitment dates of some of your other contacts. This way when the client asks you specific questions about your availability, you'll be able to answer confidently and without hesitation. At this point, the client can respond in a number of ways.

Client: *"I'm sorry. We're already booked for that period, but why don't you send us a press kit and a CD and we'll keep it on file for next year."*

That's a long no! Press kits and especially CDs have an amazing ability to disappear in a year's time. Don't send one. I have never had a callback from an allegedly "filed" press kit.

You: *"I'd be glad to send you our brochure for your information. Would you be so kind as to tell me when you will be booking your next season? I'll recontact you, and if you feel like you're still interested at that time, I'll send our press kit and CD."* (*No fool you! In any case, it's good promotion to send a letter and brochure.*)
-OR-
Client: *"We'd love to have you, but our budget is already spent for this year."* (*This is a short no.*)
You: *"Too bad. Maybe next time. When are you booking your next season?"*

After the client gives you the information about the venue's lead time, note the date in your file and set a call-back alarm.

-OR-

Client: *"We'd love to have you, but we're already booked for that period."* (*This is a short no.*)

Whether the client would love to have you or not remains to be seen. It may take two or three calls to a venue before you find out if the client's interest is genuine. In any case, keep the client's name on file for the future. Ask your contact who he or she has booked, so you can get an idea who the venue is hiring and what fees it might be able to afford. Note this information in your file. Also note a call-back date in your computer file and set a call-back alarm.

-OR-

Client: *"You called at just the right time. We're working on booking that period in a couple of weeks. Why don't you send me a press kit and we'll see what we can do?"*

Congratulations. You've gained an expression of interest.

Setting the Date

This is the second of the five stages of a negotiation. In your introductory call you will have mentioned the general parameters of your tour. The purpose of this second conversation is to set a "possible" date. Don't expect to nail down a solid commitment during this second conversation. Consider your conversation a success if you talk with the client about a number of date options and if you end the discussion with an understanding of the various considerations that need to be researched by both parties before a more solidified commitment can be made.

For a number of reasons, it's rare that a date will be set during an introductory call. Generally at least one—and sometimes several—follow-up calls are necessary before you can get a commitment from a client. Depending on the venue type, these reasons can be:

- the client may have to check his or her budget and schedule to see if anything else is being considered for those dates;
- the client may want to receive your press kit and CD so that he or she can submit your offering to a higher-up or committee for review;
- you may already have a tentative gig lined up for the day in which the client is interested;
- the client may have tentatively booked another artist, but hasn't received a commitment from the artist;
- you may need to determine how your routing for the tour is working out;
- the client may not be familiar with your name and may have to check with someone else for an appraisal.

When you make your second call to a client, you should have your calendar in front of you. Be ready to discuss at least two possible dates. After you've confirmed a few more gigs and established your routing in more detail, you may find that one of the dates works out better or that you can use one of the dates to fill in an open day or one that was tentatively booked and has since become open. When you're talking with your client, declare your preference for one date over another and tell him or her why you prefer it. Also, make sure to ask if the venue has particular days they do things or that they are closed; for instance, some venues have regular events on certain weekday or weekend nights, have a "Thursdays only" event, or are closed on Sundays.

Most clients won't ask you for a fee quote at this stage. But if a client does ask about your fees during a preliminary conversation, tell him or her that you're sure you can work something out. Assuring the client that you always do your best to accommodate a client's budget because you'd rather work than have a day off will communicate to your contact that you're open to negotiation. It will also maintain an open dialogue between you and the client. After all, there's no sense discussing a fee until you know that a date is possible. Doing so may only prematurely end your dialogue.

The client will probably request that you send a brochure or a press kit and CD at this time. If the client doesn't bring this up, you should ask if having a brochure would help him or her make a decision. If the client says yes, ask if he or she would mind if you called back in a couple of weeks to confirm receipt of the package. After all, press kits and CDs are rather costly and you'd like to be sure the material arrived okay. Note the call-back date on your calendar. This gives you a good excuse to call again to see how things are progressing on their end.

If you don't have the complete address for the venue, now is the time to enter it in your contact file. Ask your client if he or she would mind giving you his or her home phone number. Having a contact's home number gives you the option of being able to reach that person in the evenings, on weekends, or during holidays. You can also leave messages both at work and at home. Whether calling at work or at home, always ask if you are calling at an inconvenient time. It is always better to give the client the option to talk to you at another time than risk having an unproductive conversation.

Ask if the client has any idea at this point when he or she might be able to make a commitment. Note the date on your calendar and then call the client a month in advance of the date. Calling back before the agreed upon date allows you to give the client more information about your routing and firmer information about the other venues that have committed, which may help to sway the client's decision in your favor. It also gives you ample time to play telephone tag and still catch the client before the deadline.

Negotiating Your Fees

The amount that a venue can afford varies greatly from venue to venue. A struggling club owner and a prosperous club owner are very different to work for—as are universities, jazz societies, and cultural institutions. Each of these venues has different budgets, needs, and expectations. When you've gotten to the point in the negotiation process when you're discussing money, you need to try to get a sense for what the venue's financial situation is. The only way to do this is to ask questions. For example, when talking to a college music department head, you might want to ask what his or her budget is. When talking to a jazz society organizer or an arts presenter, you might want to inquire if his or her concerts are supported by a subscription series. When talking to a club owner, you might want to ask how business has been lately, who some of the venue's recent bookings have been and how well they've drawn, and whether the club has a restaurant to help support its income. Asking questions about the venue also serves a second purpose: It ensures that, in your excitement to land a gig, you don't prematurely propose a fee that is out of line with what that venue would be willing to pay you—either too high or too low.

SAMPLE SCRIPTS

After the client expresses an interest in your group and you have determined that there is a good chance that there are some dates that are mutually compatible, he or she may jump right into the financial negotiation process.

> **Client:** *"Sure. We'd love to have your band play for us. How much are your fees? I'd like to know if we can afford you before I say yes."*

If possible, resist the temptation to give a fee quote at the beginning of a negotiation. This is a crucial juncture in the negotiation process. Because you've gotten a nibble, you may get exited and either over- or underquote yourself. So try to delay giving the client a direct response to this question. Below are three alternative answers to the client.

> **You:** *"We don't have a set fee because there are many variables that affect our fee. However, what you can afford is our primary consideration."*

This shows the client that you're considerate of the venue's financial condition and are willing to negotiate.

> **You:** *"We don't have a set fee because there are many variables that affect our fee. One of the variables is how many days you want us to work. The more days you want, the lower the fee per day will be. How much work you want us to do per day is another variable. A third variable is how much support work we will have while we're in your area. At this time I still don't have a sense for how much support work we will be doing, but that will dictate how flexible we can be in order to make a gig happen."*

This kind of response throws the ball back into the client's court. The client has to think a moment about what he or she wants you to do. The client's response will give you a slight indication of what the budget is. At this point, the conversation can go in a number or directions. You can either wait for your client to respond or you can ask him or her outright about the budget.

> **You:** *"How big is your budget?"* -OR- *"What do you usually pay?"*

This is a ballsy move. This kind of response *really* puts the ball back into the client's court. A more gentle approach is to wait for the client to respond to your question about how much work he or she wants you to do. While the client is thinking about how much work he or she wants from you, you should have your fee schedule in front of you and quickly give it the once-over to familiarize yourself with your fees.

> **Client:** *"We'd like you to do [such and such] for us."*
> **You:** *"We usually charge [x amount of dollars] plus hotels for that. Does that seem like a fair price to you?"*
>
> -OR-
>
> **You:** *"We usually charge [x amount of dollars] plus hotels for that. How close do you think you can come to that figure?"*

At this point you're into the give-and-take of negotiating. Your fee quote may or may not be acceptable to this particular client. When I'm talking with a client with a good sense of humor, I sometimes take a humorous approach at this stage. For instance, when the client asks me what we charge, I'll say, "Well, somewhere between what I want and what you want to give me."

> **Client:** *"I'm interested and that sounds like a fair price. Why don't I check my budget and schedule, obtain approval from the powers-that-be, and get back to you."*
> **You:** *"Great. Should I send you a press kit and CD to help the higher-ups come to a decision? When do you think you might have an idea when you could confirm the date?"*
>
> -OR-
>
> **Client:** *"Our new budget for that period is not in yet. I'll call you when it's in and let you know where we stand financially."*
> **You:** *"Sure. When is your budget going to be confirmed?"*

When you get the date from your client, note it in your file and set a call-back alarm. A lot can happen between an initial call and a budget deadline.

> **You:** *"Do you mind if I call you a little while after the deadline to check on the status of our project?"*

Asking this question absolves the client from having to remember a callback and maintains an aggressive position. It's always good strategy to have a solid reason to call back. If a client insists that he or she will call you, it could be fine, but he or she could also be giving you a "long no." You need to know if you have a viable lead or not. If, by the date of the callback, you don't hear from the client, wait a week to be sure that you're not being a pest and call back. Clients have a lot of other things on their minds besides your gig and a callback from you keeps you fresh in their mind.

> **Client:** *"We're having a committee meeting on [such and such a date]. I'll get back to you after the meeting."*
> **You:** *"Do you mind if I call you a little while after the meeting to check on the status of our project?"*

Again, taking responsibility for the callback maintains an aggressive position. This is a particularly good idea in this scenario because meetings are often delayed and you want to stay on top of things by calling the client back.

If a client's offer is too low for you to accept, he or she could be lowballing you—trying to get you to work as cheaply as possible. Surprisingly, some clients have no idea what it takes to keep an organized band on the road. They might be offering a low fee simply out of ignorance. In this case, you might consider actually explaining to your client how much you have to pay your band and how much it will cost to get to the gig. A number of times I have felt a gig slipping away until I explained to the client the economic reality of the situation. However, if this approach doesn't work and you still can't come to a mutual agreement, respectfully decline to work the gig, giving a good reason for doing so. Explain that your salary commitments and tour expenses won't allow you to accept the offer at this time, but that you might call the client back at a later date when he or she may be more interested.

Working for a low fee can sometimes create a lack of respect in a client's mind. If you decide to entertain an offer for a low fee, dispel that impression by explaining that you're trying to build an audience and that other gigs on your tour are paying you enough that you can afford to offer the band to this venue at a reduced fee. If you still don't get the gig, be patient. You've made a potentially valuable contact and you might eventually gain the recognition necessary to get the gig.

Making Follow-up Calls

Invariably the booking process requires you to make a lot of follow-up calls. Get ready for this. Even though your clients may say they're going to call you back on a certain date, don't count on it. They could easily forget about you, or be too busy to call you back. You may have to leave many messages. If you don't hear from a client by an agreed upon date, wait a week and call the client back.

If your client forgets to call you back, try not to take it personally. Don't take an attitude like "Hey, man, I thought you were going to call me back!" Be businesslike and polite. Running a venue is just as logistically complex as running a band and, like you, your clients are usually quite harried. Mention that your files showed that you would be receiving a callback last week and that you wanted to touch base to see how things were progressing about the project you discussed. You may still not get a confirmation date at this time. Ask your client if he or she has a firmer idea as to whether the venue will be able to commit. And, if it wouldn't be too bothersome, ask your client if you can call back again at that time. Most likely the client will appreciate having you call back because that requires less work for him or her. Make a note and call your client back again on the new date.

If you still don't get a confirmation when you call back, you may either be getting a long no or your client may be genuinely busy and may have to be recontacted again. With experience, you will develop a sense for whether a client is truly interested in your proposal or not. Often, on a callback, you'll get a secretary or assistant who takes messages for the client. That person will tell you that your client will get back to you. If you don't receive a callback, try one more time. And if no results occur, put the contact lead in a dormant file for calling again at a later date.

If your computer has an automatic dialing feature, it will automatically log the dates of all your calls. You can see how many calls you've made to a venue and how often they've returned your calls, as well as how they have responded to your messages. This can be a particularly handy feature when you're playing telephone tag with a client.

If you don't solidify a gig with a particular client, ask him or her to keep you in mind in case the venue has a cancellation. Cancellations happen often, particularly with festivals and clubs. Many times I've gotten a gig at the last moment because someone else has canceled.

If you haven't already done so, during the call-back process you should ask your client if he or she can recommend other contacts to you. Get the new contacts' work and home telephone numbers. When making your new-client files, note who recommended you, and when you call those new clients make sure to mention the name of the person who referred you. Depending on how the client reacts to your request for recommendations, you can sometimes ask the client to call ahead to the new contact for you. Even if the client's recommendations don't yield other gigs for you, you have made new personal contacts that may come in handy for a later tour. I've even had some generous clients fax me a list of contacts, which greatly increased my client database.

Getting a Commitment

The differences in commitment times from one gig and another is one of the most stressful aspects of the booking process. A tour is like a house of cards. Each gig is dependent on the others. Some venues will commit up to and more than a year in advance. This is especially true of universities, festivals, jazz societies, northern European venues, and some clubs. Others will not book until three months in advance of the gig. This second group includes most clubs and venues in southern Europe.

Venues in the latter category often appear as though they can't get their business together or that they're not interested in your proposal. There is a strong temptation to either call too many times or blow the contact off. It could work against you if you try to pressure the venue to commit to a gig, using the possibility of taking another gig as leverage. This could give them an incentive to back out of the negotiation. Instead, when trying to pressure a late-committing gig into securing a date, explain that you're concerned about routing and transportation problems and that setting a date earlier than they might under normal circumstances would alleviate your problems.

Clients miss commitment dates for all kinds of reasons. A grant that was expected may have not yet come in, or perhaps a budget hasn't yet been approved by the higher-ups. Clubs and festivals may be waiting for another band to decide whether they are coming or not before they commit to you. Department heads, administrators, and committee members aren't always available and may be bound to certain academic cycles that may seem mysterious to you. Being patient during the booking process often requires a leap of faith.

If your client gave you a date by which he or she agreed to commit and that date comes and goes without a call, wait a few days and then call back and mention that you had a note that he or she would be calling you about that time but you were too busy to call until now. This avoids giving your contact the impression that you are just waiting around for a call or that you are subjecting him or her to undue pressure.

Many salespeople are great at selling themselves and their product, but freeze when it comes to closing a deal. You may not have agreed on a fee that is exactly to your liking or there may be routing problems that have added extra expenses to your tour. However, if you have gone through extensive negotiations, sent a kit and CD, and spent time and incurred expense developing the gig, you will have to commit or you will have wasted both your and your client's valuable time. This will not create a good image for yourself as a practical businessperson. Confirm the date. Close the deal! There is always a chance that you will be able to work at this venue again in the future—for a better fee and under conditions that are more to your liking. And, as was mentioned earlier, negotiating is a process that becomes easier with time.

When you're closing a deal, you'll need time to gather information for your contact file. You should also have your client and venue worksheet in front of you when you're closing a deal. Use it to be sure you've asked all of the questions you need to know about the gig. You don't want to be calling the client back time after time because you forgot to ask for certain information.

Note the commitment date and ask your client when the contract will be sent to you. Note this information in your contact file and on your calendar. If travel distances before or after the gig are problematic, ask your client if you can have an extra day's hotel for your band. Things can move pretty fast once an agreement to commit occurs.

SPECIAL CONSIDERATIONS FOR FOREIGN OR CANADIAN VENUES When you're closing on a foreign festival or Canadian gig, don't forget to confirm that you will be paid in U.S. dollars. Canadians use the term "dollars" just like we do and Canadian currency is valued at less than American currency. So, not only can you lose out in the deal if you forget to specify U.S. dollars, but for your accounting purposes, it's less complicated to be paid in U.S. dollars. Otherwise, you will have to keep track of the exchange rate on the particular day and note the cost for the exchange in your budget. You may have to wait until the dollar goes up or down. This can play havoc with your salary schedule. You will also have to spend extra time that you could have otherwise spent resting to look for a place to exchange your money at a decent rate. (This is discussed in further detail in chapter twelve.)

When finalizing a Canadian gig, ask your contact if tax papers, working papers, visas, and a union contract will be needed. With the exception of the tax papers, each of these four documents can be initiated either by you or by the venue. Filling out and filing the visa, working papers, and union contract paperwork with the appropriate agencies will be a complex and time-consuming process. You may find it easier to have your contact initiate some of these processes.

To file your tax papers, you'll first need to obtain the appropriate paperwork. The venue can either send these papers to you or tell you whom to contact to have them sent. Once you have filled out these forms, you'll need to send them to the Canadian Treasury Department.

The U.S. and Canadian musicians' unions have worked out reciprocal contractual agreements that make it easy for artists to work in each other's countries. If your client has requested that you generate the contract, contact your local musicians' union for assistance. It will have blank contracts and will be able to advise you about any updates or changes that will need to be made to these agreements.

To apply for a visa and working papers, both you as well as your venue contact will have to submit certain documents to Canadian immigration authorities. Your local musicians' union can supply you with the Canadian immigration contact information and visa application. Although your applications will be filed on Canadian immigration's computer system, you'll want to make sure that your venue knows which border crossing you'll be using. It will save you a lot of time at the border if the applications are on file at the appropriate crossing.

Once you have your completed applications and contracts filled out, signed, and returned to you, you'll have to pay a visa entry fee at Canadian immigration when entering the country. However, if you are going in and out of Canada during the same tour, you can save visa fees by having the visa dates cover the time period of *all* of your Canadian gigs. These are called multiple-entry visas and are usually acquired and paid for at your first border crossing.

As the processes for obtaining tax papers, working papers, visa, and Canadian-venue contracts are somewhat complex and may involve deadlines for completion, make notes about when any applications and contracts are to be sent to you, when you sent materials out, and any applicable deadlines. Always make copies of the appropriate documents, and keep them with you while traveling.

Chapter 9

Managing Tour Routing and Budgets

This chapter deals with some of the obstacles you'll encounter when you're routing a tour. It may seem a bit complicated at first, but with study and experience you'll develop the skills you need to master this aspect of being a bandleader. To give you a head start, the last part of this chapter has a five-part step-by-step demonstration of how I put together an imaginary tour. This process illustrates all of the complications that can arise from routing and budgeting a tour—and gives you some of the most common solutions as well.

Tour routing and budgeting directly affect one another in a number of ways. You need to book a lot of gigs to make it worthwhile for you to go on the road. However, traveling from one gig to another costs a lot of money. So, once you decide to book a tour, you need to make sure that you book enough gigs to cover your travel expenses. You'll want to avoid excessively difficult travel itineraries (because they can exhaust you and your band members and can affect your presentation), but at the same time you need to minimize your days off (because they can weigh down the profitability of your tour). Balancing the routing and budgeting aspects of a tour often seems like a juggling act. Once you have begun the booking process, you'll find that your tour's itinerary will take on a life of its own. Establishing total control over the routing process is impossible because too many touring elements are beyond your control.

TROUBLESHOOTING TOURING CONFLICTS
Complications generally arise when you start arranging your transportation for your tour-in-progress. This happens because this is the first point where you see how your transportation costs affect your tour's budget. When you have a reasonable idea of where you're going to be and when you're going to be there, you should begin to check into your transportation routing and expenses. I usually find that I am ready to do this approximately two-thirds of the way through the booking process. Sometimes you find that you just "can't get there from here"—or at least can't get there in time. Sold-out flights, unworkable travel connections, high transportation costs, among other unpredictable factors, will add to your routing problems.

Routing problems occur on every tour. These problems may be caused by:

- disparities among commitment dates of various venues in your tour;
- a need to schedule unexpected last-minute gigs;
- conflicts between travel times and performance times, which are often not known until the tour schedule is relatively complete;
- excessive distances between gigs, which can raise transportation costs;

- too many open dates;
- the fact that other bands are often competing for the same dates, which means that certain venues may wait until the last minute before they commit to a gig.

You can solve routing problems in a number of ways. Which solution you choose will depend upon the individual circumstances of a gig, and perhaps the relationship that you have with your client. For instance, you can:

- change the date of a gig;
- fill in holes in your itinerary by asking your clients for recommendations and then scheduling additional gigs;
- consider alternative forms of transportation, which may have preferable schedules and fares, by contacting a travel agent or by searching on the Internet;
- negotiate with clients so that they agree to pay for the band's accommodations for extra days off;
- lower band members' salaries slightly for a gig or two to bring the budget in line;
- solidify weak gigs that have yet to commit;
- take alternative gigs for a date that may have been canceled.

As you're finessing the routing of your tour, you may find that you need to call back a few gigs that have confirmed to see if they have the flexibility to move dates around. Plan ahead for the fact that this may happen. When you first contact a venue and set a date, ask your client if the venue has one or two possible alternative dates. Don't be afraid to ask about changing a date. Experienced clients understand routing problems and will accommodate your request if they can. And besides, you never know, sometimes changing a date at your request also solves a routing problem that the client is having. Clients deal with routing problems on their end as well, and they are often juggling dates. On occasion, a client may even call you to ask if you can change a date. Do your best to help your client out if you can. Cooperation will help you establish a positive reputation in the business and a solid working relationship with the client. When you're considering swapping dates, keep in mind that gigs with signed contracts *can't* be changed.

Some venues are locked into dates that can't be changed. This is frequently the case with festivals. However, if the festival is a multiday event, the client may be able to juggle the day of your particular concert. Arts presenters, most nonprofits, and concert series that book a year in advance, will not be able to change their dates. Don't bother to ask. Clubs, hotels, and small concert halls have the most flexibility. If you have a signed contract and the venue has started to advertise your appearance *or* if a festival or school concert hall has no other available dates and/or booking conflicts are too formidable, you most likely won't be able to change the date. However, it is always worth a quick call to find out about the possibility of changing a date.

Nothing is more stressful than looking at your tour calendar and seeing too many open stretches of nonworking days in your itinerary. Open dates increase your expenses because you and your band members are forced either to fly home and back again in the middle of your tour *or* stay out on the road and pay hotels for days on end with no income. If you have no alternative gigs lined up for the dates that are not yet filled, do more venue research. Call your clients for the dates you've already booked and ask them to recommend other venues or new leads. Another option is to get in touch with local musicians or radio station disc jockeys in the area for new leads.

It is standard practice, when you're in the preliminary process of booking a tour, to allocate 30 percent of your tour income toward accommodation and transportation expenses. However, once you start filling in your expense column with the *actual* accommodation and transportation costs, that allocation can quickly evaporate. In order to avoid this stressful scenario, assume that you are going to stay out on the road through any open dates and estimate $100 per person, per day, for hotels for each open date. Add these expenses to your budget, and then as other gigs confirm (and perhaps also agree to pay for your hotel and travel costs), you can adjust your budget accordingly.

If either you or your travel agent doesn't have E-mail, print out your itinerary and fax it to your travel agent so the two of you can discuss where you're going and how you plan to get there. Your agent may have solutions you have not considered. Alternatively, you can save your travel agent a lot of time and yourself a lot of worry about travel schedules and expenses by going on the Internet to do your own research. Almost every airline, railroad company, and car-rental service has a Web site. By checking a few sites you can get reasonable estimates of plane and train schedules and expenses for almost any part of the world. Having this information will make discussions with your travel agent much more efficient. Print out the plane and train schedules you think would work for the segments of the tour you have booked to date and fax them to your travel agent. He or she may be able to find lower prices and special offers that aren't posted on the Internet.

Expect to have some open dates in your itinerary and plan ahead for them. Negotiate an extra day's paid hotel, either before or after the gig date, with as many venues as you can. Assure the client that if another date confirms for the open date, you won't need the extra day's hotel. If you forget to ask for extra hotel days during negotiations, you'll have to call your client back to see if he or she is willing and able to help. These kinds of situations may be awkward, but you never know until you ask.

After you've made all of the arrangements that you can to save money with your travel and accommodations, if your tour still looks as if it's going to have a negative balance, try shaving a few dollars from your bandleader's salary. Check to make sure you haven't made a mistaken entry into your budget columns. As a last resort, see if taking $25 to $50 per person off a few gigs brings the tour back into the black. If other gigs commit later, you can readjust your salary entries.

Once you've completed your initial assessment of your routing consideration, you'll have to go over your itinerary and assess the viability of each uncommitted gig. Take the weakest gigs off the calendar and budget, and see what the routing and expense picture looks like then. You may be surprised to suddenly see alternative routings you hadn't previously considered. If this is the case and if you have some flexibility to make routing changes, you'll have to call some of your committed gigs back to see if they can change their dates for you.

If you're having trouble getting a confirmation from a client, tell him or her that you're trying to keep your tour expenses down and that you need an answer by a certain date, or the cost of purchasing tickets for the tour will increase and you might not be able to afford to play the venue. I've found that this approach sometimes helps to gently prod my client into making a firm decision. The downside of this strategy is that the contact may say that he or she can't confirm at that time, and suggest that you book an alternative gig if you can. This can leave you in a position from which you have little leverage to make a counterproposal. In both types of situations the client's response is usually a good gauge of how solid his or her commitment to you is.

Occasionally you'll encounter a client who just hates to say no and will keep you hanging. Oftentimes this is an indication that the client has another band in mind for that date and he or she simply hasn't yet made a decision. The closer you get to the date of the gig the less likely this is to happen—because if your client hasn't yet made arrangements for another group, he or she will be more anxious to fill the date and will be more willing to commit to you. If you find yourself in this kind of situation, you will have to make a judgment call as to how serious your client is, and how you want to proceed. Your decision may be based on whether or not you have an alternative gig. Ask the client what the odds are that the gig will be confirmed. If you get a positive response and you don't have an alternative, hold the date. If you don't get a positive response and you have a solid alternative gig (maybe for a smaller fee), take that one. It's better to have a definite gig than to hold a date open for an engagement that's looking shaky or will never happen. If you don't get a positive response and you have no alternative gig, take the date off the calendar and leave it open. If they call, they call. If they don't, you won't have made any decisions based on the gig committing.

CREATING YOUR TOUR CALENDARS

Computer calendars are indispensable for routing tours, checking on open days, logging venue info such as fees, keeping track of event schedules, filing contact information, and readjusting tour dates. Calendars can also be used to note call-back dates, client call-back dates, and dates you expect mailings to be sent or arrive. Calendars are crucial when creating tour budgets and itineraries. When talking to a prospective client, have the calendar program up and running; this way you won't be hesitant about your tour itinerary and routing.

Keep visual track of a tour's constantly changing status by highlighting calendar dates using different colors or type, depending on the status of the gig. Enter dates that are definite in red. Enter the dates that you have contacted but are waiting to hear from in blue with a question mark. Dates that are yet to be contacted should be entered in black with a question mark. As soon as the status of a date changes, adjust the calendar and update the budget.

Try to allow no more than one six-hour driving day per week, unless it's an off day, or after the trip. Three- to four-hour drives per day are reasonable, and not too exhausting. But sometimes you'll have no choice but to accept some hard travel days.

Once, in the middle of an extensive U.S. tour, I accepted two days of concerts in two different Polish cities. The client made an offer I couldn't refuse because we had four days open in that part of the tour. We finished a gig in Columbus, Ohio, drove to the airport, flew to Philadelphia, connected with a flight to Warsaw (with a change of planes in Munich), and then drove for three hours from Warsaw to the first gig. The total travel time was eighteen hours. We arrived at the first venue about three hours ahead of the performance time, which meant choosing between eating or catching a nap. I opted for the latter. Upon awakening, I hurriedly showered, shaved, and dressed, getting to the gig just in time to play. I was so tired I could barely lift my hands to the piano, but we made a good presentation anyway. Sometimes, when exhausted by hard traveling, a presentation is all you can do, but if your band has good musical rapport, that aspect alone can carry off a successful performance.

That night we got a decent night's sleep, drove for three hours back to Warsaw, took a two-hour-long train ride to Krakow, and got to the next location with just enough time to eat and rest a little before the gig. The next day we took a train back to Warsaw, caught a plane to Louisville, Kentucky (by way of Munich and New York), and finished the last two weeks of our U.S. tour. Even though I had arranged a day off for the day after our return to the United States and had managed to book gigs for that next week that only required one to two hours of driving, it *still* took days for us to recover from that trip.

DEVELOPING YOUR TOUR BUDGETS

At the same time that you are booking your tour and drafting your tour calendar, you should also be developing your tour budget. Tour budgets help you to judge the financial status of your tour. For each tour you book, you'll have to create a separate tour budget. Oftentimes you'll need to create one or two alternative budgets to test out different ways a tour might look if you add or subtract gigs. Surprisingly, sometimes you will find that it is more profitable *not* take a certain gig because the salaries, transportation, and housing costs involved with that gig lower your tour's net income.

When I first started booking my tours, I created my tour budgets using a computer spreadsheet program with linked totals and subtotals that automatically changed as I updated the entries. A spreadsheet is only as good as the person creating it. Incorrect entries and cell links can be entered into any accounting program, no matter how sophisticated it is. It took me quite a few tours to hone my computer skills so that these spreadsheets were completely accurate. One wrong number or entry title can be disastrous, so *check, double-check*, and *triple-check* your data.

I recommend the inexpensive software program Quicken Basic by Intuit. You can find out more about this program at http://www.intuit.com. Although primarily used for home accounting, Quicken Basic has a checkbook feature that can be easily customized for use with tour budgets. I prefer this program rather than a spreadsheet program because budget entries can be more detailed and calculations are done automatically. Detailed entry titles keep track of various income sources and expenditures. Quicken Basic's handy report feature also allows you to create an accurate picture of your tour's financial status. This is helpful for checking the profitability of a tour at any point during the booking process.

Both expenses and income will come your way unexpectedly during every tour, so you'll need to bring an accounting program with you on the road to update your budget. You can then adjust those entries in your Quicken Basic program when you return. I don't carry a laptop with me when I'm on tour. Instead I use a digital diary with a spreadsheet program. Although a budget spreadsheet is time-consuming to create, it's well worth the effort and it's a good way to double-check your figures and entries.

Whether you use a spreadsheet at home and/or on the road, you can save time by creating a generic budget spreadsheet that has cell links for the income, salaries, and tour expenses and that tallies the totals for each of these categories automatically. This automatic-tally function is especially helpful, because when you add or change an entry, the program changes all of the corresponding figures. (See pages 161, 163, 165, 168, and 172 for examples of a sample tour budget spreadsheet.)

To keep track of how much you are over or under your budget, set up your spreadsheet so that it creates totals for each category as well as a subtotal for the tour balance after the salaries and expenses have been deducted. To get a long-term picture of how your band is doing, you can, at the end of each year, create another spreadsheet to analyze the band's average daily income and expenses, the average income per type of venue, and your personal and band average yearly income.

This is the information you need to enter into your tour budget spreadsheet:

Dates and City Locations of Gigs: When starting a new budget, key in your first and last dates of a tour, and all the other dates between—regardless of whether they are booked or not. If the tour becomes longer or shorter than originally estimated, it's easy to adjust your spreadsheet later.

Income from Each Gig: Enter these figures as each gig confirms. If a venue is paying your hotel and/or airfares as part of your total fee, enter the figure as income on the appropriate day and then enter a zero in the appropriate cell in the expenses column. For example, if you're getting paid $3,000 for a two-day gig and the venue is paying your hotels and transportation, you'll enter $3,000 in the income column and zeros in the hotel expense column in the cells that correspond with those two days and zeros in the dates of your round-trip airfares.

Grants: Enter any income that the band will receive from support grants in the income column.

Individual Salaries: Enter these figures as soon as each gig confirms. Pay particular attention to your pay schedule to ensure that each person is being paid the correct amount for each type of service (concert, clinic, rehearsal, radio broadcast, etc.). If you want to see how a tour looks if all the gigs you've contacted confirm, make a tentative budget by adding in the income and salaries of the unconfirmed gigs. These can be updated as new information comes in.

Total Income: This figure is the total amount of the tour income, plus grants.

Individual Salaries: This figure is the total of each individual's salary for that tour.

Total Salaries: This figure is the total of all of the individuals' salaries. This is the figure that is deducted from the total-income figure to get the travel margin.

Agents' Fees: To make sure you haven't neglected to enter and deduct these fees from your budget, enter the agent's name and fee as well as the date of each gig for which the fee is owed in the expense column. Add a final cell for total agents' fees underneath that section of your expenses.

Advance Deposits: As mentioned above, the full amount of the fee for each gig should be entered in the income column. However, if you accept an advance deposit, you will need to develop a system for notating that a portion of the income for a gig has already been received. This system should be very clear, otherwise, you may forget about the deposit and, while on tour, expect to receive the full fee as it is listed in the income column. One way to notate the receipt of an advance deposit is to deduct the advance deposit from your total income. This second total will reflect the total amount of income that you will receive when you are on the road. You can call this second total something like "road income" to distinguish it from total income. You may also want to highlight the fee for the gig (which will be in the expense column under the appropriate date) in bold—so that you have a visual reminder that this entry involved an advance deposit. Personally, I find the extra level of bookkeeping involved with advance deposits cumbersome and so I make a point of not accepting them.

Travel Margin: This category is optional. This is the figure you get when you subtract the total salaries, and agents' fees (if applicable) from the total income. This figure lets you know how much of a balance is available for transportation and hotel expenses. If your tour is in good financial shape, this figure will be between 20 and 30 percent of your total income.

Airfares: These figures need to be entered in their own column within the expenses portion of your budget. When the band is traveling together, use city and state abbreviations to notate all flights. This system also works well when personnel that live in differing cities fly to and from the first and last gigs of a tour by themselves. To keep track of how your expenses are going, use any of the many Internet airfare services to get estimates on flight costs. Microsoft's Expedia Travel Service at http://expedia.msn.com/daily/home/default.hts and Preview Travel at http://www.previewtravel.com allow you to get figures for open-jaw tickets. Using these estimates eliminates the need to bother a busy travel agent for tickets you may or may not buy. Actual costs can be reentered at the time the tickets are purchased. Don't forget—as with all of the expense subcategories—to add a total airfares cell underneath the airfares category.

Baggage Fees: These figures should include the charges for the bass and drums as well as oversize or overweight luggage. Add these costs on the line after each airfare listing. These figures vary unpredictably, and cannot be determined in advance. Some airlines will charge you baggage fees and some will not. It's always safer to estimate unknown expenses on the high end and enter the inflated fees in your tour budget. Then, while you're on tour, you can change the figure on your personal organizer and, once you get home, you can reenter the correct figures into your computer spreadsheet program. Once you've done a few tours, you'll have a pretty good idea of what your average baggage fees will be.

Van Rentals: Enter the to and from dates as well as the abbreviations for the areas where you'll be driving. You can get estimates from the Internet or by calling a rental-car agency's 1-800 number.

Gas and Tolls: Enter these costs below your van-rental costs column. Map software programs such as Route 66, Delorme, or AAA, which are available on CD-ROM and on the Maps On Us Web site at http://www.mapsonus.com, can give you reasonable estimates as to how much gas you might use on a driving tour. These resources can be especially handy to check if you're within your mileage limit allowed by the car-rental agency and how much it could cost you if you go over it.

Trains: These expenses, for the most part, will only occur in Europe. (For more information about European train schedules and Eurailpasses, see pages 208–213.)

Ferries: Call the ferry company to get an estimate of its fees.

Taxis: There may be some situations (as in foreign countries) where the venue will supply most of your local, in-town transportation. In these cases, you'll only need to use taxis for limited excursions—like getting from the airport to the hotel. Since these expenses are relatively limited, you can usually ballpark these estimates yourself. However, if the band will need to take a longish taxi ride from the airport to the gig, you might ask your gig contact to give you an estimate as to how much the ride might cost.

Transportation Total: This figure is the total of airfares, baggage fees, and all other forms of tour transportation.

Hotels: Add every date where you think you'll have to pay for your own hotels. Use your collection of hotel rate books, check on the Internet, or call any of the hotel chain 1-800 numbers to estimate your hotel expenses. If you plan on staying in a hotel that is not part of a chain, call your client for the hotel info and then call the hotel to check on its cost. Be sure to include any room taxes in the figure.

Total Hotels: This figure is the sum total of all of the individual hotel expenses. This will change as you work to lower this expense.

Miscellaneous Expenses: You never know what expenses might arise during a tour. It is a good idea to plan for some unexpected expenses. For example, you might need to rent a drum set or bass amp or fix a dent in a rental van.

Tips: These costs will include airport and train station baggage handlers and hotel bellhops. This category is optional and should appear after the miscellaneous expenses category on your spreadsheet.

Total Travel Expenses: The figure is the sum of all your travel and hotel expenses.

Tour Balance: This is the most important figure in a budget. It tells you whether your tour budget is in the red or in the black. If it is in the red, you're going to have to go back over your figures to see where you can shave any tour expenses. For instance, as previously mentioned, you may find that you have to reduce your own salary, which may mean that you will make less than the other members in your band. As a last resort, you may find that you need to reduce the other band members' salaries as well in order to bring the budget back into the black. Alternatively, if you're in the black by a moderate amount, you'll be able to take a leader's fee. If this is the case, don't forget that you have other expenses, such as those incurred running your office and booking your band (telephone bills, computer software purchases, press kits, etc.) that you'll hope to defray somewhat from a tour that runs into the black.

While booking a tour, you are probably going to make at least three tentative budgets—and maybe more if you have to refigure your tour because of cost overruns. If you know that you're going to have to draft multiple budgets, when you start to enter your budget information, enter the hard or known figures first. For instance, the amounts for income and salaries generally don't change, unless you need to lower the salaries on some gigs to bring your tour balance into the black. Use this partially drafted tour budget as the starting point for your various tentative budgets. Then, as time progresses, the softer, estimated expenses that you are experimenting with in these tentative budgets, will become harder or actual and you can make the necessary adjustments to your master budget. If a venue agrees to pay for some of your travel or hotel expenses, list those figures both in their proper expense categories as well as in the income category (next to the respective gig). Enter actual airfares as soon as you have the information. It's the only way to keep track of a tour's financial status.

Until you have your pay schedule memorized, keep it handy while entering your salary amounts into the tour budget. Pay attention to those days when you're doing clinics *and* performances, because when done on the same day the rate is generally slightly less than if the two events were spread out over two days. With a quartet, an extra $50 per musician mistakenly overpaid could cost *you* $200. Occasionally, when you're negotiating a college engagement, you may have to throw in a solo clinic to clinch a deal. It is up to you whether you want to pay yourself for these. You can always add the fees to the spreadsheet and, if a tour looks like it's going into the red, knock a couple of them off to bring a tour's balance into the black.

Figuring salaries for college residencies of two days or more is more complicated. The band could be working anywhere from two to eight hours a day, as in the case where you're adjudicating a big-band festival. You'll have to decide if you are going to pay your musicians for rehearsals with a college band. These situations will be handled on a case-by-case basis, depending on the status of the budget.

For gigs where you've negotiated a guarantee and a percentage of the admission fees, enter only the guarantee (in the income column) and the full salaries (in each individual band member's income column). If you make some money on the percentage, you can add it into your portable spreadsheet later and watch your tour balance increase. However, you don't want to assume that you're going to make money and then be caught shortchanged if the gig doesn't go as well as you had hoped it would.

Keep track of your days off by including each day off in your date and venue column. These should be visual reminders for you that you'll be incurring accommodation expenses that won't be paid for by a venue or be deflected by income from a gig. Eliminate them as the days fill in with confirmed gigs. Don't forget to enter your days off into the hotel expense column, as well. Make separate checklists for the dates and destinations of all the flights to be booked, hotels to be reserved, and vans to be rented, including the driving days per rental segment and the drive time for each trip. Pay attention to those gigs that do and don't pay for hotels, for gig days as well as for days off. Forgetting three of those days could make as much as a $1,000 difference in the tour balance. Hotels and airport car-rental agencies will add a tax and an airport surcharge to your bill. Ask about the additional charges before entering your transportation figures into the budget spreadsheet. You'd be surprised at how much they can add up at the end of a tour.

You'll also want to keep tabs on some of the expenses that can vary between the time that you make your tour budget and the time that you actually go on tour. Unless you've reserved them in advance, airfares and van-rental rates can vary between the time of your original estimates and the purchase of the tickets or rentals. Hotel rates usually stay the same. The most variable expenses will be gas and other travel expenses—for instance, the extra charges for the bass case and drum set as well as oversize or overweight luggage—and miscellaneous expenses. You won't have the actual costs for these miscellaneous expenses until you're on the road. Enter those figures as you go along.

Even though you may have solidified, to the best of your ability, all of the details of a particular tour, once you're on the road things rarely follow a planned itinerary or budget exactly. For the most part, trouble can be avoided by foreseeing potential problems before they occur. However, no matter how experienced you are, there are always variations in transportation, accommodations, and budgeting.

Don't be fooled by a tour balance figure that suggests that you're going to come home with $1,500 more than the other guys. All tour budgets, even the final one that you leave for the road with, are fantasies until the tour is over. Everything costs more than you think it will because stuff happens.

I learned this lesson the hard way. I had a tour balance of $1,500 and was looking forward to having the extra bread to offset my phone bills. We were on a tour of Europe and were doing a week in Italy (starting in Bologna), then on to Cologne, Germany, and London, England. To avoid taking the train around Europe with the damned bass case, our Italian agent sent it from Bologna to our hotel in Rome, the location of our last gig in Italy. Because our rooms were under the name of the club (it was paying for them), the hotel didn't know the names of the band members and when the bass case arrived the hotel refused responsibility for it and had it sent back to Bologna.

We arrived at the hotel and the case wasn't there. Also, the person who had refused to accept it was off for a couple of days. We had no idea what had happened to it. Even a trip to the train station gave us no information of its whereabouts. When it came time for us to leave for Cologne, our bassist couldn't fly without his bass case. So we had to send our bassist, with his bass, by a brutal, twenty-hour train ride (thankfully we had a day off between gigs) in coach class (because it was too late to get any first-class seating), while the drummer and I flew to Cologne with his suitcase.

The agent went back to Bologna to find out what had happened to the case. While we were in Cologne, the agent called to say he found the case and was going to ship it to us by airfreight. However, the airline couldn't guarantee that the case would get to Cologne in time for our departure to London. Because I was scheduled to do a solo clinic, I sent the bass player down to the airline ticket office and he managed to actually buy a seat on our flight to put his (unprotected) bass in the cabin. This is unheard of these days. Most airlines will not allow a bass in the cabin, but the flight was not full and they probably just wanted to fill another seat. We lucked out. Then I called the agent again. This time the agent told me that, for security reasons, the airline wouldn't allow the case to go in baggage without someone traveling with it. The upshot of all this was that we had to fly the agent and bass case from Bologna to London.

After paying for shipping the case from Bologna to Rome and back, the bassist's train ticket from Rome to Cologne, the extra ticket for the bass on the plane from Cologne, the agent's plane ticket from Bologna to London, and the shipping charge for the case, an airport pickup fee in London for the agent and the case, and the agent's hotel room in London, that $1,500 disappeared!

ROUTING FOREIGN TOURS

Most of the routing considerations for touring outside the United States are similar to those discussed above. However, there are a few exceptions. Fees and salaries are generally 30 to 100 percent higher in Europe than they are in this country, dependent on the state of the world economy. In many European countries, there are also entertainment taxes on performances by foreign musicians, which can be up to 50 percent of the artists' fees. Employers are responsible for paying these taxes to their respective governments. In other words, you may receive $2,000 to do a gig, but the venue may be paying $3,000 to hire you. This situation has increased employment opportunities for European musicians, but has also created difficulties for American musicians who work in Europe.

One way to get around this tax is to arrange to play a gig or two, depending on the fee, for transportation only. Because entertainment taxes are paid on artists' fees only, not transportation costs, the venue isn't penalized for paying for this expense. For instance, if your airfares for a European tour come to $2,000 and your artist fee would normally be $2,000, you might be able to have the venue send the $2,000 directly to your travel agent to pay for the tickets. The venue lists the expense as travel costs, you still are getting paid for the gig (you would have had to pay the travel agent for the tickets anyway), and it's costing the venue less to hire you.

Inter-European air travel is more expensive than interstate travel in this country. The added cost of intercountry round-trip tickets will increase your average budget another 10 percent or more than what is the normal average in the United States. Depending on a tour's budget, airplanes are used only when train or road travel is impractical. Travel by road usually means you'll have to foot the bill for the van rental and the driver's salary, as well as an extra hotel room. The most inexpensive way to travel short distances is by rail. Fortunately, train travel in Europe is superior to train travel in the United States. High-speed trains (which are called IC or intercity) are common and you have a choice of first- or second-class seating. (See chapter eleven for more information about this.) Eurailpasses offer a variety of tickets and prices that can fit most travel situations and budgets. (Eurailpasses are discussed in detail on page 208.)

Hotels can be about 30 percent higher in Europe than in the United States. As mentioned earlier, try to make tentative arrangements with as many venues as possible for an extra day's hotel (for the day before or after the gig), just in case a tour has too many days off. Most venues provide local transportation to and from airports and train stations, and between the hotel and the venue. Make sure that this is stipulated in the contract.

You can book foreign gigs from the United States, but it is best to look for regional agents in each country. Although English is becoming more prevalent throughout Europe, a European agent can help you overcome language barriers and will know more about possible gigs. He or she can also be more effective than you might be in arranging local tour transportation—as agents are more knowledgeable about local travel times and other problems, and will often reserve and pay for train tickets before you arrive. Most European Web sites that you'll be surfing for venue leads also contain extensive lists of agents in each country. You will have to research the reliability and trustworthiness of each agent by consulting with other musicians who have European touring experience. These friends will also be valuable resources for agent leads.

Even though you think you've covered every eventuality, the complications of touring are unpredictable. You never know what will happen. Every time I get on a plane for the first gig of a tour I think: *Well, let's see how it goes this time.*

Touring is always an adventure.

BOOKING AND ROUTING A SAMPLE TOUR

Before you start to book your tour, organize your information. The first decision you need to make is which area of the country you're going to book. Usually this is determined by any anchor gigs for which you have signed contracts. Remember, you can't safely book a tour around its most important gig if it's not a sure thing. In the case of this tour, you have an anchor gig in Los Angeles in mid-March. (See the first March West Coast Tour calendar on the facing page.) At this point you should have organized your touring areas and contact files into groups of contiguous geographical regions, states, or countries. These groupings can be flexible, and can be in any combination and order. Parts of one region can bleed into parts of other regions. However, here is a general breakdown of the geographic regions of our country:

West Coast Tours: Alaska (AK); Arizona (AZ); California (CA); Colorado (CO); Hawaii (HI); Idaho (ID); Montana (MT); Nevada (NV); New Mexico (NM); Oregon (OR); Utah (UT); Washington (WA); and Wyoming (WY).

Southern Tours: Alabama (AL); Arkansas (AR); Florida (FL); Georgia (GA); Kansas (KS); Kentucky (KY); Louisiana (LA); Mississippi (MS); Missouri (MO); Nebraska (NE); North Carolina (NC); Oklahoma (OK); South Carolina (SC); Tennessee (TN); and Texas (TX).

Northeast Tours: Connecticut (CT); Massachusetts (MA); Maine (ME); New Hampshire (NH); Rhode Island (RI); and Vermont (VT).

Mid-Atlantic Tours: Delaware (DE); District of Columbia (DC); Maryland (MD); New Jersey (NJ); New York (NY); Pennsylvania (PA); Virginia (VA); and West Virginia (WV).

Mid-Western Tours: Illinois (IL); Indiana (IN); Iowa (IA); Michigan (MI); Minnesota (MN); North Dakota (ND); Ohio (OH); South Dakota (SD); and Wisconsin (WI).

Once you've determined the part of the country on which you're going to concentrate, then you should organize your tour calendar and tour budget spreadsheet on the computer as well as have a map readily available. Computer map programs can determine the practicality of routing distances. However, because a map program can also take time to load, it's also a good idea to keep a manila folder on a music stand in front of your desk with a map of the United States clipped to the front, for quick reference.

Next you'll set up a March tour calendar. This calendar should include the last few days of February and the first week or two of April. Your calendar will look like a solid grid of dates—not necessarily like the kind of month-by-month calendar that you're used to seeing. The idea is to be able to see all of the dates of your tour at one glance, without having to flip pages. Personally, I like to start my weeks on a Monday. This allows me to visualize both days of the weekend at the end of the week, uninterrupted.

March, twelve months before your tour:

Let's assume that the reason you're trying to book a West Coast tour is because, a year before the tour, you managed to acquire your first anchor gig: a college festival for your quartet in Los Angeles on March 19. That gig includes a group clinic on March 20. The contract calls for a fee of $2,500, plus hotels for two days and 50 percent of your transportation costs from home to the venue. This is a good starting point because

MARCH WEST COAST TOUR/CALENDAR #1

Monday	Tuesday	Wednesday	Thursday	Friday	Saturday	Sunday
Feb 23	24	25	26	27	28	March 1
2	3	4	5	6	7	8
9	10	11	12	13	14	15
16	17	18	19 College Festival Concert, L.A., CA	20 College Clinic, L.A., CA	21	22
23	24	25	26	27	28	29
30	31	April 1	2	3	4	5
6	7	8	9	10	11	12

the total for your four salaries for the two dates will be $1,400. You've checked with your travel agent and your airfares will cost $2,000, which means you will add $1,000 to your income from the gig, making the total $3,500. You also make a note of the cost of the airfare, because you'll need to add it to your expenses later.

Take a look at your calendar. It looks pretty empty at this point. All those blank dates around the anchor gig are staring you in the face. You could afford to fly the band out there, do the gig, take the money and run, and go home after the gig. After salaries and expenses, you would come home with $450 for two days' worth of work ($350 for the two gigs, plus $100 left over after all of the expenses are paid). That's not too bad.

However, an anchor gig is a valuable resource. Don't waste it. You won't achieve your long-term goals of making a living, gaining exposure for your band, playing a lot, and keeping your band together just by taking the easy way out and doing this one gig. Consider this gig as a starting point for booking a West Coast tour.

Since you're working a year in advance, you have enough time to look for other anchor gigs, secondary anchor gigs, and support gigs that could take your band into other areas of the region. You'll need more anchor gigs so you can raise the tour travel-margin figure (i.e., the balance after salaries—and agents' fees, if applicable—are deducted from income) high enough to pay for the expenses associated with an extended tour. You'll eventually learn how to figure ballpark estimates of your tour's financial status. However, when you're putting together your first few tours, you'll need to create a tentative tour budget as soon as you have acquired enough gigs to get a rough picture of the tour. Tentative budgets can be very helpful guideposts during the booking process, though of course, you'll never be completely sure of what the tour budget will be until you've finished booking it.

Work outward from your anchor gigs. Be careful when booking the first and last dates of a tour at the beginning of your booking process. If your first and last dates are too far apart, you may find that you have too many open dates in the middle of your tour that you can't fill. If the first and last dates are too close together, you may not have enough time to do the gigs you need to do to make your tour budget work. It's safe to assume that a week between anchor gigs is okay. After you've spent a couple of weeks working on booking your anchor gigs, you'll probably get a good sense of how long your tour is going to be. Then you can start working on your first and last tour gigs. This will give shape to your tour. At this point you can call your travel agent or look on the Internet for general estimates of your round-trip airfares and what it will cost to go from region to region. Once you have that information, you'll be in a reasonable position to make the first of many tentative tour budgets. Tentative budgets help keep track of how a tour is progressing financially, and how close or far away you are from having a viable tour.

By looking at your map, you figure that you're in a good geographical position to extend the tour to southern California, as well as the Bay Area around San Francisco. Flights between states along the coast are not expensive. So you figure you can work the Northwest and maybe the Southwest as well. Try to minimize backtracking to and from regions as much as possible. Although sometimes unavoidable, backtracking can make your transportation costs too high. Your plan at this point in the booking process is to work your way down from the Northwest, through northern and southern California, and into the Southwest, assuming you can find an anchor in each region.

Next, look at your leads for other anchor and secondary anchor gigs in these areas. With your files in front of you, prepare to start shotgunning your calls. You intentionally start calling on a Monday, the worst day for reaching anybody. Nobody is in the office or at home and you leave twenty messages. Normally it might be frustrating not to get through to your clients, however, when you're shotgunning your calls, leaving messages can work to your advantage. The fewer people you have to actually talk to, the more introductory calls you can make in one day.

Later that day, a client from a college in Vancouver, British Columbia, calls you back. She just started thinking about next year's program and might be interested in hiring you. You make your pitch and ask for $2,500, plus hotel costs, for a quartet concert and clinic.

Since the venue is in Canada, you also ask her to absorb your work fees and take care of the immigration paperwork. She likes your proposal—the time of year looks good and your fee is reasonable. She thinks she can afford you but the budget for next year won't be in until the end of the school year—in May, two months from now. Note her call-back date. You ask which are the best days in the week for the gig to happen, and you find out that the college usually does concert-clinics on Tuesdays.

Because you're not sure where you'll be coming from on March 3, you and she agree upon Wednesday the fourth as a tentative date for the concert, with the clinic on the morning of the fifth. Enter these dates on your calendar, with a question mark after each one. These are good "possibles." However, looking at your calendar, you see that this gig is two weeks prior to your L.A. gig. So you ask your client for alternative dates for exactly a week later—just in case you can't fill in the open days between the two anchors. Don't enter the alternative date into your calendar until it looks like you're going to change the dates from the fourth/fifth to the eleventh/twelfth.

You now have good "possibles" lined up. So the next day, you call a Victoria lead you called before and leave a second message, mentioning the date of the Vancouver gig. You don't hear from the contact. After a week you call back again and this time you connect with the client. You mention that your band may be in Vancouver, so it would be a good time for him to take advantage of the fact that you may be nearby. The client hasn't booked that period yet and tells you that he wants your band, if he can afford it. That's a clue that the venue has some budget concerns, so you mention that you can be flexible if the Vancouver gig confirms. The client needs to know if you can confirm now. A gut feeling tells you that the Vancouver gig is solid, so you accept a verbal commitment for a fee of $1,750, plus hotel costs, for a band concert-clinic on March 6. Your contact tells you that he will send you the contract in a month. Log the venue on your tour calendar and the contract arrival date in your computer calendar program.

Things are looking good now. You have good anchor gigs for two regions. There are also jazz clubs in Canada, Washington, and Oregon that might fill in weekends here and there, but these clubs book only three to six months in advance, so you'll probably have to wait seven to eight months before you book and confirm those gigs. In any case, you call a few venues and alert them that you'll be touring nearby, asking if they'd be interested in having you perform, and when you should call them back. A Vancouver club says the college gig on March 4 wouldn't be a conflict for them and that they might want to book you on the seventh and eighth. You double-check with your client at the college in Vancouver, and she tells you it *would* be a conflict for the college, as they would be using your appearance to promote the college's newly created jazz department. You keep the club gig as a backup, just in case Vancouver doesn't finally commit.

A Seattle club is interested for March 1 and 2, and another club in Portland is interested for March 7 and 8. Seattle can commit three months in advance of the date, and Portland can commit six months in advance. You enter call-back alarms in your computer for a month in advance of the dates they told you, and send each of the venues a press kit and a CD. You enter these dates into your calendar and budget with question marks. Use question marks for gigs that look solid but have not yet confirmed.

You're almost done with your first round of calls, but you don't have any "possibles" for that three-day hole from the ninth to the eleventh. Because of the empty dates and your awareness that the clubs may not confirm, you call ten other venues to see if they'd be interested in booking you. Five never bother to answer your calls. File them away for the next time. Of the five that do call you back, three colleges say they'd love to have you, but they don't have any leftover funds in their budgets to afford your fee.

However, one of the college contacts says that he may be able to afford you for a solo clinic. You tell him you'll keep him in mind, ask how soon in advance he needs to know, and that you'll do it if your itinerary allows it. The two others finally return your calls. A college in Bellingham, Washington, tentatively offers you a quartet clinic on the third for $750 (hotels not included), pending budget approval and tells you that they will call you back in three months to confirm the gig. So you add the gig to your tour calendar (along with a question mark), and add the income to your tour budget (again with a question mark). And a college in Portland, Oregon, offers you a quartet clinic on the eighth for $1,000 (hotels not included). Because you already have a tentative club gig in Portland that may pay $1,500 for two nights, plus hotels, you commit to the Portland clinic, at this time. If the club commits at a later date, you'd be making $2,500 for that weekend, plus hotel costs.

At this point, you decide to take a closer look at the dates from the sixth through the eighth. You're concerned about travel times, so you check with your map program and discover that it takes eight hours to drive from Victoria to Portland. That's pretty rough traveling, especially if you accept the club gig that starts the evening of the seventh. But look at your options. If the club does commit, you've got a good weekend's income with hotels paid. If the club doesn't commit, you can still come to Portland on the seventh and take the night off to rest up from the trip. You'll have to pay for hotels for two nights, but it's better than having the weekend open with no income at all, especially if you have no other leads for that weekend. The first week looks good.

During the past two weeks you have also called your other contacts. A jazz society in San Jose is interested in hiring you for a concert on the fifteenth and you made an offer of $1,500, plus hotel costs. Your contact has been talking with an agent for another band that is on tour at the same time, but the agent hasn't committed yet and is asking for a much higher fee. If he doesn't commit, your contact will give you the gig. You learn that the jazz society has an annual seven-concert subscription series, and that it sells tickets to the complete series in advance. Consequently, the society needs to know who's playing when by the end of the next month, so it can meet the deadline for producing the brochures that will advertise the series. You get a commitment date of one month from now and log a callback for two weeks ahead of that. You also enter the gig on your calendar with a question mark.

For this jazz society gig, one thing is working against you and two things are working for you. The reason the society wants the other band is that it is "hot" now. That's working against you. However, working in your favor is the fact that you can tell that the client is frustrated by dealing with the band's agent because he knows the agent is juggling the best dates for his band at alternative venues, and may not commit in time for the society's advertising deadline. Also, your fee will be much less than the other band's fee. You send your client a press kit and a CD. When you call your client back, he commits to you because he liked your band's music and the agent still hadn't committed or lowered his fee.

Of course, during the interim three weeks, you make calls to other anchor gigs in other regions and yield about a 50 percent response rate. Most of your responses are divided between "expressions of interest" and "not at this time" or "no money." However, during this time you complete negotiations with three other anchor gigs. A college in Berkeley, California, commits to a concert on March 12, for $1,500, plus hotel costs. A museum in Phoenix, Arizona, commits to a concert on March 27 for $2,000, plus hotel costs. And a college in Oklahoma City, Oklahoma, commits to a concert and a clinic on April 3, for $2,500, plus hotel costs. Although the Arizona and Oklahoma gigs are a little beyond the scope of a West Coast tour, you estimate that they are paying enough for you to afford to take them. Also, your call-back alarm reminded you to touch base with your contact at the college in Vancouver, and she confirmed the concert for March 4, with the clinic on the following day.

Now your tour looks like this.

MARCH WEST COAST TOUR/CALENDAR #2

Monday	Tuesday	Wednesday	Thursday	Friday	Saturday	Sunday
Feb 23	24	25	26	27	28 All fly to Seattle	**March 1** Club Gig, Seattle, WA?
2 Club Gig, Seattle, WA?	3 College Clinic, Bellingham, WA?	4 College Concert, Vancouver, BC	5 College Clinic, Vancouver, BC	6 Concert-Clinic, Victoria, BC	7 Club Gig, Portland, OR?	8 Club Gig, Portland, OR? College Clinic, Portland, OR
9	10	11	12 College Concert, Berkeley, CA	13	14	15 Jazz Society Concert, San Jose, CA
16	17	18	19 College Festival Concert, L.A., CA	20 College Clinic, L.A., CA	21	22
23	24	25	26	27 Museum Concert, Phoenix, AZ	28	29
30	31	April 1	2	3 College Festival & Clinic, Oklahoma City, OK	4	5
6	7	8	9	10	11	12

You now have eight gigs that have committed: five anchor gigs (which pay more than $1,500 per gig) and three secondary anchor gigs (which pay more than $1,000 per gig). You also have about twenty open days to fill, and the calendar still has some big holes. This is where the stressful part of routing a tour starts to intensify, because you'll begin to wonder if you will be able to fill in those holes. You've also used up about one-third of your contacts, about thirty leads. But you still have forty leads left to fill in those twenty days. And, you've booked $19,900 worth of potential work.

June, nine months before your tour:

Even though your total income looks pretty good, it's time to make your first tentative budget to see where the tour stands financially. The first step is to set up your spreadsheet with the tentative date parameters of your tour—from February 28 through April 3. Enter the total income for each gig (in the second column of the spreadsheet), and the salaries that you plan to pay yourself and each of your band members in the cells that correspond horizontally to each gig. You haven't yet locked yourself into the dates that you're going to fly to and from the West Coast. So, you still have the option of shifting the tour dates slightly, if you find that another set of dates would work better.

Spreadsheets can be set up so that all of the totals are automatically updated each time you enter a new figure. Before you start your first tentative tour budget, if you haven't done so already, familiarize yourself with the tallying functions of your spreadsheet program. Here are the cells in the facing tour budget that have been set up to show tallies:

- The total-income cell shows the sum of the second column.
- The individual salaries cells show the salaries for each of the four band members.
- The total salaries cell shows the total salaries of all of the band members.
- The travel-margin cell shows the tour balance *before* the travel expenses have been added into the equation (i.e., the total income minus the total salaries).

At this point you can see that your tour is in good shape. You've got a travel margin of $8,300. You've already determined that your round-trip airfare to the West Coast is going to cost you $2,000. However, the L.A. college festival concert agreed to pay half of it and you added that $1,000 to your income for March 19. If you deduct your airfare costs from your travel margin, the total is $6,300. This is approximately 30 percent of your total income. You generally estimate that travel and accommodations during a tour will cost 30 percent of your tour income. By this reckoning, your tour is looking good. (See budget on facing page.)

September, six months before your tour:

Bellingham's budget finally comes in and they commit to a clinic on March 3 for $800, plus hotel costs (which is better that their original offer). The Portland club also calls you back and confirms for March 7 and 8 and agrees to pay you $750 per gig, plus hotel costs. A college in Hayward, California, commits for a clinic on the eleventh for $1,000, plus hotel costs. A month later, a private house concert confirms for the seventeenth; the client agrees to pay you $850, and the band can stay at the client's house on Redondo Beach. A hotel in San Diego commits to two concerts, on the twenty-first and the twenty-second, for $1,200, plus free accommodations. While talking with the client for the San Diego gig, you learn that there is a hotel in Las Vegas that puts on concerts every Monday night, including an NPR radio broadcast. You call the Las Vegas hotel and

MARCH WEST COAST TOUR/BUDGET #1

DATE & VENUE	INCOME	SAL:You	SAL:Joe	SAL:John	SAL:Jane
FEBRUARY					
28					
MARCH					
1 Seattle?	700	200	200	200	200
2 Seattle?	700	200	200	200	200
3 Bellingham	750	150	150	150	150
4 Vancouver	2,500	200	200	200	200
5 Vancouver		150	150	150	150
6 Victoria	1,750	150	150	150	150
7–8 Club Gig, Portland?	1,500	400	400	400	400
8 Clinic, Portland	1,000	200	200	200	200
9					
10					
11					
12 Berkeley	1,500	200	200	200	200
13					
14					
15 San Jose	1,500	200	200	200	200
16					
17					
18					
19 Los Angeles	3,500	200	200	200	200
20 Los Angeles		150	150	150	150
21					
22					
23					
24					
25					
26					
27 Phoenix	2,000	200	200	200	200
28					
29					
30					
31					
APRIL					
1					
2					
3 Oklahoma City	2,500	300	300	300	300
TOTAL INCOME	**19,900**				
INDIVIDUAL SALARIES		2,900	2,900	2,900	2,900
TOTAL SALARIES	**11,600**				
TRAVEL MARGIN	**8,300**				

find out that the person who runs the venue just had a cancellation for March 24. He's a jazz fan and knows your name. You get the gig for $1,000, free accommodations, $600 for the broadcast, plus a copy of the DAT recording. This is a good time to do a broadcast because it will be close to the end of the tour and by then your band will be tight. You will also end up with a DAT tape that can eventually be used as a record master.

By now a lot of contracts have come in for your long-range gigs, including a college clinic in Dallas (for $1,200, no hotels paid) on April 4. Also a couple of concerts in Albuquerque ($1,000, no hotels paid) and Santa Fe ($1,200, plus accommodations at the client's home), which block book together, commit about this time for March 28 and 29 respectively. Your tour calendar is now looking pretty full. It's also time to do another tour budget to see the tour's financial status at this point.

MARCH WEST COAST TOUR/CALENDAR #3

Monday	Tuesday	Wednesday	Thursday	Friday	Saturday	Sunday
Feb 23	24	25	26	27	28 All fly to Seattle	March 1 Club Gig, Seattle, WA?
2 Club Gig, Seattle, WA?	3 College Clinic, Bellingham, WA	4 College Concert, Vancouver, BC	5 Morning College Clinic, Vancouver, BC	6 Clinic-Concert, Victoria, BC	7 Club Gig, Portland, OR	8 Club Gig, Portland, OR College Clinic, Portland, OR
9	10	11 College Clinic, Hayward, CA	12 College Concert, Berkeley, CA	13	14	15 Jazz Society Concert, San Jose, CA
16	17 House Concert, Redondo Beach, CA	18	19 College Festival Concert, L.A., CA	20 College Clinic, L.A., CA	21 Hotel Gig, San Diego, CA	22 Hotel Gig, San Diego, CA
23	24 Hotel Gig, Las Vegas, NV	25	26	27 Museum Concert, Phoenix, AZ	28 Concert, Albuquerque, NM	29 Concert, Santa Fe, NM
30	31	April 1	2	3 College Festival & Clinic, Oklahoma City, OK	4 College Clinic, Dallas, TX	5
6	7	8	9	10	11	12

MARCH WEST COAST TOUR/BUDGET #2

DATE & VENUE	INCOME	SAL:You	SAL:Joe	SAL:John	SAL:Jane
FEBRUARY					
28					
MARCH					
1 Seattle?	700	200	200	200	200
2 Seattle?	700	200	200	200	200
3 Bellingham	800	150	150	150	150
4 Vancouver	2,500	200	200	200	200
5 Vancouver					
6 Victoria	1,750	150	150	150	150
7–8 Club Gig, Portland	1,500	400	400	400	400
8 Clinic, Portland	1,000	200	200	200	200
9					
10					
11 Hayward	1,000	150	150	150	150
12 Berkeley	1,500	200	200	200	200
13					
14					
15 San Jose	1,500	200	200	200	200
16					
17 Redondo Beach	850	200	200	200	200
18					
19 Los Angeles	3,500	200	200	200	200
20 Los Angeles		150	150	150	150
21 San Diego	600	200	200	200	200
22 San Diego	600	200	200	200	200
23					
24 Las Vegas	1,600	300	300	300	300
25					
26					
27 Phoenix	2,000	200	200	200	200
28 Albuquerque	1,000	200	200	200	200
29 Santa Fe	1,200	200	200	200	200
30					
31					
APRIL					
1					
2					
3 Oklahoma City	2,500	300	300	300	300
4 Dallas	1,200	150	150	150	150
TOTAL INCOME	**28,000**				
INDIVIDUAL SALARIES		4,450	4,450	4,450	4,450
TOTAL SALARIES	**17,800**				
TRAVEL MARGIN	**10,200**				

The total income for your tour is now $28,000. The travel margin is $10,200, which is still comfortably more than 30 percent of the tour income. The tour is looking good, but you don't know your transportation and housing expenses yet. However, by looking at the calendar, some transportation and hotel costs become obvious. It's time to get a more accurate picture of your touring budget by adding in your housing and transportation cost estimates.

November, four months before your tour:

Make a list of the trips that you will need to take and their respective dates and fax this list to your travel agent for estimates. At this point it looks probable that the first and last travel days will be from home to Seattle on February 28, and from Dallas to home on April 5. These dates and regions should not change too much, but if they do, you'll still probably go to and return from the same regions.

- You're going to need a van in the Northwest for the period from March 2 to 8, approximately seven days.
- On March 9 or 10 you will have to fly from Portland to the Bay Area. Assume that San Francisco will be your destination. (Oakland and San Jose are also possibilities, but more on that later.)
- You will need a van in the Bay Area from either the ninth or tenth through the sixteenth or seventeenth, approximately seven days.
- On March 16 or 17 you will fly from the Bay Area to Los Angeles.
- You will probably need a rental van in L.A. for at least four days, and perhaps as many as seven, depending on how you decide to go to San Diego. Ask your agent to price the flights from L.A. to San Diego as well as how much it would cost you to drive the rental van for that trip.
- Since the fares are cheap, you decide that driving from San Diego to Las Vegas, a six-hour drive, is not worth the effort. So you'll plan to fly for that leg of the tour as well. Date yet to be determined.
- On March 25 or 26 you will fly from Las Vegas to Phoenix.
- On the morning of March 28 you will fly from Phoenix to Albuquerque.
- You will probably need a rental van in New Mexico, but since this part of the tour is undetermined you decide not to ask your travel agent to get these quotes just yet.
- Although this part of the tour isn't certain yet, you ask your agent to price the flights on April 2 or 3 from Albuquerque to Oklahoma City.
- Late on April 3 or early on April 4 you will fly from Oklahoma City to Dallas.

Your agent gets back to you with the airline and van-rental information. Even though the flights between L.A. and San Diego are cheap, you decide to drive the rental van for that leg of the tour, since it isn't very far. Now you're ready to add your travel expenses to the tentative tour budget.

Van rentals average $50 per day. You put each estimate in its proper location. In the airfare column, add the estimates for each flight. Make sure to include an airline fee of $50 per flight for the bass, in its case. Some airlines, depending on who you get for a counter agent, will often wave the bass fare, but it's best to add it in as an expected expense and deduct it later, if you don't actually incur that cost. If you're traveling with a drum set, make sure to add overweight charges for that as well.

MARCH WEST COAST TOUR/BUDGET #3

DATE & VENUE	INCOME	SAL:You	SAL:Joe	SAL:John	SAL:Jane	EXPENSES	
FEBRUARY						AIRFARES	
28						NY–WA, TX–NY	2,000
MARCH						Bass	100
1 Seattle?	700	200	200	200	200	Portland–Bay Area	500
2 Seattle?	700	200	200	200	200	Bass	50
3 Bellingham	800	150	150	150	150	Bay Area–L.A.	240
4 Vancouver	2,500	200	200	200	200	Bass	50
5 Vancouver						San Diego–Las Vegas	240
6 Victoria	1,750	150	150	150	150	Bass	50
7–8 Club Gig, Portland	1,500	400	400	400	400	Las Vegas–Phoenix	1,000
8 Clinic, Portland	1,000	200	200	200	200	Bass	50
9						Phoenix–Albuquerque	800
10						Bass	50
11 Hayward	1,000	150	150	150	150	Albuquerque–OK City	1,000
12 Berkeley	1,500	200	200	200	200	Bass	50
13						OK City–Dallas	1,000
14						Bass	50
15 San Jose	1,500	200	200	200	200	TOTAL AIRFARES	7,230
16							
17 Redondo Beach	850	200	200	200	200	VAN RENTALS	
18						WA	350
19 Los Angeles	3,500	200	200	200	200	Bay Area	350
20 Los Angeles		150	150	150	150	L.A.	350
21 San Diego	600	200	200	200	200	Gas & Tolls	75
22 San Diego	600	200	200	200	200	TOTAL VAN RENTALS	1,125
23							
24 Las Vegas	1,600	300	300	300	300	TOTAL TRANSPORT	8,355
25							
26						HOTELS	
27 Phoenix	2,000	200	200	200	200	3/9	300
28 Albuquerque	1,000	200	200	200	200	3/10	300
29 Santa Fe	1,200	200	200	200	200	3/13	300
30						3/14	300
31						3/16	300
APRIL						3/18	300
1						3/23	300
2						3/25	300
3 Oklahoma City	2,500	300	300	300	300	3/26	300
4 Dallas	1,200	150	150	150	150	3/30	300
5						3/31	300
						4/1	300
TOTAL INCOME	28,000					4/2	300
INDIVIDUAL SALARIES		4,100	4,100	4,100	4,100	TOTAL HOTELS	3,900
TOTAL SALARIES	17,800						
						TOTAL TRAVEL COSTS	12,255
						TOUR BALANCE	-2,055

Hotels can average $300 per night for four people. Right now you have thirteen open days in your schedule. These could add up to hotel expenses of $3,900—without counting the gigs for which you weren't able to negotiate hotel costs to be included. At this point, it looks like you are going to be $2,055 over budget. Although this doesn't look very encouraging, don't start to worry yet. Other gigs will still commit at later dates.

You figure that you will have one day a week off. However, you still need at least six to nine more gigs that *either* don't include hotels but pay at least 30 percent more than your salaries *or* pay your minimum salaries and hotels. Your final bookings will probably end up being a mix of the two.

About a month before the tour commences, you will need to make another tour budget that includes all of your late-committing gigs, and as much accurate information about your hotel and transportation expenses as possible. You'll call every hotel for its actual costs. And you'll have printouts of all of your airfares and van-rental expenses faxed to you by your travel agent.

December, about three months before your tour:

You've now got about fifteen leads left—some that look good and some that don't. It's time for you to recontact those late-committing gigs. The club in Seattle commits for two nights, on March 1 and 2 for $700 per night, plus hotel costs. Another club in San Francisco commits on March 9 for $600, and they have a four-bedroom apartment that the band can use. You just shaved $100 from your hotel expenses. How? Because the gig is paying $200 less than your base salary ($800), you'll have to make up the $200 shortfall from the tour budget. Instead of paying $300 for a hotel on an off day, that day is now only costing the budget $100.

A Napa Valley winery that puts on jazz concerts one Friday every month commits for March 14 at a fee of $800, but no hotels. A club in Santa Barbara commits for the sixteenth, but can only offer a guarantee of $400, plus the door and hotels. This saves $300 on the hotel, but you can't be sure that you'll make more than the guarantee. So you come out even on this gig because you have to make up the $400 shortfall on the salaries. But you still figure that it is worth your while to take the gig. There's a chance that you will make more than the guaranteed $400. And even if you don't, it is better to play and gain the audience exposure than to sit in your hotel room. You never know, this gig might lead to something else. Stranger things have happened.

At this point, you've deducted almost three days worth of hotel expenses ($800) from the budget, but you've also added another hotel expense for the gig in Napa.

Looking at the tour from March 1 to 22, the tour itself seems okay. The only period that's looking difficult to fill is the last week of the tour in Texas and Oklahoma. However, you've used up most of your leads by this time and are getting worried. Time for more research. You call the Dallas college back to ask for any leads and find out about a club in town that books national groups on Fridays or Saturdays. The club isn't booked yet and your contact likes the idea that you're doing a clinic the day before (it will help the draw), so she books you for April 5 for $800, plus hotel costs. She also mentions two other clubs that the club block books with in Houston and Fort Worth. You give the venues a quick call and they eventually book you on March 31 and April 2 for $800 each, plus hotel costs.

You've still got four days off for the last two weeks of the tour, but you luck out by finding a new jazz club in Denver. Your client there books you for two nights (March

MARCH WEST COAST TOUR/CALENDAR #4

Monday	Tuesday	Wednesday	Thursday	Friday	Saturday	Sunday
Feb 23	24	25	26	27	28 All fly to Seattle	March 1 Club Gig, Seattle, WA
2 Club Gig, Seattle, WA	3 College Clinic, Bellingham, WA	4 College Concert, Vancouver, BC	5 Morning College Clinic, Vancouver, BC	6 Clinic-Concert, Victoria, BC	7 Club Gig, Portland, OR	8 Club Gig, Portland, OR College Clinic, Portland, OR
9 Club Gig, San Francisco, CA	10 Day Off	11 College Clinic, Hayward, CA	12 College Concert, Berkeley, CA	13 Day Off	14 Winery Concert, Napa, CA	15 Jazz Society Concert, San Jose, CA
16 Club Gig, Santa Barbara, CA	17 House Concert, Redondo Beach, CA	18 Day Off	19 College Festival Concert, L.A., CA	20 College Clinic, L.A., CA	21 Hotel Gig, San Diego, CA	22 Hotel Gig, San Diego, CA
23 Day Off	24 Hotel Gig, Las Vegas, NV	25 Club Gig, Denver, CO	26 Club Gig, Denver, CO	27 Museum Concert, Phoenix, AZ	28 Concert, Albuquerque, NM	29 Concert, Santa Fe, NM
30 Day Off	31 Club Gig, Houston, TX	April 1 Day Off	2 Club Gig, Fort Worth, TX	3 College Festival & Clinic, Oklahoma City, OK	4 College Clinic, Dallas, TX	5 Club Gig, Dallas, TX
6 All fly home	7	8	9	10	11	12

25 and 26) for $1,500, and she has a hotel sponsor that gives the club rooms gratis. Your calendar is now looking like this. (See above.)

January, about one month before your tour:

Your tour is almost done, you think!

It's time to do a final budget. This involves finalizing your transportation and accommodations and using accurate figures for all tour budget entries. You'll need to look at your calendar and budget spreadsheets at the same time. You'll also have to go over your notes and contracts and double-check which gigs pay for hotels. Considering that you have to enter in all of the new data as well as call hotels, airlines, and van-rental companies (unless you can get your travel agent to do it for you), this process will probably take you at least a day or two. Open up your spreadsheet program and enter and delete amounts as you go along.

MARCH WEST COAST TOUR/BUDGET #4

DATE & VENUE	INCOME	SAL:You	SAL:Joe	SAL:John	SAL:Jane	EXPENSES	
FEBRUARY						AIRFARES	
28						NY–WA, TX–NY	2,000
MARCH						Bass	100
1 Seattle	700	200	200	200	200	Portland–Bay Area	500
2 Seattle	700	200	200	200	200	Bass	50
3 Bellingham	800	150	150	150	150	Bay Area–L.A.	240
4 Vancouver	2,500	200	200	200	200	Bass	50
5 Vancouver						San Diego–Las Vegas	240
6 Victoria	1,750	150	150	150	150	Bass	50
7–8 Club Gig, Portland	1,500	400	400	400	400	Las Vegas–Denver	1,000
8 Clinic, Portland	1,000	200	200	200	200	Bass	50
9 San Francisco	600	200	200	200	200	Denver–Phoenix	1,200
10 DAY OFF						Bass	50
11 Hayward	1,000	150	150	150	150	Phoenix–Albuquerque	800
12 Berkeley	1,500	200	200	200	200	Bass	50
13 DAY OFF						Albuquerque–OK City	1,000
14 Napa	800	200	200	200	200	Bass	50
15 San Jose	1,500	200	200	200	200	TOTAL AIRFARES	7,430
16 Santa Barbara	400	200	200	200	200		
17 Redondo Beach	850	200	200	200	200	VAN RENTALS	
18 DAY OFF						WA	350
19 Los Angeles	3,500	200	200	200	200	Bay Area	350
20 Los Angeles		150	150	150	150	L.A.	350
21 San Diego	600	200	200	200	200	Gas & Tolls	75
22 San Diego	600	200	200	200	200	TOTAL VAN RENTALS	1,125
23 DAY OFF							
24 Las Vegas	1,600	300	300	300	300	TOTAL TRANSPORT	8,555
25 Denver	750	200	200	200	200		
26 Denver	750	200	200	200	200	HOTELS	
27 Phoenix	2,000	200	200	200	200	3/10	300
28 Albuquerque	1,000	200	200	200	200	3/13	300
29 Santa Fe	1,200	200	200	200	200	3/14	300
30 DAY OFF						3/18	300
31 Houston	800	200	200	200	200	3/23	300
APRIL						3/28	300
1 DAY OFF						3/30	300
2 Fort Worth	800	200	200	200	200	4/1	300
3 Oklahoma City	2,500	300	300	300	300	4/4	300
4 Dallas	1,200	150	150	150	150	TOTAL HOTELS	2,700
5 Dallas	800	200	200	200	200		
						TOTAL MISC. EXPENSES	0
TOTAL INCOME	33,700						
INDIVIDUAL SALARIES		5,950	5,950	5,950	5,950	TOTAL TRAVEL COSTS	11,255
TOTAL SALARIES	23,800						
						TOUR BALANCE	-1,355

Enter your new gig's income and salaries. Then enter your hotel expenses. You have days off on March 10, 13, 18, 23, and 30, and April 1. After you check your venue work-sheets, you discover that the gigs on March 14, 28, and April 4 aren't paying hotels. You'll have to pay hotels for only nine days. (See left.) But your tour budget is still more than $1,000 in the red.

It's time to start checking actual rates for the hotels for which you are paying. At this point you'll also scrutinize the expenses for each day of the tour to see where you can shave $25 here to $300 there. You'd be surprised at what you can save by thinking about what's going on each day. There will be some negative surprises as well. This will be discussed more in depth later.

Start with your first hotel expense date on the calendar-budget and enter the new information into your budget as you go along. The band is staying at the San Francisco club's apartment for the gig on the ninth and you arrange to stay there on the tenth as well, saving $300 from your hotel expenses. When you check in with the client in Berkeley, he reserves rooms the thirteenth on his credit card and gets you a corporate rate of $50 per person. Enter $200 for March 13.

Checking your publicity notes, you notice that there is a radio station in Los Angeles that might do a radio interview at 9:00 A.M. on the morning of the concert (March 19) to promote your appearance at the college festival. Call the festival to arrange it for you, but mention that you'll be a three-hour drive away from L.A. on the day of the inter-view. Ask if they can pay for the hotel on March 18, so you can drive down a day ahead of time to make the interview the next morning. That saves another $300 on March 18.

You're really trying to shave that budget now. After staring at your notes and cal-endar, you realize that the San Diego gigs on March 21 and 22 are in a hotel. Call them back and arrange free rooms for the day off on the twenty-third. Delete another $300 from your hotel costs.

On March 28, you get hotel rooms for 50 percent off with your Quest Card Membership at $60 per person. (For more about this, see chapter ten.) Enter $240 into the budget for that day.

In Santa Fe, on March 29, you forgot that the band is staying at the client's home. Arrange to stay there on the day off after the concert, too. Deduct another $300 from the budget. The hotels on April 1 and 4 fall into place, using AAA discounts at $220 and $260 per night, respectively.

Your tour balance is now in the black $125, but you're not done yet.

Now you need to scrutinize the travel section of your budget to see if there are any places where you might be able to shave off some costs. You decide to start by looking at the transportation for the Texas–Oklahoma segment of your tour. How are you going to travel from Santa Fe to Houston to Fort Worth to Oklahoma City to Dallas, and what is it going to cost? Time to go back to your map program to see how many flights you can avoid taking by driving the last week of the tour.

Santa Fe to Houston is a thirteen-hour drive. You'll have to fly and add that leg of the trip to your budget. Luckily, there are inexpensive $75 flights to Houston. Add another $300 to the airfare column in Budget #5 and $50 for the bass. Houston to Fort Worth is a six-hour drive. That's okay. Fort Worth to Oklahoma City is three hours. No problem. Oklahoma City to Dallas is another three-hour drive. Driving the last week is doable. Because you are renting the van in Texas and returning it in Texas, there are no one-way charges. You'll have to add another seven-day van rental ($350) and gas expense ($50) to the budget. Your tour suddenly went into negative numbers by $625.

It's time to rethink your situation. The question to answer now is which one of these gigs is costing more than it's earning? After staring at your calendar and spreadsheet a while, you begin to wonder if you can you afford to do the Denver gig. Better do another alternative budget, leaving the Denver gig out of the tour, to see what happens to the budget. This means that there will be an added expense for hotels for the two additional days off as well as the airfares from Vegas to Phoenix.

In Budget #5, reenter the airfare from Las Vegas to Phoenix, which is $1,000, and delete the $1,200 airfare from Denver to Phoenix. Delete the income and salaries from the Denver gig as well. The tour balance jumps up by $300. It looks like you're going to have to cancel the Denver gig. Call the Denver gig and explain your transportation problems and cancel the gig. You'll have it on file for another tour.

Any more ways to cut down on your expenses?

Looking back at your venue worksheet you remember that the Vegas gig on March 24 is a hotel. Calling the Vegas client back, you learn that hotel rooms in Vegas are cheap, only $35 per person, per night. You could stay in Vegas for the twenty-fifth and twenty-sixth for $280—which is $320 less than your standard estimate of $600 for two nights. Not bad, but why not see if you can shave the budget even more? Looking at the calendar, you notice that you could go to Phoenix on the twenty-sixth, and avoid traveling on the day of a gig. You also observe that on the twenty-seventh, the clinic in Phoenix is at 11:00 A.M. Just to be sure that all is well, you go back on the Internet and discover that you can't get any flights to Phoenix early enough on the morning of the twenty-seventh to get you there in time. You have to leave Las Vegas on the twenty-sixth. Checking your venue worksheet for this gig you note that the college is giving you rooms sponsored by a local hotel that supports the college music program by supplying free hotel rooms to visiting artists.

Call the Phoenix client and explain that you can't get from Vegas to Phoenix in time to make the morning clinic. After apologizing for the mix-up, explain how the tour routing changed since the time the gig was negotiated. Ask your client if she can give you an extra day's rooms. No problem says the client. You've just saved another day's hotel expenses.

However, the van expenses for the Northwest, Bay Area, and L.A. were only estimates, so you'll have to tighten those up. Let's look at the Northwest rental first. Oops! If you arrive in Seattle on February 28, as planned, you'll have to pay an extra day's hotels that you didn't notice, and account for it in your hotel budget. Change your plans to fly into Seattle early on March 1.

You don't need a van for March 1 and 2, because the hotel is within walking distance of the gig. The club has no van to pick you up at the airport, but the airport is close to the city and has minivan taxis that will only charge $30 to take you to your hotel. By not renting the van until you need it on March 3 to drive to Bellingham, you also save $80. You've been estimating the van rentals at a rate of $50 per day. You'll need that van for the six-day period, from the third through the ninth, and the rental company has a special on for a weekly rental at a rate of $275, with no extra charge for a one-way rental from Seattle to Portland. Change your estimate for that period from $350 to $275.

Notice that I just put the general term "Bay Area" in for the next leg of the tour. That's because there are three major airports in the Bay Area from which to choose: Oakland, San Francisco, and San Jose. You'd think that flying into San Francisco would be the obvious choice, but there are other considerations. It's $20 cheaper per person to fly from Portland to Oakland than to San Francisco, and the rental-car agencies at the Oakland airport don't charge the 18 percent airport tax and surcharge that San Francisco does. You save $65 on the van rental and $80 on the airfares. There are also no one-way rental fees from picking a van up at one airport and dropping it off at either of the other two. The seven-day rental for March 9 to 15 is $300.

Be sure you time the flights in and out of each area carefully so that they correspond with the time of day of the van rentals. For example, time your flight to Oakland so that you don't arrive too early in the day. You want to rent the van late enough in the day so that you can return the van in San Jose in time to avoid an extra day's rental charge. If you pick up the van at 11:00 A.M. and return it at 1:00 P.M., you'll have to pay the extra charge. An extra day's charge is not prorated and can cost anywhere from $50 to $90. As you'll be renting another van when you get to L.A., you could end up paying for two days of van rentals on the same day.

The L.A. van rental is pretty straightforward, except for the end of the week. Do you need the van in San Diego? It seemed like you would need to rent the van for ten days, from the sixteenth through the twenty-fourth, to get to the airport for your flight to Las Vegas. That could be a seven-day rental plus two extra days on the twenty-third and twenty-fourth, at an extra cost of $70 per day. However, careful scrutiny and some research paints another picture. A more economical approach is to rent the van for a seven-day rate of $350 and drive to San Diego (one-ways rentals are okay). The hotel in San Diego has a courtesy van that will take you to the airport on the twenty-fourth. So you can turn the van in on the twenty-second, and avoid the extra two days' charge. You didn't think about those extra days when you did your earlier budgets, so the rental figure for that period stays the same.

Are you through with all the expenses and travel considerations? Not yet. What about getting to and from Canada?

The ferry fees are $15 for the van and driver and $5 for each additional passenger. Add $60 (round-trip) to the miscellaneous expenses row. For the ferry from Victoria (Vancouver Island) to Port Angeles, add $30 more to the miscellaneous expenses. And for the Ferry to Seattle, add $15 to the miscellaneous expenses.

The tour is booked. The budget is now $575 in the black.

This is the way your tour budget and tour calendar look now. (See following pages.)

However, five of the flights you take don't charge you for the bass, so in the end you take home an additional $250. Not too bad, considering.

The process for booking tours is similar in foreign counties. The differences are the language problems, currency-exchange rates, lead times, higher airfares, and higher fees.

MARCH WEST COAST TOUR/BUDGET #5

DATE & VENUE	INCOME	SAL:You	SAL:Joe	SAL:John	SAL:Jane	EXPENSES	
FEBRUARY						AIRFARES	
28						NY–WA, TX–NY	2,000
MARCH						Bass	100
1 Seattle	700	200	200	200	200	Portland–Bay Area	500
2 Seattle	700	200	200	200	200	Bass	50
3 Bellingham	800	150	150	150	150	San Jose–L.A.	240
4 Vancouver	2,500	200	200	200	200	Bass	50
5 Vancouver						San Diego–Las Vegas	240
6 Victoria	1,750	150	150	150	150	Bass	50
7–8 Club Gig	1,500	400	400	400	400	Las Vegas–Phoenix	1,000
8 Clinic, Portland	1,000	200	200	200	200	Bass	50
9 San Francisco	600	200	200	200	200	Phoenix–Albuquerque	800
10 DAY OFF						Bass	50
11 Hayward	1,000	150	150	150	150	Santa Fe–Houston	300
12 Berkeley	1,500	200	200	200	200	Bass	50
13 DAY OFF						Albuquerque–OK City	1,000
14 Napa	800	200	200	200	200	Bass	50
15 San Jose	1,500	200	200	200	200	TOTAL AIRFARES	6,530
16 Santa Barbara	400	200	200	200	200		
17 Redondo Beach	850	200	200	200	200	VAN RENTALS	
18 DAY OFF						WA	275
19 Los Angeles	3,500	200	200	200	200	Bay Area	300
20 Los Angeles		150	150	150	150	L.A.	350
21 San Diego	600	200	200	200	200	TX–OK–TX	350
22 San Diego	600	200	200	200	200	Gas & Tolls	125
23 DAY OFF						TOTAL VAN RENTALS	1,400
24 Las Vegas	1,600	300	300	300	300		
25 DAY OFF						MISC. EXPENSES	
26 DAY OFF						Taxis	30
27 Phoenix	2,000	200	200	200	200	Ferrys	105
28 Albuquerque	1,000	200	200	200	200	TOTAL MISC. EXPENSES	135
29 Santa Fe	1,200	200	200	200	200		
30 DAY OFF						TOTAL TRANSPORT	8,065
31 Houston	800	200	200	200	200		
APRIL						HOTELS	
1 DAY OFF						3/13	200
2 Fort Worth	800	200	200	200	200	3/14	300
3 Oklahoma City	2,500	300	300	300	300	3/25	140
4 Dallas	1,200	150	150	150	150	3/28	240
5 Dallas	800	200	200	200	200	4/1	220
						4/4	260
TOTAL INCOME	32,200					TOTAL HOTELS	1,360
INDIVIDUAL SALARIES		5,550	5,550	5,550	5,550		
TOTAL SALARIES	22,200					TOTAL TRAVEL COSTS	9,425
						TOUR BALANCE	575

MARCH WEST COAST TOUR/CALENDAR #5

Monday	Tuesday	Wednesday	Thursday	Friday	Saturday	Sunday
Feb 23	24	25	26	27	28	**March 1** All fly to Seattle Club Gig, Seattle, WA
2 Club Gig, Seattle, WA	3 College Clinic, Bellingham, WA	4 College Concert, Vancouver, BC	5 Morning College Clinic, Vancouver, BC	6 Clinic-Concert, Victoria, BC	7 Club Gig, Portland, OR	8 Club & Clinic, Portland, OR
9 Club Gig, San Francisco, CA	10 Day Off	11 College Clinic, Hayward, CA	12 College Concert, Berkeley, CA	13 Day Off	14 Winery Concert, Napa, CA	15 Jazz Society Concert, San Jose, CA
16 Club Gig, Santa Barbara, CA	17 House Concert, Redondo Beach, CA	18 Day Off	19 College Festival Concert, L.A., CA	20 College Clinic, L.A., CA	21 Hotel Gig, San Diego, CA	22 Hotel Gig, San Diego, CA
23 Day Off in San Diego, CA	24 Hotel Gig, Las Vegas, NV	25 Day Off in Las Vegas, NV	26 Travel Day and Day Off in Phoenix, AZ	27 Museum Concert, Phoenix, AZ	28 Concert, Albuquerque, NM	29 Concert, Santa Fe, NM
30 Day Off	31 Club Gig, Houston, TX	April 1 Day Off	2 Club Gig, Fort Worth, TX	3 College Festival & Clinic, Oklahoma City, OK	4 College Clinic, Dallas, TX	5 Club Gig, Dallas, TX
6 All fly home	7	8	9	10	11	12

Chapter 10

Arranging Travel and Accommodations in North America

When you're booking a tour, reserve a few days and nights just to work on transportation. Expect to spend a lot of time on the Internet and on the phone with your travel agent. Or, if you're making the travel arrangements yourself, plan to spend a lot of time calling the airlines, hotels, and van-rental companies. Once your travel agent has finalized your travel itinerary, he or she can fax you reservation sheets for the flights, van rentals, and hotels. These sheets will be invaluable when it comes time for you to create your itineraries and finalize your budget estimates. Review the reservation sheets carefully for accuracy, and alert your agent immediately if you discover any errors. Keep these sheets on file.

As we discussed in chapter nine, at a certain point in booking a tour, you're going to need to calculate an estimated tour budget—*even though all of the venue commitments will probably not be committed yet*—just to see if the tour is looking economically feasible. I usually do this about two months before the first date on the tour. This process allows you to spot any financially weak points during the tour and to make any necessary routing, transportation, or accommodation changes to improve the profitability of your tour. Since you'll need to have real expense figures when you draft these near-to-final tour budgets, you'll need to have the travel agent's cost estimates on hand. Try different scenarios with alternate budget spreadsheets to see if there may be other ways to route your tour that would be more economical.

ENHANCING YOUR QUALITY OF LIFE WHILE ON THE ROAD

Transportation, routing, and hotel considerations are complex and fraught with potential for mishaps that can affect tour budgets as well as your quality of life while on the road. To minimize the potential for mishap as best you can you must pay scrupulous attention to every detail of the business of travel *before* you leave for your tour—because this is when you can best solve the problems. Quality of life on the road has a direct bearing on a band's social interaction as well as its ability to perform. Striking a balance between maintaining a good quality of life and sustaining the economic viability of a tour will be a real challenge for you as the bandleader. These issues arise most visibly when you're dealing with your travel arrangements.

Large geographical leaps from venue to venue can be expensive and exhausting. They are expensive because flights for long distances are often costly. They are exhausting because excessive traveling depletes each band member's personal energy (which, you remember, is his or her most valuable asset while on the road). This in turn affects performance quality as well as the band members' abilities to interact well in the intimate and stressful environment of the road. There is no sense going on tour if upon arrival at an engagement your band is too tired to play well. Your capacity to fulfill the challenging demands of being a bandleader and conducting business with your clients on the road will also become severely diminished if you don't maintain certain quality-of-life standards. So, be vigilant when you're making your travel arrangements.

ARRANGING AIR TRAVEL

One of the many hats you will be required to wear as bandleader is that of "expert travel arranger." Air travel will inevitably be one of the biggest travel expenses of each tour. Therefore, your ability to find and book timely *and cheap* flights will directly affect the ultimate profitability of your tour. Luckily, with the advent of the Internet it is a lot easier to find cheap flights than it used to be. The Internet allows you to do research during nonbusiness hours. So, if you wake up in the middle of the night worrying about how you're going to schedule that flight from Las Vegas to Tucson, you can hop on-line and find a deal that will ease your mind. I tend to use the Internet as a first source for information. Once I find flights that work with my schedule and itinerary, I fax the information to my travel agent so that he can iron out the details.

Working with Travel Agents

Travel agents want your repeat business. As a result, I've found that they work harder, go out of their way for a client more frequently, and are more concerned about a client's budget than other sources. They are also usually more aware of special programs that airline carriers offer, and they have personal relationships with airlines' ticket agents that come in handy—especially when you have special requests, which you often have when traveling with a band.

It may take time for you to find a true professional who comprehends the complexities of a touring band's transportation requirements. But once you do, it will be worth your while to cultivate a good working relationship with him or her. Survey other musicians and booking agents and ask them about their travel agents. Test a prospective agent by having him or her reserve a trial tour and then call one or two more agents and have them do the same. Once all the quotes are in, compare prices, quality of service, and each agent's willingness to work hard. The major factors to consider are the agent's awareness of your budget concerns, expertise, and depth of patience.

A qualified agent holds appointments from the International Air Transport Association (IATA) and the Airlines Reporting Corporation (ARC). These qualifications indicate that he or she has met the financial and professional requirements that the airlines deem necessary to trust him or her with blank air tickets. Other affiliations to look for are membership in the American Society of Travel Agents (ASTA) and the Association of Retail Travel Agents (ARTA). Many qualified travel agents have the initials CTC (Certified Travel Counselor) after their names.

My travel agent is a magician. There have been countless times that I've called him in a panic after doing an estimated budget that made the tour look like it was going to go over budget. His patience and knowledge of the travel business has saved countless tours from financial disaster. I couldn't function as a bandleader without him.

Your travel agent can be your best friend, or your worst enemy. You'll have to work closely with him or her when it comes time to arrange your tour transportation. So be mindful of maintaining a positive working relationship. But always remember that good travel agents are usually overworked. Stay on your agent's good side by showing that you have a firm grasp of the realities of travel, and a healthy respect for his or her time.

Only you possess the basic information about where and when you're going, and what you're doing on a tour. In order for your agent to dependably work on your travel plans you will need to give this information to him or her as succinctly as possible. How well your agent is able to function directly depends on how accurate the information you give him or her is. If you forget to mention a crucial piece of information, the arrangements that your agent makes for you may not actually suit your needs.

Transmitting the mass of information necessary to make tour travel arrangements, verbally, by phone, is time-consuming and leaves you open to communication mistakes. Before I was fluent with the Internet, I used to type a list of the travel dates, gig times, and destinations, which I then faxed to my agent for further discussion. Even though I *thought* I was being thorough, I often left out important details. Now, I print out a copy of my calendar and fax it to the agent along with any details and instructions that I feel are relevant. This ensures that we're on the same track when we finally do speak.

Since only you know the times you need to arrive at your destinations, you can save your agent a lot of time by researching your flights on the Net. Print the relevant pages and fax them to your agent, who can then reserve and order them for you—and maybe even find less expensive fares for these same flights. Ask your agent if a flight looks like it will be full. Don't take a chance on being assigned an uncomfortable seat. Reserve those much-coveted aisle or window seats in advance and get to the airport early. Save all of your faxes to your agent in a manila folder, along with your contracts. You'll need the arrival and departure times later, to let your venues know about airport pickup and drop-off times.

At the time that you're scheduling your travel itinerary, your tour calendar should be fairly complete, showing all of the dates you've booked thus far, as well as any open or unconfirmed dates. My computer calendar has icons for planes, trains, and cars, which I use to highlight my travel days. That way I have a clear picture of each travel day, and the form of transportation I'll be using. Use your checklists to make sure every flight and van rental has been included. Note any TBCs (gigs to-be-confirmed), their expected confirmation dates, and the cities to which you'll be flying or driving.

There are a number of travel concerns, peculiar to touring musicians, that other travelers may not share. For example:

- All of the airplanes that you take must be large enough to handle the bass case. Some planes might be big enough, but have baggage doorways too small to accommodate the bass. Especially confirm local flights in the United States as well as all planes in Europe.
- In Europe, flights on Fridays through Mondays are busier than midweek flights. Don't assume you'll be able to get seats on a flight and then wait too long to check availability.

- Flights from major to minor cities in Europe are less frequent than similar flights in the United States. Often there may be only one flight in the early morning (no sleep for you if you had a late gig the night before), and another one in the early evening (which might get you in too late to make your gig). Some days there may be no flights to your destination.

As long as you discuss your needs with your agent *in detail*, the travel planning process should run smoothly. And if you do encounter problems when you're setting up the travel plans for your tour, remember that you can alter your tour to meet your travel restrictions. For instance, if you find that you can't fly into a smaller European city on the day that you had hoped, you may need to keep some dates open as travel days (for which, hopefully, you can get your venue to pay).

In addition to making arrangements for air travel, your travel agent can also make arrangements for van rentals and hotels. You might want to take the time to go on the Internet to do your own research, and then relay the information to your agent. However, if you find that you're crunched for time, that is a relatively easy job for your agent.

Making Your Own Airline Reservations

Although I personally like to work with a travel agent, making your own travel arrangements has some benefits. The primary one is speed. Solidifying your own travel plans is a one-step (or close to a one-step) process. Working with a travel agent is a multistep process. When you work with an agent, you need to prepare your travel notes, send the material to your agent, confirm the details with the agent over the phone, give the agent time to work out your arrangements, receive and review the tentative arrangements, and respond to the agent—either with an okay or with adjustments. If you're working against a tight deadline, you may find that doing the reservations yourself is less stressful than trying to work your needs into an agent's (already pressured) schedule.

Keeping airline travel expenses to a minimum will always be a priority—but this is especially true when you're starting a new band. Whether you fly coach-, business-, or first-class will depend on your tour budget. In most cases, assume you'll be flying coach-class, unless your band has a name recognition value that would permit business- or first-class travel. The availability of business-class service is growing, and although these fares are more expensive than coach-class, this level of service is more personal and provides the traveler a larger baggage allowance. For foreign travel, the increased baggage allowance alone can result in significant savings. However, for domestic travel, the money saved on baggage will probably not outweigh the higher costs of traveling business-class.

If you decide to make your own travel arrangements, you need to know where you can turn for good, cheap travel information.

TICKETING AND INFORMATION SERVICES Airline tickets as well as van rentals—and in some cases hotel reservations—can be arranged and purchased from a variety of sources, including airlines, discount houses, travel services, travel clubs, the Internet, and (as was previously discussed) travel agents. The quality of these services can vary greatly, and the cost of airline tickets may change daily. Many factors affect the prices of fares.

Busy air routes between major cities are often less expensive than less-traveled routes between smaller cities. Off-peak-season fares are usually cheaper than high-season fares and vary according to the destination. Summer is not an off-peak season when you're traveling to Europe, but it is when flying to Australia. Purchase-by dates, which are discussed later in this chapter, also affect pricing. Determining when will be the most opportune time to buy a ticket is often a judgment call.

Here are the most helpful sources of ticketing information:

Airlines: Airline ticket agents have the same flight information as travel agents, but an airline representative will not work as hard as a travel agent to find practical, inexpensive flights (and, of course, airline representatives only have information about their particular carrier). Airline ticket agents also tend to be restricted by company policies and aren't as flexible as travel agents. Fare quotes from airlines tend to be higher than from agents because airlines have an interest in making a profit for their employers, and the information is often not consistent—calling an airline three times may elicit three different fare quotes. However, as good travel agents are often busy, airline agents can be a good and quick source for basic information about flight times, routings, and seat availability.

Discount Houses: These sellers, which are often refered to as "consolidators," deal in bulk with discounted tickets that they have purchased from the airlines. Consolidators are sometimes accessible to the general public, and they often offer the cheapest tickets you can buy. The downside to purchasing airline tickets through a discount house is that the tickets are usually nonchangeable, nonrefundable, and very restrictive, plus discount houses don't always have tickets for all carriers. Buy discount tickets only if your itinerary is firmly set and changes are not expected.

The first year I had my trio on the road, before I discovered my travel agent, I bought three tickets to Europe from a discount ticket house. Upon checking in at the gate, I discovered that the fares were cheap because I had unknowingly purchased wait-list tickets. Noticing how crowded the gate was with departing passengers, I started to get nervous about making the flight. Luckily, the "Shmooze Meister," bassist Todd Coolman, was with the band at the time. We double-teamed the ticket agent with our good-guy (Todd) bad-guy (me) routine. The combination worked and we made our flight. But now I go over every ticket I buy with a fine-tooth comb. Since that experience, I have only used discount tickets purchased through a travel agent. Be sure to ask about the restrictions on any tickets that you buy through a discount house. Some consolidators advertise their services in newspaper travel sections and travel magazines and you can contact them yourself, but it's safer to use your travel agent to handle this type of ticket.

Travel Services: American Express and AAA are two of the main travel services. These services are tourist-trade oriented and, while they may be very helpful for the nonbusiness traveler, their representatives may not have the patience or the expertise that is necessary to understand the complex needs of the touring musician.

Travel Clubs: Advertised in newspapers, travel clubs most often sell charter flights. Though the tickets that are available through travel clubs are inexpensive, they're unpredictable. Departure and return dates can be delayed or even canceled. Charters don't offer the scheduling flexibility you require as a touring musician.

The Internet: One of the easiest ways to access schedules and prices is through the Internet. Microsoft's Expedia Travel Service, at http://expedia.msn.com/daily/home/default.hts, is one of the best and fastest on-line travel sites. Its travel-agent link will search for fares for any date, at any time—one-way or round-trip—and list them from the cheapest to the most expensive, on every airline that travels your route. Departure and arrival times, number of connections, and total travel times are also listed for each flight. The site also lists purchase-by dates, and a combination feature that allows you to do open-jaw tickets and multiple flights. (Open-jaw tickets will be discussed in detail later in this chapter.)

Some other handy on-line ticketing services that offer different features are:

- http://www.lowestfare.com
- http://www.reallycheaptickets.com
- http://www.travelocity.com
- http://www.delta-air.com/womenexecs
- http://www.previewtravel.com/Home

Although the Internet is an excellent tool for researching your flight schedules, it's best to use a travel agent to finalize the complex details of touring transportation. Use the Internet to quickly research and access the information you'll need to know about your travel possibilities.

Mastering Ticket-Purchasing Strategies

Over time, you'll work out a system with your travel agent so that the two of you will efficiently coordinate your efforts. You'll never know as much about the business as your travel agent does. However, becoming familiar with certain essential ticket-purchasing strategies will help you communicate more effectively with your agent. The six most common ticketing strategies for the traveling musician are:

- avoid canceling or changing purchased tickets;
- use open-jaw tickets;
- use Saturday stay-over tickets;
- avoid one-way tickets;
- avoid having a third party make your travel arrangements;
- maximize free mileage.

Being familiar with these six strategies will not only help you communicate more efficiently with your agent, but it will also help you maximize your agent's efforts.

AVOID CANCELING OR CHANGING PURCHASED TICKETS At a certain stage in the process a tour takes on a life of its own, frequently changing its shape from what you had imagined in the beginning of the booking process. Accordingly, your travel arrangements will have to change with it. Sometimes a late-committing gig will come in that will require you to drastically change your travel arrangements in order to accept it. Depending upon how expensive it is to change your travel itinerary, you may or may not be able to accommodate the late gig. Changing the date or destination of an already-purchased ticket often involves penalties that can be expensive and prohibitive—unless, of course, the income from the late-committing gig warrants the extra expense.

One of the most frustrating aspects of booking a tour is the disparity of commitment times among different venues on your tour. Festivals and cultural venues may confirm a year or more in advance, while clubs may only confirm from two to six months in advance. There will be a cutoff point in the booking process of every tour, where you will have to decide whether or not you are finished booking. Oftentimes this cutoff point is dictated by the ticket purchase-by dates.

I've booked some tours that changed shape three times. At these moments you will need a patient travel agent. Many times, I've shortened a tour and found that the changes have *improved* the tour budget. Sometimes canceling a gig eliminates extra travel expenses, extra days off, or extra hotel expenses (i.e., lowers the tour's net expenses), whereby actually improving the entire tour's financial profile.

When you get information on flights—either from the Internet or from your travel agent—check the date on which prices may change as well as the date by which the tickets need to be purchased. Don't expect your agent to keep track of this information for you. Purchase-by dates have a direct bearing upon the need to receive final commitments from late-committing venues. However, purchase-by dates may vary from airline to airline. Some airlines have no purchase-by date at all, others may require that you pay for tickets within twenty-four hours of making the reservation. To avoid losing a good deal, make sure you ask about the stipulations.

It may happen that you will purchase your "outside" tickets (i.e., your tickets from home to the first gig and from the last gig to home) before you purchase the "inside" tickets (i.e., your venue-to-venue tickets). The first and last dates are the most important dates of a tour. Set the first tour date as soon as possible. The airplane ticket for your first date usually cannot be changed. You can often change the date of the last flight. However, this often involves a penalty (often from $25 to $75). Many smaller airlines have no purchase-by dates. It's possible to wait a little longer to buy tickets with these carriers, but if you wait, you risk losing seating availability. When you're making inquiries about a flight, check the seating status. If the flight looks relatively full, reserve the seats, but wait on the purchase of the tickets if you can.

Generally, the farther in advance you reserve and purchase your tickets, the less expensive they will be. Of course, if you anticipate a price war or your travel agent has inside news of an impending price reduction, you will probably want to wait to buy your tickets. But, in general, it's safer to reserve your tickets in advance. That way you are sure that you will have the flights, seats, and prices you want—as long as you buy the tickets by the purchase-by date. Tickets can be reserved seven, fourteen, twenty-one, and thirty days in advance, or longer. The only drawback to charging tickets too far in advance is that you may end up having to pay for the tickets before you receive income from the tour. Unless you have a cash reserve to pay these charges in advance of a tour, you must pay attention to the timing of your ticket purchases.

USE OPEN-JAW TICKETS When routing a tour, keep in mind that it's possible to buy open-jaw tickets. This type of ticket allows you to travel from a home airport to the first city of a tour and return to the home airport from a different, last city of tour. Open-jaw tickets are not applicable if the distance between airports within the open section is greater than either the outgoing or the returning leg of the trip. An open-jaw ticket would be okay, for example, if you left from New York and flew to Chicago, then flew from Indianapolis back to New York—as the distance from Chicago to Indianapolis is less than either the outgoing or the returning flight. Conversely, if you flew from New York to Chicago with a return to New York from Los Angeles, you would not be able to use an open-jaw ticket—as the distance from Los Angeles to New York is greater than the distance from New York to Chicago (i.e., the originating flight).

USE SATURDAY STAY-OVER TICKETS If your tour is going to last longer than a week, take advantage of discounted round-trip, Saturday stay-over fares. These stay-over fares are considerably cheaper than round-trip fares that leave on Sunday and return home on the following Saturday. For a short, within-the-week tour that starts on a Sunday or Monday and ends on a Friday (and therefore has no Saturday stay-over), see if you can get your client at the tour's first gig to pay an extra day's hotel cost so that you can fly out on Saturday rather than on Sunday. Using this strategy, you can create a stay-over at the end of the week as well.

AVOID ONE-WAY TICKETS Oftentimes, depending on routing considerations, you'll find that you can use short round-trip and open-jaw tickets within the brackets of a longer open-jaw ticket. If this is not possible, you may be forced to buy one-way tickets, even though they are costly. Two flying strategies can reduce the expense of one-way tickets. An inexpensive way to fly one-way is to buy a round-trip ticket, with a return date that includes a Saturday stay-over, even though you don't plan to use the return part of the ticket. This can often be much cheaper than an ordinary one-way ticket. Some airlines will credit the unused ticket to another flight for a later tour, within a year of the original purchase. Confirm this with your travel agent. A second way to avoid the high costs of one-way tickets is to use any of the smaller, no-frills airlines. These kinds of airlines often have low fares, whereby one round-trip ticket costs the same as two one-ways. In this case, the one-way tickets are not cost-prohibitive.

AVOID HAVING A THIRD PARTY MAKE YOUR TRAVEL ARRANGEMENTS Having a venue arrange your air transportation is logistically impractical. Introducing a third party into the mix makes travel even more complex—especially for you, if you end up as the go-between with the venue and your travel agent. When a third party gets involved, glitches often occur that can cause problems for other parts of your travel arrangements. This is because the third party will not know the complex details of your travel schedule. When you're negotiating with a venue that will pay your band's airfares, because tour itineraries are so complex, try to keep control of all of the travel arrangements yourself. Ask your client if you can arrange the travel and either have the venue pay for these expenses in advance or reimburse you at the time of the engagement. Explain to your client that the engagement may be part of an ongoing tour and that the band won't be going to/from home from/to the gig. Explain that the ticket prices will be based upon the rates it would otherwise cost the venue to fly your band from your home base to the venue and back—no more. Look up those flights on the Internet, print them out, and fax them to your client ahead of the gig so that the reimbursement can be approved and waiting for you when you receive payment for the engagement.

MAXIMIZE FREE MILEAGE Band personnel should register with every available airline's free mileage plan and report their frequent-flier numbers to you. Keep these numbers on file. Make it clear to the band members that free miles earned from the tickets, van rentals, and hotel charges were earned from the band's tour budgets—and, therefore, are band property. These free miles are restricted for use for future band tours only, not for personal travel. Free tickets can make many a tour economically viable.

Phone companies such as AT&T, MCI, and Sprint are a great source for free mileage. Spending $400 to $600 a month on long-distance phone calls to book tours will quickly earn you points toward travel. You can easily earn thousands of miles with these plans. However, don't wait too long to transfer mileage credits from these accounts to partner airlines, because it can take up to three weeks to credit your account and you can't buy a ticket until you have the credit in your account. After you make the transfer, call the airline and confirm that earned mileage has been credited to the appropriate account.

Partner airlines, car-rental companies, and hotels can also help you earn extra free miles. Keep a list of these partnerships on a computer file. When you are making arrangements to rent a car or van, ask if you can earn any free mileage from the rentals. Keep track of how many free miles you have accumulated by entering and updating earned mileage in an airlines transportation data file on your computer.

Airlines allot only a certain number of seats per flight for frequent-flier passengers. Ensure that seating is available by reserving frequent-flier flights at least two months in advance of a tour. If you're traveling on or near a holiday, check to make sure that there aren't black-out dates (dates on which you can't use this kind of ticket) for the flights in which you're interested. The only drawback to frequent-flier tickets is that carriers will often route you on less-direct flights, which require multiple connections. This can make a trip longer and more tiring than taking a direct flight.

Avoid ticketing confusion by making all frequent-flier reservations yourself. To do this, you'll need each band member's certificate numbers. However, each of the members of your group will have to redeem his or her own mileage certificates by calling the airline him- or herself. Inform your band members of the airlines, flight numbers, and times—either by phone or, even better, by mail, fax, or E-mail. If you do this by phone, have each band member repeat the information back to you to confirm its accuracy. Frequent-flier certificates are also redeemable by mail. It takes up to six weeks to receive them, however, for a reasonably small fee ($25 to $50) the tickets can be expedited and sent via Federal Express. In order to do this, the tickets have to be purchased in person at the airline ticket office by each individual. Identification will be required.

Managing Your Baggage and Equipment

Implement a one-bag rule when you go on tour. Each member should bring no more than one suitcase on the road. Excluded from this rule are any instruments, carry-on shoulder bags, and boxes of CDs. This rule will help you avoid needing to pay over-weight charges and is especially crucial when you're flying to and around Europe. (This will be discussed further in chapter eleven.) Also, carrying excessive baggage increases the wear and tear on your body. Except in Europe, where curbside check-in counters are nonexistent, use curbside check-in counters whenever possible.

Because of the longer check-in time required for unusual or oversize luggage, the bassist (and the drummer, if he or she is traveling with drums) will probably have to arrive at the airport earlier than the rest of the group. In order to check in the instrument he or she will need to have his or her tickets on hand. Unless your bassist (or drummer) has a credit card on hand to pay for oversize or excess baggage (never use the term "overweight"), you will need to arrive at your originating airport at the same time that he or she does (in case there's an extra charge for the bass and/or drums). If you are departing from different originating airports, ensure that your bassist (and drummer) has a credit card to pay the excess baggage fee him- or herself. Also, remind him or her to save the receipt so that you can do a reimbursement later.

If your band members are experienced road rats, they can be trusted to check in their own baggage. However, when traveling with inexperienced band members, check in the baggage yourself, or oversee the check-in and collect all of the baggage-claim tickets. Here is the method that I find most efficient:

Before checking in, do a baggage count. It's the easiest way to keep track of your baggage. Baggage-claim tickets are often stapled to the ticket cover. Don't throw ticket covers away until all of the baggage has been collected at your destination. If your baggage gets lost, you will need your baggage-claim ticket in order to recover it. Make sure that every bag has a name tag. Whenever you're flying nondirect, multiple flights, losing a bag is always a concern. Recovering lost baggage can be a time-consuming and frustrating process—especially if you are on a tight travel schedule. There'll be long, slow lines at the lost-baggage counter if a flight has misdirected more than one customer's bag. It's difficult to arrange for a lost bag to be forwarded to you at the right city, on the right date, when you're performing a series of one-nighters. So, when your tour involves a lot of air travel, it is prudent to have an extra copy of your itinerary on hand—just in case you need to give it to a baggage agent. Oftentimes you will be given a general contact number, where the agents will not be familiar with your situation, so make sure that you write down the agent's name and the phone number of the lost-baggage counter where your claim was filed.

Finally, each band member is responsible for his or her own tickets and carries them while traveling. If the tickets are lost or misplaced, the band member will be responsible for replacing them at his or her expense. Excess baggage receipts and airline tickets will be needed for tax purposes. Collect them as each leg of a tour is completed.

CARRY-ON BAGGAGE Although enforcement can vary from airline to airline, most airlines allow two pieces of carry-on luggage per passenger. The maximum dimensions per bag for carry-on luggage are generally forty-five linear inches (i.e., the sum of height, length, and width). There's generally a seventy-pound weight limit per item as well. Not everything that you carry with you is considered a carry-on. For instance, personal items—such as purses, overcoats, umbrellas, a reasonable amount of reading material, canes, small cameras, binoculars, and crutches—are not counted as carry-ons. However, laptop computers and briefcases *are* counted as carry-ons.

Sometimes a carrier will not accept two carry-on bags in the cabin if too many passengers have too much luggage to be accommodated by the amount of available overhead storage. If you show up late and there's no overhead storage space left, your carry-ons will be checked at the gate. Planes are usually loaded from the rear to the front of the plane. If you've reserved seats in the rear of the plane, you'll be among the first to board, and you'll be sure to get your carry-ons in the cabin.

There are certain items that you should *always* pack in your carry-on luggage. If you take medication, always pack it in a carry-on—even for short flights. In the event that your flight is delayed or that the airline loses your luggage, you won't be caught without it. Don't pack passports, tickets, and important travel documents in checked baggage.

When you're flying with a bass, its case, and a small bass amplifier, take the amp on the plane as in-cabin luggage. The bassist can then bring a shoulder bag and amp into the passenger cabin (as his or her two pieces of carry-on luggage), and store the amp in an overhead compartment. Often the bass case (with the bass inside) and suitcase can be checked as baggage, without incurring an extra charge for the bass. (This situation will be discussed later in this chapter.)

When in doubt, don't try to sneak your guitar or saxophone on board at the last minute. Notify airline personnel before boarding. They may be more flexible than you think they will be. If you're really desperate and don't want to check in the instrument, insist on its high value or fragility, or declare it as a priceless antique.

SEATING STRATEGIES FOR MAXIMIZING STORAGE SPACE Bulkhead seats offer extra legroom, but no underseat storage. Emergency-exit rows have extra legroom, but underseat luggage must fit securely to ensure that the exit isn't blocked. Emergency-exit seats are often difficult to book in advance; if you can't book them in advance, book a seat just behind the emergency-exit row and see if you can change your seat when you arrive at the check-in counter. Or, if the flight is not too full, take a chance and try to change after the doors have closed but before you start taxiing for takeoff. When arranging for emergency-exit seats, check that you have been given the seats that recline. Sometimes the seats near the emergency exit don't recline. Some emergency exits have two rows of seats—of which the more forward of the two don't recline. On some planes, emergency-exit seats may be at the bulkhead. Check. There is a lot of competition for these seats, so it's best to arrive at the airport earlier than usual if you want to try to get them.

If a flight is looking crowded and you have a lot of carry-on luggage, ask for a seat in the rear of the plane. In most cases, passengers in the rear rows are boarded first and, therefore, get their luggage in the overhead compartments first. Once the overhead compartments are full, however, passengers are often required to check in their carry-on luggage. Confirm with the gate agent whether or not the plane will be loaded from the rear before you make your request, however. Otherwise you might find that your strategy has backfired.

THE BASS CASE Touring musicians know that the bass and its case are the bane of every traveling band. You used to be able to buy an extra ticket for the bass so that you could bring it on the plane and put it in a bulkhead seat. Increased airline security measures and improvements in lightweight-plastic bass cases have made this an impractical approach to bass transportation. Basses and their travel cases now commonly go under the plane as checked baggage. Luckily, this is a less-expensive approach than buying a seat for the bass. Unless you can slip a baggage checker at a curbside check-in counter a tip to get the case on the plane for you, the case will have to be checked in at the ticket counter. Inexperienced ticket agents often get uptight when they see that big case. Arrive early at the airport. Allot extra time to check in the equipment. It will be difficult enough to get your equipment on the plane. You don't want to feel pressured because of lack of time.

Most experienced bassists have developed a technique for coping with confused or inexperienced airline ticket agents. Some agents will only go by the rules and some will be quite flexible. If there is a choice of agent check-in lines to select from, observe the agents to see how they are reacting to their customers and try to determine which one might be the most accommodating. Don't stand the bass up. Lay it down so it won't appear big. Until things go wrong, adopt a relaxed, friendly, and self-deprecating attitude. (For a more detailed and highly effective strategy about how to check in the bass and its case, see pages 203–205.)

In the early 1970s, I had the good fortune of working with the Cannonball Adderley Quintet. It would be impossible to find a more professional bunch of road rats than the guys who were part of this band. On the road from forty to fifty weeks a year, they had flown in and out of most of the major airports in the United States so many times that Cannonball was on a first-name basis with most of the airport curbside baggage handlers. We would arrive at curbside and you'd hear Cannonball greeting the handler with a "Hey, Bill" or "What know, Jack," shaking his hand and communing with him. Where we had played and where we were going was always the subject of conversation. Cannonball's great sense of humanity always carried the day. He would slip the handler $20 and the bass case and the baggage would disappear and be put on the plane personally by the handler, bypassing the check-in counter and any excess-baggage fees. I don't think Cannonball ever paid an excess-baggage fee while I was with the band.

When you're organizing your travel details, have your travel agent check on the size of the plane—especially when you're booking connecting or no-frills flights to smaller cities. Some baggage compartments are too small to carry the bass case. If the flight is fully booked, the airline will give priority to its passengers' luggage over the bass and will send it on a later flight. While you're at the gate and waiting for your flight to board, try to see if you can watch the plane being loaded. Most gates have windows through which you can see if the bass and drums are being loaded on the plane. If your equipment is bumped from a crowded flight, you will invariably spend an inordinate amount of time on the telephone locating the equipment and making sure it will be where you need it and at the right time—and it may ultimately arrive at your destination too late to be of use. This can be an exhausting and frustrating experience. If you don't see your bass being loaded, inform the gate personnel of the problem. If they don't adequately address your concerns, ask to speak with the pilot or captain. Explain that you are performing a concert and that you can't afford to have your instruments arrive at your destination later than you do—because this will impede your ability to perform and may result in your being sued (which implies that the airline may also be subject to a suit). This should convince the airline of the importance of loading your instruments.

Troubleshooting Potential Air-Travel Problems

When making your travel arrangements (as well as once you're on the road), you'll want to pay particular attention to the two aspects of travel that are potentially problematic: winter travel and changes in time zones.

Before you leave home, as well as during a tour, stay up-to-date on weather and travel conditions—both in your departure area as well as in your various destination areas. Watch the Weather Channel on cable television. Or log on to the Weather Channel's Web site at http://www.weather.com and enter the zip codes of your departure and arrival destinations.

Keep an eye on the internal destinations of your tour as well. You don't want to violate any contracts or lose income from a gig because you couldn't get there. If it looks like there's going to be trouble with delayed flights and missed connections, call your next venue to work out a possible solution. You may have to cancel a gig, and absorb the loss of tour income, because of bad weather. You might also incur the additional time and expense of changing hotel reservations, plane tickets, van rentals, and airport pickups and returns.

Changes in time zones are potentially problematic when you're driving state-to-state in the United States or flying country-to-country in Europe. Do your research before you make your travel arrangements. Keep a time-zone map handy or check the time zones with your clients. Your travel checklist has a section on time zones to remind you of these questions when you're talking with a venue.

THE RISKS OF WINTER TRAVEL During the winter months, check the layover times between connecting flights. Assume that there will be delays—either taking off from your origination point or landing at your connecting airport. If you're worried about the possibility of inclement weather, take an earlier flight so that your layover will be longer. This will help to ensure that you can make the connecting flight, even if your first flight is delayed by bad weather.

If you can, arrange to travel to your first destination a day ahead of time, especially if the gig is an anchor gig and there are short layover times between the flights that will get you there. It may be safer and cheaper for the tour to have an extra day off than to take a chance on being unable to get to a gig that is financially crucial to your tour. Analyze the tour budget and routing to see which travel days may best be left open under these circumstances. Try to get the venue to pay the extra day's hotel. Explain that you want to be sure that you can make the engagement. They will usually be understanding. If they don't agree to pay, have them reserve the hotel rooms for the extra day and pay for them out of the tour budget.

Except in rare cases, I avoid touring during the months of December through February. It can be frustrating and costly. A case in point was during the historic blizzard of 1978. While in the midst of playing a series of one-nighters, my quintet was stuck in Bloomington, Indiana for five days. We were stranded in a Holiday Inn that was running out of food, with one thousand dollars a day of income going down the drain. When we played the gig in Bloomington, people came to the concert on snowshoes and skis.

I was on the phone six hours a day for five days, building up a hefty telephone bill, trying to find a way out of there. I finally found a train to a town that had an airport that was open, and we managed to continue our tour. Because I always guarantee my band's salaries while on the road, the storm cost me $5,000. The tour went into the hole and I came home in debt.

Whenever possible, when taking gigs during winter months, accept work only in geographical areas that are noted for good weather. For instance, try booking in the southern states during these months or Japan and Australia (because our winter is their summer). South America, Italy, Spain, Africa, and Portugal are not noted for seeing much snow during the winter.

Sometimes it is worth the chance to take a gig during bad-weather months if you can book a direct flight to the city where the venue is, and if the venue is within easy driving distance from the airport. However, even though you've taken these precautions, still keep an eye on the weather reports. And always leave plenty of time for the drive.

One December, we did a week's tour of the Northwest that involved two drives across the Cascade Mountains. The U.S. Park Service had electronic warning boards along the highway to alert you if unsafe snow conditions were in effect. In unsafe conditions, they only allow you to drive on the mountains if you have snow chains on your tires. Otherwise you have to pull over on a rest area or find a motel to stay in until conditions improve. We were continuously tuned in to the weather reports on the van radio. Fortunately, the garages and gas stations in the area sell snow chains that can be turned in on the other side of the mountains, for a refund. Luckily, we had no snow emergency, but at moments it was a pretty nerve-racking drive.

KNOW YOUR TIME ZONES With U.S. travel, as with foreign travel, you need to be mindful of changes in time zones. Avoid being late for an engagement by confirming the time zone the venue is in and noting the time zone of the venue on your venue worksheet. Airlines list departure and arrival times in local time zones. Some states, like Indiana, have zone lines that zigzag wildly across the state.

Late one afternoon my trio arrived at Indianapolis airport to fly to a gig that was going to be in Louisville that evening. I figured the amount of time it would take to collect our baggage, rent the van, and drive from the airport to get to the gig on time. While the guys were collecting our baggage, I took the shuttle bus to the rental agency to pick up the van. When I arrived, the agent was on the phone coping with an irate, dissatisfied customer who would not get off the phone. There were also two other people ahead of me, impatiently waiting in line. I always leave a little extra time in my calculations, so I knew I was still cool. Finally, after a half-hour delay, the agent got off the phone. The elderly couple in line before me had never rented a car before, asked a million questions about the process, and needed directions to their destination. That took another twenty minutes. I eventually got to the counter, aware that the cats were waiting for me and probably beginning to worry about why I wasn't there. I rented a seven-passenger minivan and took off for the terminal. Upon trying to pack the van, we discovered that it was too small to hold the luggage, the bass case, and three guys. We unpacked and I drove back to rent a different model, but was told that it was the only minivan left in the lot. I looked across a field and noticed another van-rental company. So I turned in the original rental and ran across the field to the other company, which informed me that it had no vans available.

So I ran back to the first company and was greeted by a new agent, who then told me they had a nine-passenger van that was available at twice the price. The previous agent had never mentioned it. I cried the blues about the situation and the agent gave it to me for the same price as the minivan. I boogied back to the terminal to pick up the cats, who at this point had been waiting there for two hours. We packed the van and took off. Although the schedule was now a little tight, the speed limit was 75 mph and we figured that if we didn't stop for anything, and checked into our hotel rooms after the gig, we'd make it on time. What we didn't find out until we arrived, *an hour late*, was that there was an hour time difference between Indianapolis and Louisville. We ended up having to play the gig in our traveling clothes.

Coordinating Canadian Air Travel

Air travel to and from Canada has similar complications as foreign travel. However, it is easy to overlook some of these things, since psychologically Canada doesn't seem "foreign." But don't be deceived. Details concerning customs and immigration, contracts, work permits, taxes, and equipment will demand your attention while you're booking the gig as well as when you're traveling. You'll need an extra bit of patience when you commit to Canadian gigs.

When flying to Canada, research at what point you will have to go through customs and immigration. This could occur at a Canadian stopover or at your final destination. If customs and immigration are at a stopover, allow at least two to three hours between connecting flights. It can take that much time to process your work permits, equipment, and baggage through customs. Before you leave for a Canadian gig, confirm with the venues that the necessary paperwork has been submitted to the immigration officials and that it will be on file upon your arrival. If it is not on file, the venue will need to send someone to customs and immigration to file the contracts. Make sure the venue filing your papers knows your Canadian entry point. Even though the immigration officials will have the information on their computers, it will take twice as long to get your paperwork finalized if the papers aren't at the entry point when you arrive.

To ensure that the customs process moves as smoothly as possible, have copies of all contracts, NR-16 forms, Non-Resident Tax Waiver certificates, and proof of citizenship (passports, birth certificates, citizenship papers, or voter-registration cards) as well as the itinerary and equipment list on hand. The imbalance in currency-exchange rates and import taxes between Canada and the United States has created a dual situation wherein articles that can't be inexpensively purchased by Canadian citizens in Canada are illegally purchased in the United States, imported, and sold in Canada—for a higher price than if they were sold in the States. Conversely, because things are generally less expensive in Canada, American citizens can buy some articles more cheaply than they can in Canada. If you are leaving Canada without an equipment list, customs officials could legally impound your equipment, assuming it was purchased in Canada. The list should be as detailed as possible. Note weights, sizes, identifying marks, and serial numbers of all of your horns, guitars, drums, and cymbals as well as the bass, bass case, and amplifier. Upon entering the country, have the customs official date stamp the list to prove that you brought the equipment into the country legally. Have this list on hand for all foreign travel. A more official approach is to fill out a Certificate of Registration, Customs Form 4455 (020984), and have it signed by a customs officer upon exiting the United States at the Canadian border.

If you expect to be going in and out of Canada more than once during a tour, request a multiple-entry work permit. You will have to pay the fee for this permit upon entering Canada. Have the correct amount of cash or a credit card with you. As of this writing, the permit fee for an individual is $125, and for groups of two or more it is $250. (For more information about the paperwork required to work at Canadian venues, see page 142.)

ARRANGING GROUND AND WATER TRAVEL

At first, renting a van or car may seem like an ordinary and simple procedure. However, there are some aspects of renting a van that will meet the needs of a touring band that are different than renting a car for personal use. Since, as the bandleader, you have the welfare of a tour at stake, you can't afford to learn all of the various rental idiosyncrasies as you go along. Use your travel agent to rent vans and cars. He or she will have all the information about rates, one-ways, mileage charges, and discounts, and can fax you confirmation sheets.

You should have your travel agent initiate the rental process *after* you have reserved or bought your plane tickets, because the rental agencies will ask for your pickup and return times as well as your flight numbers. Pay attention to the timing of a rental return and your next flight. Check the flight's departure time and allow enough time to drive back to the airport, return the rental, and then check in for your flight.

Have your venue information ready for access on the computer when renting a van. Calendar and contact info should be in front of you while talking with your travel agent. Be aware of an engagement's start times, how long it will take to rent and pack the van (allow an hour for this), and any drive times involved.

This section addresses the issues of transportation by ground and water; train travel is not included in this section. Train travel in the United States cannot be compared with foreign train travel. Trains in Europe are considered to be "the people's" method of travel and they are geared to include the ordinary traveling citizen. The ordinary citizen in the United States tends to travel by road or air, since gas and national airfares are much less expensive here than in Europe. European trains offer much more routing flexibility, cover more destinations, and are less expensive than U.S. trains. Most U.S. train fares are as expensive as airfares. (For more information about train travel, see chapter eleven.)

Van-Rental and Driving Strategies

The purpose of a tour budget is to try to keep your expenses as low as possible. Although you will be renting vans throughout the touring process, be alert to the days and times for which van rental is not absolutely essential and avoid adding this expense to your budget if it isn't necessary. For instance, the first gig of a tour segment may be in the same city as the airport at which you will arrive. If it is, you can save a day's rental fee by arranging for an airport pickup by the venue. Rent the van on the day after your engagement and turn it in at the next or originating airport. This strategy comes in handy when you're renting a van on a weekly basis, with extra days beyond the seven-day rate. Extra days are charged at an expensive daily rate.

Sometimes a tour routing works out so that your band will end a tour segment in a different state and airport from the one at which you arrived. If this happens, check on the possibility of renting a one-way van. Although one-way *car* rentals are now inexpensive (with an average of a $100 drop-off fee), renting one-way vans is becoming more restrictive. Many companies will not allow vans to be dropped off out of state. However, some neighboring states, such as Washington and Oregon, may allow interstate drop-offs. If returning the van to its origination point would involve an impossible drive time, consider the alternative of renting two cars and taking advantage of an interstate, one-way drop-off option. The drop-off and rental fees will not be much more than the price of a van rental.

If it is not possible to either rent a one-way van or rent two one-way cars *and* if the engagement is the last of a tour, I often send the band home from the nearest airport and drive the van back to its origination point myself. There is no sense keeping the band members on the road any longer than necessary.

Watch out for mileage charges. They add up rather quickly. Most rental agencies offer 100 free miles per day. Some have higher rates, with no mileage charge. You'll have to do some quick calculations to see if a van rented at a low rate with mileage charges will be cheaper than a van rented at a high rate without mileage charges. You'll need to estimate your mileage to make this decision. Map software programs come in handy in this respect.

Consider acquiring a computer program called Route 66 from the Netherlands-based company by the same name. They can be reached by phone at (011-31-318) 554724 or on the Internet at http://www.route66.nl or at http://www.magicroute.com. This program creates maps, written directions, and estimates of cost, miles, and drive times for trips between any points in the United States for all but the smallest towns. European map programs are also available.

The Internet's Maps On Us Web site at http://www.mapsonus.com offers complete and accurate driving directions to any city in the United States. You can also get door-to-door directions by entering the addresses and zip codes.

A city street map will come in handy while you're on the road. Most venues will send you a map upon request. The best book for city maps is the *Trucker's Atlas for Professional Drivers* (American Map Corporation, 1999), which costs $19.95. It covers most U.S. cities.

One of the best buys in the world is membership with American Automobile Associate (AAA). If you are a car owner, join AAA. The services they offer can be invaluable to the touring musician and are well worth the minimal cost. One of their most valuable services is Triptiks. Triptiks are strip maps that contain suggested travel routes, drive times, and estimated mileages and are invaluable when renting a van with a mileage charge. AAA also provides large-scale maps of the states in which you will be driving. Call any AAA office and inform them of your route. Complete strip maps will be mailed to you in ten days or fewer.

AAA membership also has other benefits. As an AAA member, you will receive a 10 percent discount for food when you show your AAA card at many on-highway restaurants. AAA will also send you discount cards that are good for up to 10 percent off of rentals with Hertz and Avis. For an additional fee, you can upgrade your membership to AAA Plus, which not only supplies you with free American Express checks—like their regular program—but it also offers twenty-four-hour Global Travel Emergency Assistance. This is an exclusive hotline number that can be used anywhere in the world to obtain assistance for serious travel-related difficulties—such as lost passports or airline tickets, stolen cash, medical emergencies, or legal problems. AAA Plus offers free passport photos at any branch, as well as many other valuable services. They also sell a CD-ROM with detailed maps of every location and route in the United States. Call your local AAA branch for additional information about their services.

Discount cards for National Car Rental can be obtained from the musicians' union. Thrifty Car Rental offers a discount of 10 percent for those who are more than fifty-five years old. Many other discount offers can be found through various organizations, such as AARP. Keep your eyes open for these deals. Discounted corporate rates are also available at car-rental agencies, if the band's business is set up as a corporation.

Here's another handy money-saving trick that works if you haven't used your credit card to reserve a van: Make your van reservations ahead of time. Upon arriving at the destination airport, don't immediately mention that you have a reservation. Rental companies often have cancellations and rate changes. They lose money with unrented vehicles. You may be able to get a lower rate than you had originally arranged. Ask the agent if he or she has any vans available that day, and the rate. If the rate is lower than what you had originally been quoted, rent the van on the spot. You may be able to save as much as $100 on a weekly rental. However, this strategy will not work if you confirmed a reservation with your credit card, as the agencies usually require a twenty-four-hour advance notice for a cancellation.

Also, if you have time and the counter lines aren't too long, survey a couple of other rental companies for available vans. In most airports, the rental counters are all in the same gate area. You might be able to get a better deal than your original rental company offered. Again, this strategy only works if you didn't reserve the original rental with your credit card.

Create a computer data file for the airlines and car-rental services you'll be using most often. A 1-800-number telephone book is a good source for most of these contacts, except for the smaller, regional, or lesser-known rental companies. Most travel Web sites have links to major car-rental companies. Bookmark them on your browser for easy access.

There may be an occasion where van rentals from national van-rental companies are booked, the agencies have no vans available at the airport, and your agent has no further rental information. If this happens to you, check with your venue contact to see if there are any smaller, local rental agencies at that particular airport. Many airports have local rental companies about which travel agents won't necessarily know. Venue contacts can give you the phone numbers of local rental companies by looking them up in their local Yellow Pages. Once you have booked your plane reservations, contact these local rental companies to see which ones have the best rates. Note rates and mileage charges, if any, in a data file, so the information doesn't get mixed up or lost. If you get a good rate, book it. If you get another good rate from another company, book it as well. After you decide which company to use, call back later and cancel the other bookings.

Rental companies quote prices without taxes and airport surcharges. Airport surcharges and taxes can be as high as 18 or 20 percent, and can add up to seriously affect a tour budget. Always ask about the taxes and surcharges that will be applied to your rental and include them as part of the rental fee in your tour budget estimate.

Take special note of the time of day that you plan to rent your van, as well as the time of the flight on the day that the van is being turned in. Overtime fees after the first hour can be anywhere from $10 an hour to another full day's rental fee. Therefore, you can sometimes save a day's rental fee by leaving for your flight a few hours earlier than you might have otherwise. Allow extra time for returning the van, and avoid undue pressure and stress by planning to turn the van in at least one and one-half or two hours ahead of a flight.

Depending on the size of the airport, it will take at least forty-five minutes to pick up the van after a flight arrives. If your flight arrives at 12:00 P.M., you'll be picking up the van at approximately 12:45 P.M. For a 4:00 P.M. flight on the day of a van return, with the drive time to the airport being two hours, you'll need to leave the hotel by 12:30 P.M. This will get you to the airport at 2:30 P.M. with plenty of time to check in. However, a full day's rental will be charged for that hour and three-quarters, because the van was rented at 12:45 P.M. and returned an hour and three-quarters *after* the original rental time. Leaving the hotel at 10:45 A.M. could save you as much as $40 or $50. Most experienced road rats prefer to arrive early for all flights, the philosophy being that it is better to wait at an airport rather than rush to catch a flight.

When filling out a rental form, you'll have to decide if you want to refuse the insurance. This is the most expensive kind of insurance that exists. And your own automobile or home insurance may cover the rental of a van or automobile. Credit cards often carry excess insurance that covers losses above and beyond the limits of any other insurance. In other words, if you do $4,000 worth of damage to the rental vehicle, your home or automobile insurance may cover $3,000 worth of damage, and your credit-card insurance may cover the remaining $1,000. You'll want to double-check on the terms of your own insurance and the fringe benefits that are offered by your credit cards before you leave for a tour, so that you know whether or not you can confidently turn down the rental insurance. Even if your credit card doesn't carry extra insurance, always use a credit card to rent a van, as you will avoid the large cash deposit that would otherwise be required. Avoid the additional charge for extra drivers as well.

Vans can vary greatly in capacity—accommodating from five to nine or more passengers. Most vans these days carry seven passengers. For your purposes, a seven-person van can usually hold up to four people, their luggage, instruments, and the bass case. Consequently, the one-bag rule is really an important consideration. Ask your agent to confirm that there will be enough room for the band's baggage—including the drums and the bass case—behind the last row of seats, and that the last row folds down. Some of the newer seven-passenger vans are not long enough to accommodate the length of the bass case. A larger van may be required. Don't be caught short by arriving at the rental agency only to discover that the van is too small.

Packing baggage and equipment is an art. Experienced road rats can find a way to pack most vans, but there is a cutoff point as to the number of people and the amount of baggage any van can comfortably and safely hold. Good rear viewing from the driver's seat is a must. It should be stressed to your band members that no matter who is behind the wheel, everyone is driving the van and all must share driving responsibilities with the driver.

The bass case will be the largest baggage item. Avoid driving with the bass case, wherever possible. If you're flying into and returning from the same airport, it may be practical to store the bass case for that segment of the tour at the airport. Check if the airport has baggage-storage services or airline-cargo storage facilities. Since you will be traveling on the same airline, the cargo facility may store the case—as a courtesy or for a small, daily fee. If the airline uses a local independent storage service for its cargo flights, ask for the telephone numbers of the storage service. The service may be able to meet the incoming flight to pick up the case, or you may have to drop it off on your way out of the airport. When balanced against concerns for comfortable and safe driving conditions, the minimal charge and minor inconvenience for this service is well worth it.

An alternative to the scenario described above is to leave the bass case at the first venue or first hotel of a tour segment, and pick it up on your way back to the airport. Confirm that someone will be around at the time that you return. Double-check your contact's availability a day or two before you return to pick up the case. When none of the above possibilities are options, a local musician, preferably a bassist in the area, may be able to store the case for you. If your bassist doesn't happen to know someone in the area, you can ask the venue to recommend a local bassist for you.

Be advised that some major car-rental agencies have implemented checks on their renter's driving records. If your driving record has too many moving violations (usually three or four) within a two- to three-year period or a DWI violation, you could be refused a rental. Make sure your driving record is up-to-date and has a minimal number of violations before you rent a vehicle on the road.

Venue-Supplied Local Transportation

The objective of a tour budget is to keep expenses low, so free transportation is always the best transportation. Scrutinize an itinerary for those situations where ground transportation may be supplied by a venue. Look for situations where you can save on van-rental fees, gas, and tolls by arranging for a series of venues that are within two hours of each other. These venues can then either pick up the band at a preceding gig or drop off the band at a following gig. This strategy is called piggybacking. If a venue agrees to piggyback for you, make sure that you give your client accurate hotel information and directions. It is also advisable to ask each venue if it provides airport pickups and drop-offs. If they do, make sure they are informed of arrival and departure times, and get the phone numbers of your drivers.

If the venue has arranged to supply all local transportation for you, make sure that the driver knows what time to return to the hotel to pick you up for the sound check or gig. Add fifteen minutes in front of the pickup time to make sure that he or she arrives on time. It is better to have the driver wait for you than to have you wait for the driver.

Contact each upcoming venue client at least a day before your arrival. If for some reason you can't do that, contact the client as soon as you get into your hotel room. Things may have changed since the last time you spoke and the client may be getting nervous if you haven't called him or her before you left home for the tour. If you don't already have this info on your itinerary, you may need directions to the venue, drive times, and sound check times. If directions to the venue are complicated, you will save a lot of wasted time and energy driving around looking for a hard-to-find location by arranging to have the client, or an assistant, come to the hotel to guide your van to the gig.

When you're doing morning or afternoon solo college clinics, make arrangements with your client to have a student pick you up and drop you off at your hotel. Get the driver's name and phone number. You may also need to pick up a check for your performance fee and get to a local bank to cash it before the gig. It's a time and energy saver to have someone who is familiar with the locality drive you to the bank and back to your hotel. And most of the time the students really enjoy the opportunity to hang out with a working musician.

Driving and Taking Ferries in Canada

Driving in Canada is much the same as driving in the United States except for the previously mentioned border considerations. Allow extra time at customs and immigration for processing your paperwork. The same paperwork and documentation that is required for flying is necessary when you drive. Be prepared to have your van searched. Musicians are easy targets for border searches—as we are still perceived as being drug addicts and alcoholics. It should be stressed that no illegal substances should be brought across any border.

It's illegal to bring CDs into Canada without declaring them as items to be sold for profit. If you do declare them, you may have to pay an import tax. Some musicians take the chance and decide not declare them and instead hide them in the van, but if your vehicle is searched and the CDs are found, you could get into some trouble. Pleading ignorance of the law rarely gets you anywhere with customs officials. It is better to take the high road and declare the merchandise and pay the small tax.

If you're traveling from Washington state to Vancouver or Victoria *or* if you're traveling between Vancouver, Victoria, or any other of the islands in that area, you will have to take a ferry. Research the ferry departure, arrival, border clearance, and travel times very carefully. There are two ferry companies that service the area, and they have summer and winter schedules: The British Columbia Ferry Corporation (1-250) 386-3431 and The Victoria Clipper, Inc. (1-206) 448-5000 or 1-800-668-1167. Be sure you are getting the appropriate schedules when arranging ferry travel in the summer for the fall season—or vice versa. Ferries are busier at certain hours and on certain days of the week—as in the summertime or on holiday weekends.

During holiday weekends, the wait in line can be as long as five hours. On these occasions, cars will often arrive the night before an early morning ferry to ensure a place in line. Monday mornings and Friday evenings are the busiest times, with trucks transporting goods to and from Canada. To be sure you get on the ferry you want, and don't get bumped to a later one, arrive at least an hour in advance. Add a half an hour to your estimated travel time for customs and immigration. Also, add the time for travel from the ferry to the final destination. The cost for ferry travel includes the price of the vehicle and a minimum number of passengers. Extra passengers are charged at an additional fee.

ARRANGING HOTEL ACCOMMODATIONS

Most tours will include a mix of top- to poor-quality hotels. The kind of hotels you stay at will depend on your tour budget and the budgets of the venues that are paying for your hotel rooms. One day you could be staying at the Hilton. The next day you could be crashing at the Ajax Motel. It's strange, but it always seems like it works out so that you get to stay in the best hotels for the shorter times and the worst hotels for the longer times.

There are certain prerequisites for decent accommodations:

- The rooms should be clean, with smoking and nonsmoking options.
- The hotel should have twenty-four-hour phone services (some motels in smaller towns will have no phone service after 10:00 P.M.), an elevator (some motels don't have elevators to the second floor), parking facilities (free or paid), a restaurant or nearby access to one, and dry cleaning and laundry services. For longer stays, it is an added convenience and a real money-saver if the hotel has a refrigerator and laundry room.
- The rooms should be equipped with a television, phone, fax, and modem hookups, if needed, and large beds, ideally queen- or king-size.
- The hotel should be close to the venue (no more than a half hour's drive away) and should have discounted room rates (AAA or Quest).

Arrangements for hotels can be made either by you, your travel agent, or the venue. If he or she is not too busy, your travel agent can do it for you and save you a day's work. Your travel agent will have all of the information listed above at his or her fingertips and will be able to send you a complete itinerary—with hotels, flights, and van rentals (including accurate costs)—and save you a lot of extra work. When you get this material from your travel agent, double-check the itinerary. Anyone can make a mistake. But a mistake in an itinerary can cause a lot of trouble.

If you decide to let the travel agent make these arrangements for you, let him or her know what your budget is and fax a list of when and where you'll be staying. The only problem with using a travel agent to make these arrangements is that he or she may not have the time to personalize your arrangements to your needs—such as arranging smoking and nonsmoking rooms. It has been my experience that good travel agents are very busy and they will have enough to do booking your flight and making your car-rental reservations. Having personalized hotel accommodations is important to quality-of-life issues. You might want to handle those arrangements yourself. That way you'll be sure that things are done right and that the band members will be happy.

When booking your own accommodations, always have your client and venue worksheet and credit card info on hand. After you make your reservations, note your confirmation numbers on your tour itinerary. And always guarantee your reservations with a credit card, especially if you are going to arrive after 6:00 P.M.

When making reservations, ask the hotel clerks if the hotel honors any discounts or frequent-flier partnership miles. One of the best discount programs is Quest Membership Services, which offers a 50 percent discount at many hotels, in various price ranges, in most areas. They can be reached at 1-800-704-8199. The Quest card also offers a 25 percent discount at hotel restaurants that participate in the Quest dining program, as well as rental-car discounts. There is an initial fee of $90 and a yearly membership fee of $40, and each member has to join. But if you travel a lot, the benefits are well worth the expense. Reservations depend upon availability, and there may be black-out dates.

Most hotel chains will send you booklets with complete information about their rates, locations, and available services. Although you'll have to ask for an updated booklet each year, it's worth having these booklets on file.

Hotel Reservations Network, which can be reached at 1-800-964-6835 or on the Internet at http://www.hoteldiscounts.com or at http://www.180096hotel.com, books hotels at up to a 65 percent discount in most major cities. There's no membership fee and reservations depend upon availability. If you're on the Internet, you should also check the bookmarks page on my Web site (http://www.upbeat.com/galper) to download links and E-mail addresses of most hotel chains where you can make on-line reservations directly.

If your hotel reservations are being booked by the venue, make sure to ask your client if the rooms will be listed under your name, the group members' individual names, or the venue's name. Also, make sure that you get the confirmation numbers. If you don't, something like the following could happen.

A number of years ago my trio was performing at a jazz club at the Disney World outside of Paris. We arrived at the hotel after a hard day of traveling and were ready to check in to get some much-needed rest before the gig. The promoter had arranged the room reservations for us, but when we arrived at the check-in counter, our reservations could not be found. It took three hours for the hotel clerk to find our reservations. They were under the name of Mr. Hal Galpertrio. It was just too funny to get upset over.

Check-in Procedures

Compare your arrival times in the area with your check-in times at the hotel. If you arrive too early, your band could be sitting around the lobby for hours waiting for the hotel personnel to make up your rooms. If you know that you will be arriving before the check-in time, request an early check-in in advance. This doesn't always work, especially when a hotel is fully booked the previous night, but at least it puts the odds in your favor—especially when favored hotel guests try to check in before you. If all the rooms aren't ready, and it looks like you're going to have a long wait, don't let the hotel put the band members and their luggage temporarily in the first room that becomes available. You'll be out of sight and out of mind. It is much better for you to have a bunch of disgruntled musicians with their baggage hanging around, moaning, giving dirty looks to the clerk at the front desk, looking at their watches, and clogging up a lobby. It inspires the clerk at the front desk to get your rooms prepared and get rid of you.

When you're driving from the airport to the hotel, keep your eyes open for restaurants, fast-food services, Laundromats, dry cleaners, drugstores, twenty-four-hour convenience stores, supermarkets, and shopping malls. You never know when you might need the services of one of these types of businesses—and it is better to have scoped them out than to try to randomly hunt for them when the need arises.

If the hotel has a restaurant, check its hours of operation. If it doesn't, ask the front-desk clerk to recommend one in the area. A fast-food restaurant may be your only chance to eat if you've checked in late and don't have much time left before the gig. It seems like someone always needs a drugstore, and a supermarket can be a handy solution to the problem of finding something to eat after a gig, especially since most restaurants are closed after 10:00 or 11:00 P.M.

Getting your laundry and dry cleaning done while you're on the road is a major consideration. Hotel laundry and dry-cleaning services are more expensive (because the hotel adds its surcharge) and take more time than outside services, plus they may not be available on weekends. A drop-off Laundromat can come in handy. Sometimes, with a little schmoozing, you can get an outside dry cleaner to process your clothes twice as fast as the hotel.

The better hotels have bellhops who will bring your bags to the room. Although the services of a bellhop are a luxury when you have the time, if the hotel is very busy and your schedule is tight, you could be waiting for up to an hour for your luggage to show up. Better to use that time to get something to eat or grab a much-needed nap. Always take a luggage carrier with you when you're traveling, and use it to bring your bags to your room.

Your bass player will probably think of it but, if not, ask if the hotel has a safe place where he or she can store the bass case. It can take up considerable space in a small hotel room. If you are driving to other gigs in the area and plan to return to the hotel at a later date to take a flight to another region, ask the front-desk clerk if he or she will store the case for you until you return. Leaving the bass case somewhere can make packing a van a lot easier. If neither the airport nor the hotel will store the case for you, the venue might provide an alternative. Just be sure to confirm that someone will be there when you get back to pick it up.

When checking in, even if the venue is paying for the rooms, don't put down cash deposits for incidentals such as telephone, restaurants, and laundry. Some of your band members may not have credit cards. It's more efficient and less time-consuming to guarantee each member's incidentals using your own credit card. Advise the check-in agent that charges for incidentals will go on each individual's bill, but that you will pay all room and tax charges. Be sure that the hotel has correctly listed each musician's name and room number. You don't want to be getting someone else's call from home at an inopportune moment. Make a list of each musician's room number on the back of the hotel's business card. This system serves a double purpose. It allows you to contact your band members quickly if there are any plan changes, and it ensures that you always know exactly where you're staying—if somehow you get stranded someplace and can't remember the name or address of your hotel. Tell each member the "lobby call" time (i.e., the time the band will be loading for an airport, train, or gig) before he or she leaves for his or her room.

There may be times, as when you're traveling in Europe, when it will be desirable for you to pay for your room with cash in local currency. (This will be discussed further in chapter eleven.) If you decide to pay for your room with cash, tell the front-desk clerk that you will be guaranteeing the rooms with your credit card, but paying in cash at check-out time. This will help ensure that they don't accidentally run the room charges on your credit card. When the venue is paying the rooms, double-check with the front-desk clerk that the rooms have already been paid for, or that they have the client's credit card—or, in the case of a college or arts presenter, a voucher from the organization on file.

Some of the more up-scale hotels charge fees for parking. When making your hotel reservations, ask about this so you won't have any unexpected charges on your bill when you check out. If the hotel has a valet service that is responsible for parking your van, call down to the concierge at least half an hour ahead of your departure time. If the hotel is full, you could have your band members standing around waiting for your vehicle to be delivered.

Telephone calls that are charged to your room can be very expensive, as hotel surcharges are often added to each call. Check the telephone information card, which most hotels display by the phone, to see the rates for local and other outside calls. Some hotels will charge as much as a dollar for a local call. Make your band members aware of this as well.

Long-distance calls should be charged to your personal long-distance carrier's 1-800 number. If you routinely use this option, you'll pay less for your calls and you'll have a record of your tax-deductible road calls from each hotel on your home phone bill. Contact your carrier to find out about its 1-800 long-distance access number and always carry a card with that information.

Observe good hotel safety measures. Leave your television on whenever you're not in the room.

Check-out Procedures

After the gig, you should confirm with your client, or driver, any travel arrangements you've made for the following day. Once you get back to the hotel, you should confirm with your band members when the next day's lobby call time will be—even if it's listed on the itinerary. Even better, do this when the gig ends, just in case some of the musicians go off on their own.

The next morning, allow yourself fifteen extra minutes to get to the desk to check out the band before the lobby call time. When leaving your hotel room to check out, never leave your door open. Someone could come into the room and cause damage, for which you will be responsible. Go over the hotel bill carefully to make sure you don't have any unnecessary charges. Don't hesitate to ask about any unusual charges. Sometimes hotels make mistakes—for instance charge you for a phone call that a previous patron made. Make sure all of the musicians have paid for their incidentals. When paying for your rooms with cash, you should tear up your credit card receipts (for the deposit) as well as the hotel's carbon copies of the receipts.

Chapter 11

Arranging Travel and Accommodations in Foreign Countries

Traveling in Europe is very different from traveling in the United States. Even if you're an experienced stateside traveler, you will probably need to do some research before you plan a European tour—especially if it is your first time going there. Many informative travel guides have been published. You may consider purchasing one or more of these guides while you're planning your tour, or before you leave the country. They can be very helpful with logistical information, as they often list inexpensive hotels and restaurants, locations of American Express offices and other helpful agencies, as well as basic, foreign-language phrases. You'll save yourself money (and have a much better selection from which to choose) if you purchase these books in the United States, rather than once you're on the road.

One of the major differences between stateside and European travel is air travel. Although most European countries are within easy flying range of each other, flying between foreign countries is more expensive and complicated than flying from state to state in the United States. Because of the expense factor, many bands either drive or take trains for intercountry European travel. Luckily, train travel in Europe is less expensive, more efficient, and oftentimes (if you are taking large, intercity trains) more comfortable and faster than train travel in the United States.

ARRANGING FOREIGN AIR TRAVEL

When booking overseas flights pay particular attention to time zones. Most flights from the East Coast to Europe leave late in the afternoon (between 5:00 P.M. and 9:00 P.M.), and flights from the West Coast leave in the morning (between 6:00 A.M. and 11:00 A.M.). Flights from either coast arrive in Europe the morning of the next day. Depending on whether you depart from the East or West Coast, when flying to Australia or Japan the in-flight time can be between twelve and twenty-four hours, and during the trip if you fly westward (which you generally do), you will cross the international date line. When crossing the international date line from the west to the east, you gain a day. When flying from the east to the west, you lose a day. So, if you leave Japan and fly to the east, you can actually arrive in the United States the day *before* you left.

Certain cost-cutting devices exist that can lower your European intercountry airfares. Many of the major European airlines have flight-coupon programs. Policies vary depending on the airline, however, the general idea is that your flight from the United States must be to the airline's hub city: Air France to Paris, KLM to Amsterdam, Lufthansa to

Frankfurt, etc. By flying to the airline's hub city, you become eligible to purchase one-way ticket coupons to, in some cases, more than 130 cities in Europe for $110 to $140 per flight, per person. The first flight to the next destination has to be confirmed and booked from that airline's hub city. Also, to qualify for these fares, at least two people have to fly together and each traveler must purchase a minimum of three flights. In some cases, the airlines offer the option of buying up to twelve coupons for each person. The coupons are valid for two months after your first flight. Consolidated discount tickets are often not eligible for this plan, nor are frequent-flier tickets.

Since intercountry fares often cost up to $450 per person, per flight, these flight coupons can amount to a considerable savings—even if you don't have an engagement in the airline's hub city. For instance, it may be economically beneficial to fly to the hub city for the first day of a tour, arrive in the morning and catch a later flight (using your coupons) to get to the city of your first gig. There is one catch to these coupons. Most flights will not go directly to your final destination and will have to connect with secondary flights through an airline's hub city. You could be flying KLM from Zurich, Switzerland, to Milan, Italy, but you'll have to fly north to Amsterdam to connect with the Milan flight. Countries are close together in Europe and layovers are shorter than in the United States, so the extra flying time usually is not that much of a consideration. Even if you have to use two coupons for your flight, at $120 per coupon the final cost will usually be cheaper than the direct regular fare between most cities.

Be forewarned that some European countries, such as France and Italy, have strong unions. When you fly with airlines from these countries the potential for impromptu strikes by airline pilots, air-traffic controllers, and baggage handlers is ever present. These strikes can cause havoc with your travel plans. However, except in Italy, unions are required to register strikes under certain guidelines, and they are often scheduled in advance for a specific date and time—like next Thursday for twenty-four hours. Your travel agent may have advance notice.

Two particular strike experiences come to mind.

My trio had just finished a segment of a European tour in France and we were about to depart from Paris. Arriving at the airport, we were informed that the air-traffic controllers had just gone on a twenty-four-hour strike and no one was getting out of Paris that day. Luckily, it was a travel day and we didn't have a gig that evening. There was—as there often is in European airports—a hotel counter where people make reservations for hotel rooms in the area. It was very early in the morning and most of the other travelers were groggy and stunned about the interruption in their travel plans.

To beat the rush, I hustled over to the hotel counter and managed to find three inexpensive rooms in three separate hotels. I then proceeded to the rather lengthy ticket line and arranged reservations for the next day's flight. We were able to check in the bass in advance. So we shared a cab to our respective hotels and enjoyed a day of rest in Paris. The extra cost for the hotel rooms and cab didn't help the tour budget (which is why I always leave in an extra amount for emergencies), but the next day we made the gig without any additional disasters.

In another situation, I was traveling in Italy with the Phil Woods Quintet. We arrived at Rome's Fiumicino Airport to catch a flight to Milan, where we had a concert that evening, only to find that the Alitalia pilots had gone on strike for an undetermined amount of time. The indomitable road manager, Peter Hjuits, was with us. Peter got us on a Swiss Air flight to Lugano, Switzerland, and then we embarked on a three-hour train ride to Milan. However, when we boarded the train we had to put the bass on the train's baggage car. Unbeknownst to us, at the Swiss-Italian border the baggage car was separated from our train because of customs. So when we arrived in Milan we discovered that the bass wasn't on our train. Peter, who loves a problem, waited around the Milan train station for the next train to bring the bass. Meanwhile we checked into our hotel to eat and rest. When the train finally arrived, Peter brought the bass to the hotel. We made the gig that night.

European flights can be canceled without notice. If this happens, you can try to work it out with the airport counter personnel, but they are usually swamped with other passengers who are trying to solve the same problem you have. If the differences in time zones allow it, call your travel agent and have him or her resolve the problem at that end. It will get done faster, cheaper, and with less stress and fewer complications for you. The same goes for those, hopefully rare, moments when a ticket gets lost.

Many venues provide transportation to and from an airport, using their own vehicles and personnel. To avoid any travel problems, you should urgently insist that your venue contact stay with you until you have checked in your baggage and received your boarding pass. Your contact will know the language, and will frequently be familiar with the local airline personnel, and can be considerably helpful in overcoming unforeseen problems.

Managing Your Baggage and Equipment

European airline rules governing the fees for oversize and overweight luggage are more stringent than those enforced by American airlines. Excess-baggage fees are so high that if overweight charges were paid on every flight, a tour could be bankrupted. Avoiding the expense of excess-baggage fees is an art. Most experienced European roadies earn their salaries because of their skill at avoiding these fees.

When touring with the Phil Woods Quintet in Europe, the agent we were working for used the services of "the king of the roadies," a man from Amsterdam named Peter Hjuits. This tireless and dedicated man loved the challenge of taking a band on the road. As he was always working in the background, I'm not privy to all of his secrets, but he had some techniques of which I am aware. We would always give him some CDs to use as "grease for the wheels" (not a bribe, but a gift for good treatment) when coping with resistant airline personnel. Peter was always pleasant and personable. Having traveled in Europe for so long, as a roadie, with so many bands, he was known by most personnel in many airports. When Peter traveled with us, Phil never had to pay excess-baggage fees and saved hundreds, if not thousands, of dollars.

European airlines check bags either by the amount of weight allotted to each person or by the number of bags allowed per person (as in the United States). To minimize your potential for being charged baggage fees, when checking baggage and instruments at a ticket counter, collect all of the tickets and check in the band as a group. This way, the airline will consider the total amount of weight or number of bags allowed for the group as opposed to the individual amount allotted per person. This will allow you to check more baggage than if you checked in as individuals. For example, four people traveling as a group may be allotted seventy pounds of checked baggage each. The total allotment for the group will be 280 pounds. If three 40-pound suitcases are checked in individually and then the bass player checks in one 70-pound bass plus one 40-pound suitcase, then ninety pounds of free, checked baggage would be wasted (with the first three band members), and the bass player would have to pay overweight fees for the bass. However, if you check in as a group, the extra ninety pounds from the first three musicians would more than cover the extra weight of the bass case.

Ask about check-throughs when checking baggage and equipment for foreign travel. Baggage can often be checked through to your final destination, especially when transferring from an international carrier to a national airline. This avoids the necessity of carrying any luggage and equipment from one plane to another, or, even worse, from an international terminal to a national terminal. Inquire where and when you will be going through customs. Trying to recover baggage inadvertently left sitting on a tarmac, or in customs in a foreign country, is an exercise in futility best avoided by being attentive and curious. It is possible that airline employees at the originating check-in counter may be misinformed. Double-check by asking a steward on the plane if he or she knows when and where the baggage will be going through customs.

When baggage and instruments have been checked onto a national airline, it may be possible for you to observe the plane being loaded from the windows at the gate, while the plane is waiting to board. If it's a crowded flight and a smaller than usual plane, watch to see if the bass and its case are loaded. When there are crowded flights, airlines will sometimes send an oversize piece on a later, less-crowded flight. The airline personnel will know nothing about the fact that you are trying to make a concert date that evening. If you don't see the bass being loaded, inform the gate personnel of the problem. They may be helpful or not. If they're not, remember that, as on a ship, the pilot or captain of an airplane has the final say as to what does or doesn't go on a plane. Ask to speak to that person and explain the situation. This will be your court of last resort. Explain that you have a concert to perform and if you can't honor the contract you'll lose income and be sued. This indirectly implies that the airlines may be subject to a suit as well. Protest that you also don't feel comfortable about leaving a $10,000 instrument in the airline's care. This should persuade the airline personnel to prioritize your instruments.

Most U.S. airlines charge between zero and $75 to ship the bass and its case. However, the expense of flying the bass to Europe can cost anywhere from $75 to $175—and to Japan it can cost $300 or more. Don't bother calling an overseas airline for cost estimates of its excess baggage fees. You'll receive three different answers from three different people, none of which may be applicable upon arrival at the airport. Airlines are not accustomed to handling musical instruments. Assume that the bass will cost $175 each way for transcontinental European air travel. Overweight charges for inter-European air travel are unpredictable—as the same airline in different countries will enforce the rules inconsistently. You could fly Air France from Bologna, Italy, to Paris, France, one day with no overweight charges and the next day fly from Paris, France, to Madrid, Spain, on the same airline and be charged $200. Leave those cells open in your budget spreadsheet and digital diary, but allocate an extra sum for these charges in your tour balance. Enter any overweight fees in your digital diary spreadsheet as you go and count your blessings if you are eventually charged less than what you had allocated.

A common reaction of many inexperienced airline personnel is to immediately short-circuit upon seeing a bass case. Be prepared for this reaction at all times. To keep overweight charges to a minimum, an understanding of the mentality of the personnel you are interacting with is essential. From 1990 to 1993, we had the good fortune to have bassist Todd Coolman playing and traveling with our trio. Todd is not only one of jazz's premier bassists, but is also a past and present master of coping with, and understanding, the mentality of inexperienced airline personnel. Todd has offered the following much-appreciated strategy for inclusion in this book. Bandleaders, drummers, and bassists will, for all time, be appreciative of his contribution.

A Four-Part Strategy for Checking in the Bass

This strategy is laid out in four stages. Hopefully, you will have success after stage two or stage three and won't have to resort to the tactics in the last stage. When traveling in Europe, you will have less control of the situation than you will if you are in the United States because of language barriers. However, since European fees for overweight baggage tend to be so much higher than American fees, it is worthwhile to familiarize yourself with this process and use it whenever possible—especially if you have found an airline person who is willing to negotiate with you in English.

The success of this strategy is dependent on your understanding of the psychology of the people with whom you are negotiating. Airline employees are bound by company rules and regulations, many of which can be altered on the spot only by a higher official who has the authority to make independent decisions. As in any corporate environment, lower-level employees are hesitant to accept responsibility for making decisions, especially if they think they will get in trouble for doing so. For the most part, you will be dealing with lower-level employees when you approach a ticket or check-in counter.

Each employee has a work record that is used to evaluate his or her job performance. These employees try to avoid taking any action that might negatively affect their records. Conversely, they want you to know that they're in charge of the situation, and that they're able to exert their authority. Their reaction to your circumstances can also depend upon their mind-set that particular day. If the agent's dog died that morning, or spouse left town with the kids and the savings, you're not likely to get a very cooperative response. If a substantial number of difficult travelers have checked in that day, you may not get a great response either. To catch an agent at his or her best, try to arrive at the airport a little earlier than usual. If you are one of the agent's first customers for a flight, he or she will be more likely to be cooperative than if he or she has already checked in a dozen or so hassled travelers with individual concerns.

STAGE ONE It is advisable to repair and clean up your bass case once a year. A good-looking piece of luggage may be treated better than a scruffy looking one. Likewise, you should also think about your own appearance when flying. After a week or two on the road, you can easily arrive at an airport looking ragged, tired, and impatient. Try to avoid looking like you don't want to be there. In the truest sense, airport demeanor is a performance. Your appearance and attitude are important. Start setting good vibes from the minute you arrive at the airport. When the baggage handler brings your luggage to the counter, ensure that the counter person you have selected to work with sees you tip well. At this stage, appear pleasant, presentable, and cooperative. Dress like a professional. Greet everyone with a smile.

If the airport is busy and the agent is under pressure, commiserate with him or her. Comment on how hard the agent is working and how overworked he or she must be. Or if airport activity is slow, express your understanding of how boring the job can sometimes be. Demonstrate your sympathy and understanding that the last thing the agent probably needs is to be coping with the complications created by a bass case the size of a small truck.

STAGE TWO Make sure that the bass case is lying down. Don't bring it up to the counter until you're asked to do so. Position it a short distance away, or near a big post, and surround it with your other baggage, so that it appears smaller. Avoid using terms like "weight" or "overweight." Instead, always say "oversize." Ideally, you don't want the agent to put the case on a scale. If weight becomes an issue and the agent is inexperienced, he or she will think of sending the case the most expensive way possible—air cargo. This is to be avoided at all costs.

If the agent seems flustered by the situation or starts to take an uncooperative stance, mention that you've had lots of experience traveling with the bass and that he or she is not the first person to see the case as a problem. Pleasantly assert your wish that the case be shipped on the plane as an oversize item. Offer to sign a limited-release waiver, which would absolve the company of any responsibility for damage to the bass. This informs airline personnel that you are an experienced traveler with a working knowledge of the system. Inform the agent that you have your own insurance for the bass as well.

STAGE THREE If you still encounter resistance, don't looked bugged—yet. Declare that the agent's resistance to sending the bass as an oversize item is a highly irregular problem, something you have never experienced with other airlines. If you've already traveled with this airline on this tour and weren't charged for the bass during those flights, show the agent your tickets for the previous flights and argue that if the airline's baggage policy is consistent, you shouldn't be charged now. Ask the agent for an explanation of the specific problem.

Communicate to the agent that you are trying to work with him or her, and ask if there are any alternative ways to resolve the situation in a mutually satisfactory manner. Instead of using the words "I" or "you," use "we." For example, asking "Why can't *we* work this out?" is less confrontational than asking "Why can't *you* work this out?"

Often inexperienced airline personnel aren't aware of all the rules. Because of their inexperience, they don't want to take a chance on violating unknown company rules. If they don't know the answer to a problem or question, they will often just say "No." Ask your agent if he or she is certain that this decision is standard policy, and would he or she please check with another airline employee or official. A more experienced company official or employee at another counter can absolve your agent of the responsibility of making a decision—and tilt the scales in your favor.

STAGE FOUR If a satisfactory resolution has yet to occur, ask to speak with the highest-ranking supervisor on duty at the moment. When the official arrives, apologize for taking up his or her valuable time and assure the official that you are aware that he or she has more important things to do. This lets the official off the hook a little. Explain that you are asking for help. You are trying to carry on your business and he or she is your last remaining resort. If speaking with this high-ranking person doesn't lead to a resolution, it's time to get irate.

At this point, you have nothing to lose. Point out that in your experience of years of traveling you've never received such an uncooperative response from airline personnel, and you expect airlines to be of service to those with special needs. Explain that if every flight were like this, you would have been out of business years ago. Ask the official if there is any way this situation can be resolved. If the answer is still "No," escalate. Inform the official that you have no choice but to ask for his or her name or business card. Demand that the official give you the names, addresses, and telephone and fax numbers of his or her direct superiors—the head of customer relations and the president of the airlines. Assert that you will contact these higher authorities immediately and advise them of the official's unnecessarily antagonistic and uncooperative treatment. In an effort to keep his or her work record unblemished, the official may finally be motivated to act in your favor. If not, pay the money and follow through on your threat. The airline company could, after the fact, compensate you in some fashion.

It can also be effective to divide the above tactic between two members of the band—using a good cop, bad cop approach. The good cop can give the bad cop a breather by introducing a note of reasonableness into the negotiations from time to time, which may alleviate some of the tension of the situation. The good cop can apologize for the bad cop's behavior, restating things in a less confrontational manner.

When coping with resistant airline personnel, you can sometimes adopt the "Ugly American" tactic. To be sure, a polite and respectful attitude is universally appreciated. However, when traveling and working in foreign countries, there can be certain situations, when, as a last resort, acting loud and arrogant can achieve better results than being polite and understanding.

Many Europeans have experienced the wrath of insensitive American tourists so often that they are conditioned to expect such behavior—even to the point of not being satisfied until they have elicited such a response. They can then justify their preconceptions about the general crudeness of American travelers. When pushed by uncooperative airline personnel, I have often enjoyed playing this role, and have found it to be quite effective, if used judiciously. This tactic can also backfire. But if nothing else has worked, you may have nothing to lose by trying it anyway. If it doesn't work and you look like you're getting deeper into trouble, you can always walk away, calm down, and come back and apologize.

Excess baggage charges in the United States are usually paid at the check-in counter. However, in Europe, if all else fails, you may have a final court of last resort. Overweight charges are paid at a separate counter. When you go to the counter to pay the charge, look bugged. Explain the situation. The official at this counter has the power to change the rules, including the authority to charge you nothing at all.

I've seen Todd use the preceding strategy repeatedly and with great success. Although there were times when nothing worked, most of the time we avoided paying overweight charges for the bass and its case.

Customs and Immigration

The new European Common Market agreements have resulted in the easing of many travel restrictions for member countries that are signatories. So it is now easier to pass through customs and immigration than it used to be. However, you'll still have to cope with certain restrictions for those countries that are not Common Market members.

Make it band policy that all luggage and equipment should be collected from baggage claim at the same time and that everyone should wait for all band personnel so that you can all be processed through customs and immigration together. This ensures that everyone is on hand. It also ensures that everyone is available to assist any band personnel that might be in trouble.

Air travel in Europe can be more complicated than in the United States due to the fact that most foreign airports have higher security measures in force than we have here. Drum and bass cases are often scrutinized by customs officials. If you are stopped and your equipment is searched, be patient and cooperative. Adopting a negative attitude will only make things more difficult.

Passports, Visas, Work, and Tax Papers

Whenever you travel internationally, you need to have a current passport. At least three months before you plan to leave for an international tour, confirm that all band members have updated and valid passports. If one of your band members doesn't have a passport, or if his or her passport has expired, passport applications and renewal forms can be downloaded from the Internet at http://travel.state.gov/passport_services.html or mailed from your local passport office. Make sure that you give yourself ample time to obtain or renew your passports. Although there are ways to speed up this process slightly (like sending the passport office a prepaid Express Mail envelope for your passport's speedy return), you don't want to be caught short of time.

Before you leave for your tour, make sure that you have some extra passport-size photos of each of your band members on file, in case you need them for visa applications. Also, make sure that you have everyone's passport number and information on file. Enter this information exactly as it appears on the passports. Some countries insist that the information on a visa should match the passport information word-for-word, otherwise entry into that country could be refused.

Policies regarding travel visas vary from country to country. Visas are not required for travel to Canada, Mexico, the Caribbean Islands and most Western European countries. To be safe, ask the tour promoter if visas are required for an engagement to enter the country. For those countries where visas are required, contact the embassy of that country for a visa application form, and apply at least two months in advance of the gig. For information on countries where visas are needed for entry and departure, the U.S. government publishes a pamphlet that is updated yearly entitled "Foreign Entry Requirements," which is available for $.50 from the Consumer Information Center, Department 363F, Pueblo, Colorado 81009. Or you can call (1-719) 948-3334.

Policies regarding work and tax-exemption papers also vary from country to country. Some countries require you to file work papers at immigration. Your local promoter or venue operator generally processes these papers so that they're on file when you arrive at immigration. Work papers require the following information about each band member:

full legal name, address, phone number(s), birthday and birthplace, Social Security number, age, passport information (i.e., the passport number and the state in which it was issued), and the name and address of the venues you're working and the individual and total income of your gigs in the country. Some countries have limits on earnings. Canada has a yearly per person limit of $10,000. Italy does not allow you to take more than $12,000 out of the country. If you're lucky enough to have earned more than $12,000 as a band for that leg of the tour, distribute the money among your band members until you pass through customs and immigration.

Each U.S. resident is responsible for filing taxes on income earned in foreign countries. However, some countries—such as Italy and Germany—have tax treaties with the United States that may require you to fill out tax-exemption forms to avoid being double-taxed—once by each of the two countries. (This is discussed further in chapter twelve.) Your local promoter should have this information and will let you know what you have to do to avoid being double-taxed.

Certain countries in the Far East have very harsh drug rules. In some countries the death penalty is observed for possession of illegal substances. When they receive applications for travel visas, some of these countries may inquire with the U.S. Embassy and law enforcement officials as to whether the applicant has a police record. A record of a drug arrest, no matter how old, could create problems for a band member when he or she is trying to acquire a visa for several of these countries. If you or one of your band members has a record of a drug arrest, contact a lawyer and have the record expunged. This is neither a difficult nor an expensive process. Considering the higher performance fees that can be earned in these countries, it is well worth the effort and expense.

ARRANGING FOREIGN GROUND TRAVEL

Foreign van-rental rates are similar to U.S. rates. Since foreign air travel is expensive, it is often financially beneficial to rent vans and drive from venue to venue. Your decision to fly or drive is dependent on the following factors: how many people are in the band, the distances between venues, the amount of equipment being carried, and your tour budget. You may find that driving is a viable option—especially if you're carrying a lot of equipment, if your group is larger than a trio, and if you're traveling to neighboring countries.

Driving in Foreign Countries

Driving in foreign countries is markedly different from driving in the United States, mainly because of language problems. For this reason, self-driving is usually avoided. When touring abroad, it is customary for bands to hire a driver who also functions as a roadie. If you hire a driver, you will incur the added expense of the driver's salary as well as an extra hotel room (from $60 to $100 per day), unless you can negotiate for the venue to pay for the extra room. Experienced drivers' salaries can vary between $100 and $150 per day. So, the cost to you (including hotels) for an experienced roadie could run between $1,120 and $1,750 per week. This expense will have to be balanced against what it would cost to fly the band between major cities, and the potential excess-baggage expenses for the equipment and luggage.

Sometimes a European agent will arrange and pay for a driver out of his or her fee. If this is the arrangement, of course, the agent's fee will be higher than if this fee wasn't being paid. Alternatively, you can pay for the cost of the driver out of your tour budget directly. In either case, you will be paying for it. For short tours, renting a van can be a pleasant way to travel—especially if your group is not too large. You will see more of the country than you would by flying, and you will have more control over your travel times as well as your meal and rest stops.

Taking Trains

Except for the high-speed trains in the Boston–New York City–Washington, D.C. corridor, most U.S. train travel can be dismissed as being an impractical and an expensive way to travel. U.S. train schedules and routing are limited and the costs of domestic train tickets are high. European trains, however, are totally different. European trains offer a wide variety of classes of high-speed trains that allow travel to almost anywhere in comfort, and at a lower cost than flying. Using a Eurailpass is the least expensive way to travel by train in Europe. For information, contact Rail Europe, by mail, at 2100 Central Avenue, Suite 200, Boulder, Colorado 80301; by phone, at 1-800-438-7245; or on the Internet at http://www.raileurope.com.

Rail Europe offers a wide variety of train passes, including the Eurailpass, Eurail Flexipass, Eurail Saverpass, and the Europass. These plans offer the most affordable fares for the touring musician. If you're planning to travel within a single European country, you should consider a single-country Eurailpass, such as the BritRail Pass, the France Railpass, or the Italy Rail Card. The variety of plans and fees offered are too numerous to mention here. Which plan you select depends on how many days of train travel are required (and in some plans, how many countries you travel to) within a fixed time period. These plans offer first-class tickets only. First-class cars offer the option of making advance seat reservations for an extra fee. Some high-speed trains will *only* accept reserved tickets. During the low season months, advance reservations may not be needed, but during the summer it may be wise in certain situations to spend the extra amount, about $10 per reservation, per person, to ensure seating availability. You'll want to gauge each trip individually and decide whether the reservation is required, because at $10 per seat reservation, per trip, you could be adding a hefty extra expense to your budget if you indiscriminately reserve seats for every train that you take.

Some plans, like the Eurail Flexipass, include savings on train surcharges and free or discounted fares on ferries, steamers, or boats. Depending on which pass you buy, there may be some minor restrictions. Check the details of each pass carefully before you purchase your ticket.

When booking European tours, there have been a few occasions when I had the possibility of extending a tour one day beyond the travel period allowed by my fourteen-day Eurailpass. After doing alternative budgets with and without the extra day, each time I discovered that the ticket fees and added salaries that we would incur if we accepted the additional gig made the extra day's work not worthwhile. If you're not planning on making many train trips within a tour, it might be more economical not to buy travel passes. Before you decide whether or not to purchase a travel pass, compare the cost of your trips against the cost of the passes. You can access foreign train information for any country on the Internet at the CTU Railway Page at http://www.cvut.cz/home/railway.htm.

Train configurations should be taken into consideration when you're reserving seats. Open-seated first-class cars will often have a row of double seats on one side of the aisle and a row of single or double seats on the other side of the aisle. These seats can often be turned around by pressing a pedal under the seat, which offers travelers the choice of facing each other or being back-to-back. The advantage of having seats facing each other is that you may be afforded the extra comfort of being able to take your shoes off to rest your feet on a magazine on the empty seat opposite you.

Many trains have enclosed cabins that seat six people per cabin, three per side, with an aisle outside the cabin. These cabins are quieter than open-seated cars and offer more privacy and leeway to use air-conditioning, open the windows, or close the curtains to block any viewing from the aisle. They are also much better for sleeping than open-seated cars. Check if your train has cabin seating or not. Many travelers prefer to have cabins by themselves, if they can get them. There are ways to avoid being cramped in a cabin with too many people. For instance, if there are three of you traveling together, you may consider configuring your reservations so that two of you are seated in the outside seats on one side of the cabin, with the middle seat on that side empty, and that the third person is seated in the middle seat on the other side. This way, as described above, each of you has the option of stretching your legs. You're playing the odds in an effort to stay comfortable, but there is no guarantee that these seats will stay open. However, noting the reservation configuration in your cabin, subsequent travelers may try another cabin with fewer inhabitants and baggage, as well as a more comfortable seating configuration.

When a seat is reserved, it will have a little card holder above it (or in the case of a cabin, outside the cabin door) with a card in it noting which segment of the trip has been reserved. If a seat is not reserved, the card holder will be empty. Reserved or not, if the train is crowded, you be will expected to allow access to an unoccupied seat to any traveler who requests it.

Tickets contain information about the train designation, arrival and departure times, car and seat number, and whether the train has a dining car, snack bar, or traveling food cart (which generally sells sandwiches, coffee, and soft drinks). You will want to make sure that your train is designated as an IC (intercity) train. Trains without the designation "IC" will be slower, local trains that have more stops than intercity trains. In addition, nonintercity trains are usually second-class and no seats can be reserved. Getting on and off nonintercity trains with your baggage and equipment while traveling at rush hour will be a hassle. So, even if you have to wait a little bit longer for the next intercity train, the wait will be worth it—as the trip will be more comfortable and you're also likely to arrive at your destination sooner than you would if you took the nonintercity train.

If you have a day off or your itinerary has a day or two gap in it and there is a lengthy distance from one gig to another, you may consider purchasing tickets for a sleeping car on an overnight train. This strategy can save you a lot of money on hotel bills as well as on airfares. Depending on where you are traveling and whether you select single or double first-class accommodations, the prices can range from $38 to

$148, and reservations are required. Compared to the rigors and expense of air travel, sleeping cars offer privacy, comfort, and economy of price.

Being able to understand the posted train information is a prerequisite if you want your train travel to run smoothly. Most train station mezzanines have large, overhead boards that list all the trains for that day, their designations, track numbers, arrival and departure times, and whether the train has a dining car or not. There are also large (usually yellow) cardboard charts posted on the station walls that offer a total picture of train-travel information for that season. These charts can come in handy to double-check train tickets, and find the correct platform.

Larger train stations have many platforms, each of which often has two numbered tracks (one on either side). Reconfirm which track and side of the platform you should be on to make your next connection. Don't depend on the overhead sign on the platform for this information. It lists only the next train that is scheduled to arrive at that track and it changes as each train leaves the station. Your train and its arrival time will not show up on the overhead sign until it is the next one coming.

Rather than rely on the overhead platform signs for train information, check to see if there is a standing board at the end of each platform. This is common for many European countries. The standing board will list that day's train information for the facing track on each side of the board. It will also show where each car will be positioned when the train stops at the platform, and will picture a schematic of color-coded cars, with car numbers on them, that corresponds to the car configuration of the train. You'll also notice on the board that one of the letters from A to E is over each car; these correspond with the large letter you'll see hanging over the track. To avoid getting on the wrong end of the train when it pulls into the station, look up your car number and what letter it will stop at on the platform. The train will stop exactly where posted. After a while you'll get so familiar with the system that you'll be able to position yourself at the exact place where the door to your car will be when the train stops.

First-class cars are often at one end of the train, and second-class cars at the other. Whether the first-class cars are at the beginning of the train or at the end is up to the whim of the powers-that-be, and their position can change from train to train. If there is a dining car, it will usually be between the first- and second-class cars.

When traveling by train, you'll need to pay extra careful attention to the boarding time of your train. For intermediate stops at smaller stations you might have only three minutes to get on or off a train. Negotiating a crowded platform without knowing which is the correct car, with your luggage carts and equipment in hand, will be very difficult. If you're on the wrong end of the platform, don't board where you are. You'll probably have to run to the correct car, but the conductors will be watching what's going on on the platform and won't let the train pull out until all passengers are completely boarded.

The importance of knowing where your car is was memorably brought home to me while playing a European tour with the Bobby Hutcherson–Harold Land Quintet in the early 1970s.

It was rush hour and although we had reserved seats, we arrived at the train station late, and didn't have time to check the board to see where our car and seats were located. As a result, when the train came we inadvertently got on the train at the wrong end. The train was full and had cabin seating. The aisles also had pull-down seats for those who couldn't get cabin seats and they were full of people and their luggage.

We were traveling with a bass, bass amp, drum set, luggage, and Bobby's vibes, which were packed in six or seven fiber travel cases. In our haste to get on the train, we piled all of our baggage and equipment in the space between the train car and the baggage compartment at the end of the train. Bobby left the four of us in that space and went looking for our cabin. After twenty minutes of winding his way back and forth through ten cars filled with travelers he returned to show us to our cabin. In total we had sixteen pieces that we had to carry from one end of the train to the other. With five men, that meant three trips to accomplish the move.

The first trip we carried our burdens—bumping, squeezing, and pushing our way down the crowded aisles. Most of the people, thinking this was an isolated inconvenience, just turned in their seats, or if standing, sucked in their bellies, giving us dirty looks as we passed by them.

However, when the people in the aisles saw us returning empty handed, their looks changed. There were ten cars filled with worried faces. We picked up our second load and retraced our steps—through all the mumbling and grumbling travelers, most of whom, to avoid being jostled by our passing, unwillingly rose from their seats and moved their luggage to ease our passage. As we got to the end of each car, we could see behind us the multitude of relieved passengers readjusting their luggage and clothes, happily regaining their not-too-comfortable perches. They were glad to see us go, and all wore relieved expressions on their faces.

Things started turning ugly when the aisle passengers saw us returning empty-handed for a second time. They couldn't believe it. Tension filled the air. Testy conversations, accompanied by angry body language, started loudly emanating from these poor travelers who were trying to get home after a hard day's work.

We had, unfortunately, saved the bass, bass amp, bass drum, and other big pieces for the last trip. As much as we may have wanted to, we could not slink past the other travelers unnoticed. Upon entering each succeeding car of weary passengers, we were greeted by an in-unison groan, which swelled up with the mounting tension. Ten cars, each with a group groan. By the time we finished with our chores, we had to have been the most hated men on earth!

There is a downside to train travel: Because there is a shortage of baggage porters in most train stations, you will have to carry your own baggage most of the time. Traveling with a lot of equipment can be tiring, and sometimes impractical. Some train itineraries may include as many as four trains in a day. This could entail lifting a forty-pound suitcase up and down from the overhead luggage racks eight times before reaching your final destination. This can be avoided, depending on the configuration of the train cars. Some cars have luggage storage space at the end of each car, or space between the seats, where most of the luggage can fit. A first-class cabin offers privacy and comfort, but will have overhead racks that involve lifting. Open-seated cars will have overhead racks, and maybe storage at each end of the car.

One problem with train travel will (again) be the bass, and maybe its case. To avoid carrying the bass case with you throughout each leg of your tour, ship it by train to the location of your last venue and arrange to have it either picked up at the station by the venue or stored in the left-baggage department at the train station. Alternatively, if you are starting and ending your tour in the same city, the bass case can be stored in the left-baggage department at the originating station and picked up again upon your return. When traveling by train, the bass itself can be put in the space at the end of a car, across the overhead racks in a cabin, or in an unoccupied seat—depending on the available storage space on the train. Some trains have open sections for passengers who are traveling with bicycles that, if empty, can also be a handy place to put the bass. However, you may be required to put the bass in a baggage car.

Most small-town train stations have no elevators, porters, or handy moving-baggage strips, such as can be found along the side of platform stairs of the larger train stations. Without these amenities, transferring baggage and equipment from one platform to another is physically challenging, especially if transfer times between trains are tight. These factors can increase your risk of missing a train, or being totally exhausted by the time you arrive at your final destination. Always ask the conductor for the platform and track number of the next train. Know which stop precedes yours, and immediately after you pass the next-to-last stop, position yourself with your bags at the train doors—so that you are in position before other passengers start to line up to get off the train.

On our first European trio tour in 1990, we had one train transfer that allowed us three minutes between trains. The agency that booked the tour sent three of its people to the train station so that they were already there when we arrived. The first person held the next train from leaving while the other two (and a porter) helped the three of us move our luggage to the next train with a luggage cart. This highly orchestrated affair was successful—and we actually wouldn't have been able to get on the train without the help of these three people. As it was, the last bag got on just as the train was ready to pull out of the station.

Even if you don't think that traveling by train for your entire tour makes the most sense for your particular circumstances, you might find that taking certain trains is more economical than flying. The new Eurostar train, which travels in the Chunnel (the tunnel under the English Channel), is a convenient and relatively inexpensive way to travel from London to either Paris or Brussels. There are now eleven London–Paris round-trip trains daily. As of this writing, second-class fares are $120 one-way or $240 round-trip, and first-class fares are $172 one-way or $342 round-trip ($290 with a Saturday stopover), including meal service. There are also six London–Brussels round-trip trains daily. Schedules and prices are, of course, subject to change. You can find out more information about the Eurostar by calling (011-44-1233) 61 75 75 or by checking the Internet at http://www.eurostar.com.

Discounts for the Eurostar may be available for persons holding a BritRail Pass, Eurailpass, Europass, or France Railpass. You can get discounts of 33 percent in coach and more than 20 percent in first class. With this discount (and as of this writing), an unrestricted Eurostar trip by coach costs $83 (London to Paris) or $79 (London to Brussels). Eurostar trains require reservations and have fares as low as $67 each way if purchased fourteen days in advance with a Saturday stopover. As always, quoted prices are subject to change.

One of the most worthwhile books on road travel is the book *Guide to the Road for the Touring Musician*, by David Liebman (Jamey Aebersold Jazz, 1994). You can order this book directly from Jamey Aebersold Jazz, either by calling 1-800-456-1388 or by accessing the company's Web site at http://www.jazzbooks.com. *Guide to the Road for the Touring Musician* only costs $5.95 and is a must-buy for anyone aspiring to be a road rat—especially if you expect to travel in Europe. David covers many aspects of life on the road, including safety and health issues as well as packing, jet lag, eating, sleeping, and road etiquette.

ARRANGING FOREIGN HOTEL ACCOMMODATIONS

Hotel accommodations work differently in foreign countries than they do in the United States. Many hotels have a long history of service that is based on generations of experience. However, the range of the quality and cost of hotels is much wider in Europe than it is in the United States. Don't accept any hotel that is rated with fewer than three stars. If you are making the arrangements yourself, language barriers often mean that you don't have as much advance information about the details of your accommodations as you do when the venue acts as a mediator. This is all the more reason why it is critical to stay at the better-quality hotels where your comfort levels are better ensured. Although things are changing, rooms in Europe are generally much smaller than they are in the United States. In fact, I once had a hotel room in Germany that was so small, I couldn't open my suitcase!

Hotel accommodations are usually arranged either by a promoter or by the venue. If this is the case, make sure you have communicated your band's preferences to your contact. Things like whether you want a smoking or a nonsmoking room—or whether your room will have a shower or a bathtub—directly affect your quality of life while you're on the road. Taking a few minutes to anticipate these needs in advance will make a huge difference once you're actually there.

Check-in Procedures

European hotel check-in procedures are similar to those in the United States. They differ in only minor details. Hotel restaurants keep track of your meals and you will rarely be asked to sign a check after a meal. Just showing your room key will suffice. Serving times at hotel restaurants are very restricted—generally from 6:00 A.M. to 9:00 A.M. or 10:00 A.M. for breakfast, from 1:00 P.M. to 3:00 P.M. for lunch, and from 7:00 P.M. or 8:00 P.M. to 9:00 P.M. or 10:00 P.M. for dinner. In general, tipping is not necessary; it is included in the bill. It is the custom, however, to leave some small change on the table after a meal. Some of the newer and more expensive hotels have twenty-four-hour room service, but watch out for the cost.

Generally, telephone charges in Europe are much higher than in the United States. If you don't pay careful attention to the telephone charges that are in effect, you might be surprised by a large hotel telephone bill when you're checking out. Never use a hotel phone switchboard to make long-distance calls to the United States. Most American telephone companies offer a wallet card with a list of the phone numbers to use in each country so that you can call home when you're on the road. If you use one of these long-distance cards to call home, you will be charged to your home phone bill at the same rate as if you were calling from the United States to Europe. Many hotels in smaller towns have a trunk service fee that they charge to connect you to the nearest major telephone hub. Ask the hotel personnel if they have these fees. If so, you might wait to make your calls until you get to a bigger city.

Beware of using hotel laundry and dry cleaning services. They are twice as expensive as in the United States and they take longer. One-day service is almost nonexistent. You might get lucky and find a Laundromat near the hotel, but it will probably not have drop-off service and you'll have to do the laundry yourself.

As a case in point, I was on tour in Italy with my trio, and we had a couple of days off in a hotel in Catania, Sicily. I thought I'd take advantage of this hiatus to get a little dry cleaning done and sent eight handkerchiefs, eight pairs of underwear, and eight T-shirts to be laundered. Two days later, there was a knock on my door and three hotel maids were standing in the hallway—one with the handkerchiefs, one with the underwear, and one with the T-shirts. All of the items were neatly ironed and folded and were carried in their separate baskets. You would have thought the hotel maids were carrying the Crown Jewels. I should have been alerted by this royal treatment that something was wrong. But when I checked out I was totally surprised to find a charge of $80 for laundry on my bill. Needless to say, I fussed and fumed to the best of my ability, but the powers-that-be were unrelenting. I know when I've been had, so I grudgingly paid the bill. This is when I learned that you don't have to go to Central Park to get mugged!

Check-out Procedures

If your performances were paid in local currency, you'll save money on exchange rates by using that currency to pay the hotel charges when you check out. It's a convenient way to get rid of any local currency you're holding, especially if you are going to another country that day. If you don't have enough currency to pay the total bill, you can split the bill between the currency and your credit card. Try to avoid paying your hotel bill with U.S. currency (i.e., American cash) because hotels have the most expensive exchange rates of any of the services that exchange money. Instead, pay your hotel charges with your credit card. All charges should be in the local currency. Your credit-card company will obtain the lowest exchange rate possible on the day that the debt was incurred. If you pay all of your tour expenses with an American Express Gold Card, you'll also add a tidy sum to your frequent-flier program.

Chapter 12

Organizing Your Tour Finances

As a bandleader and small-business owner, you will become highly skilled at managing your finances. As you will soon discover, running a business under "normal" circumstances can be a complex venture. However, running a business while on the road—and, therefore, while away from your normal financial resources and support systems—can be tremendously challenging. The best remedies for this challenge are forethought and planning. Thinking through what your needs on the road will be *before* you actually leave will save you a lot of time—and many headaches as well.

PREPARING FOR YOUR TOUR
All start-up businesses incur credit-card debt. That is one of the risks involved with beginning and running a business. Managing your finances is a large part of any business. However, if the techniques in this book prove successful, you'll soon be *touring* with your band. And for all practical purposes, that means that you're going to have to manage your finances while you're away from your normal support systems and out of your normal routine. In many different respects, this is a challenging venture.

One of the biggest challenges of going on tour is handling your income as well as your expenses. This sometimes involves carrying large amounts of cash with you while you're on the road. Since this is a risky venture, one of your jobs as bandleader will be finding ways in which you can eliminate (or at least reduce) the risks involved with working in cash. Another one of your major challenges will be managing your debt payments carefully while you're on the road—so that you make your payments on time and don't incur additional fees as a result of late payments. These are both big challenges. However, some basic organization—especially before you leave for your tour—will help you manage these responsibilities.

Managing Your Credit Cards
It is very difficult to take a band on the road without using credit cards. Credit cards come in handy for all sorts of situations—reserving hotel rooms and rental vans, for instance. They help to reduce your dependence on cash (which is a major safety feature). And, when you're traveling abroad, credit cards can help you secure the best exchange rate for paying tour expenses.

The two most common credit-card companies are Visa and MasterCard. Although it is often called a credit card, the American Express card is actually a *charge* card, meaning you have to pay off your balance each month and can't carry over debt from one month to the next. Of the three major cards, I prefer American Express, for two main reasons. First, since you have to pay the American Express card off each month (or risk losing your card privileges), your purchases don't incur any interest charges. Second, because you're not carrying debt from month to month, you don't have to

make debt payments (as you do with credit cards). Making debt payments is an inefficient way of managing your money—since you often are only paying off the interest of
your purchases and not paying off the purchases themselves. Relying upon the
American Express card—at least primarily—can help you be realistic with your
expenses. As with any of the credit cards, using an American Express card (rather than
cash) is a good idea because it provides you with an accounting at the end of the year
that is very helpful at tax time.

Another benefit of using the American Express card is that you don't have a credit
limit. This can come in handy when you're on the road—especially when you're
putting down a guarantee. If you use a Visa card or MasterCard to guarantee your van
rental, for instance, in order to ensure payment of services these companies will deduct
the amount of the rental from your credit limit *before* you actually pay it. You could be
on the road, needing to pay another bill, and discover that you can't use your card to
pay the bill because you've already reached your credit limit. You aren't charged interest for these advance deductions, but to avoid running out of credit, keep track of how
much there is left on your card after you make these kinds of reservations.

For example, if your Visa card or MasterCard has a $3,000 limit and you use it to
purchase $2,000 worth of airplane tickets before the tour, you will have $1,000 worth
of credit available for van rentals and hotels while you're on the road (assuming that it
was "clean" when you started). However, if you also reserve vans and hotels in advance
and they amount to $1,000, the amount of these reservations will be deducted from the
card before you pay for these services. Your credit limit will have been used up—even
before you leave for your tour.

Pay close attention to your credit-card billing cycle. Before you leave for your tour,
try to anticipate how much money will be on your card and figure out when you will
have enough tour money to pay off the card account, and make arrangements so that
you can send in the payment before the due date. Not paying a debt on time could
leave you on the road with a card you can't use. For instance, if you purchase your
tickets too far in advance and don't have the money on hand to pay for them before
you leave for the tour, you will probably find that your card is shut off when you're
touring. To avoid this scenario, check with the company to find out the first date of
your billing cycle, and note that essential information in your credit-card data file.

Whenever possible, try to coordinate the purchase-by dates of your airline tickets so
that the charges are billed to your card after the first day of your new monthly billing
cycle. That way, in the scenario described above, the tickets would have gone on the
cycle that overlaps with the tour and that portion of your bill would have been due a
month later. You'll also want to note the first date of your billing cycle on your computer calendar and your itinerary—especially if the due date occurs while you're on the
road. Making charges on or after this date will give you an extra month to pay for them.

As mentioned earlier, one advantage of using the American Express card is that it
has to be paid off at the end of each monthly billing cycle. But another advantage is
that, as you receive performance fees, you can make payments (or prepayments) on the
card at any American Express office while you're on the road. This helps avoid the possibility of losing your cash while traveling. Making these kinds of payments helps you
get tour expense money out of your hands as soon as possible. However, in an effort to

discourage money laundering, American Express limits cash payments on its accounts to $1,000 per day. You can go beyond this limit by purchasing postal money orders or bank checks to pay off any money owed in excess of the $1,000 limit. Although generating postal money orders or bank checks involves some extra time and expense on your part, it is worth the effort, as American Express will accept postal money orders and checks of any amount. Make sure to get receipts for every payment.

Pretour budgets are never 100 percent accurate and often your road expenses will differ from the figures in your final budget to some degree. Your monthly credit-card statement will come in handy for updating your tour budget when you get home.

The American Express card, especially the American Express Gold card, offers many extra services that other cards do not. The company's baggage-insurance plan is inexpensive and well worth the cost, because airline reimbursement for lost baggage will only be a small percentage of what your bag and contents are actually worth. As of this writing, the American Express Gold card also has one of the best free-mileage plans of any credit card. For every dollar that you spend with the card, you receive a free mile. As transportation costs can be from 25 to 30 percent of a tour's budget, tickets bought with free mileage can be used to make a financially tight tour possible. Frequent-flier plans change often. Check with the company to confirm any policy changes.

When you take a band on the road, you are responsible for the well-being of each of the band members.

Traveling around the world with no financial resources to get you out of trouble, if trouble occurs, is risky. In addition to the American Express card, you should always carry a Visa card or MasterCard that has a high credit limit and that is clear of any charges. This card should be reserved for use in emergency situations only. You never can predict what will go wrong on the road and you should have the financial backup of one of these cards to cope with any emergency. If an emergency does occur, it is the lesser of two evils to "bite the bullet" and absorb the debt that is necessary to get yourself, or a band member, out of trouble. Road emergencies can sometimes be the end of a band. You may never have to use this card, but it does lower your stress factor to know it's there.

Visa cards and MasterCards are tempting to use for touring expenses because the account can be paid off over time. If you are like many musicians and don't have a large cash cushion, this can be a risky proposition. You may get home and, because of an emergency, have to use some of the cash that was allocated to pay off your card account to solve a domestic problem. This can result in a hefty credit-card tab that may take a long time to pay off.

I made this mistake when first touring with my own band in 1990. Using both a Visa card and a MasterCard to pay for my transportation for a fall tour, I returned home to discover that my furnace had died and I needed to buy one immediately or I would be out of heat for the winter. The new furnace cost me $4,500. The following spring, upon returning from a tour, I had to replace the motor in my car with a rebuilt engine. That cost me another $2,500. As things were a little financially tight at the time, both times I paid for these expenses with cash that had been earmarked for paying off my band's transportation and hotel expenses. I ended up with $7,000 on my cards, and it took me years to pay it off.

When using a Visa card and a MasterCard, you'll also have the additional expense of the interest on the cards. Although credit-card interest is generally not tax deductible, interest on the cards could be tax deductible *if* the charges were for business expenses. Every business that uses loans to finance business expenses is allowed to deduct the interest on its loans as part of its cost of doing business. Check this with your accountant. However, if you plan to do this, then it is wise not to mix business and personal expenses on the same card—otherwise you'll have to pay your accountant to untangle these accounts at tax time.

Using the Foreign Entertainers' Tax to Your Advantage

Many European countries impose increasingly expensive foreign entertainers' taxes on venues and promoters that hire non-European performers. These taxes can be as high as 50 percent of the performance fees. In other words, if your fee is $1,000, the venue may have to pay an additional $500 in taxes to its government. This could bump your overall cost to a point where the venue can't afford to hire you. However, the interesting aspect of this situation is that the venues only have to pay a tax on the performers' *fees*, and not on the other expenses that the venue might incur when bringing a band in for a gig.

You can turn this aspect of the tax law to your advantage by employing the following technique: If you're asking $1,000 for a performance fee, but a 50 percent tax makes the gig too expensive for the venue to hire you, tell your client that you would waive the fee for the gig *if* he or she would wire $1,250 to your travel agent to pay for your round-trip airplane tickets. Arrange this well in advance of your tour, before your agent charges the tickets to your credit card. The venue doesn't have to pay any entertainment taxes and, therefore, saves $250 on the tax. You add $250 to your fee and your contract reads that you're playing the gig as a showcase.

Declaring Independent-Contractor Status

Independent-contractor status is another tax issue you may or may not encounter as a bandleader. The issues are complicated and not clearly defined, as, at this writing, the musicians' union, the American Federation of Musicians, is lobbying Congress to pass an equitable independent-contractor law and loosen the regulations that govern whether or not someone qualifies for independent-contractor status. If this law is passed, the number of classifications that will need to be proven to obtain independent-contractor status will be reduced from twenty to three. Although the current list is quite subjective and liable to interpretation, the more a business can show it doesn't control an existing relationship with a worker, the easier it is to argue a case for independent-contractor status.

Tax and money savings are the primary considerations for choosing to pay the band either as employees or as independent contractors. Businesses that use independent contractors as opposed to employees don't have to:

- pay any federal or state payroll taxes;
- pay unemployment taxes, which, when combined, can add up to 15 percent or more of your expenses;

- cover the independent contractors under any retirement or fringe-benefit plans, such as medical or insurance plans;
- pay workers' compensation, which can exceed 33 percent of your overall payroll;
- file quarterly payroll tax returns, workers' compensation audits, and/or yearly W-2 forms.

It can be risky for a business owner to claim independent-contractor status for a worker—especially if that worker is considered by the IRS to be an employee. The penalties can be costly if, at a later date, the IRS challenges you and your workers can't prove true independent-contractor status. Discuss with your band members whether they'd prefer to be classified as employees or as independent contractors. If they choose to be classified as employees, this classification may have a negative effect on your total band finances and individual salaries—as you'll have to pay all of the items listed above and that in turn will require that you reduce the band members' salaries.

If you are claiming independent-contractor status for your workers and your payments exceed $600 per calendar year, you'll have to file a form 1099 for each worker, otherwise the penalties can be costly.

Although it may or may not result in any protection, consider making independent-contractor agreements with each of your band members. Contact your local union for the classification list and an update on the status of the new bills now being considered in Congress. Also check with your attorney and accountant to avoid future problems with the IRS.

MANAGING YOUR FINANCES WHILE ON THE ROAD

As a bandleader you will have to deal with numerous financial concerns. These concerns include getting paid, handling cash, paying your band, sending income home, sending foreign currency home, exporting and importing cash, exchanging foreign currencies, organizing your tour documents, and keeping receipts. This section will give you an overview of the many strategies that you can take to help manage your finances while you're on the road.

Getting Paid

There are two common ways to get paid while you're on tour: by cash or by check. Which option you choose will depend on how your business is set up and how you want to pay your band. Generally, salary payments are made at the time that performance fees are collected. However, the timing of these payments may also be dictated by how much cash you, as the bandleader, need to keep in reserve as a safeguard against any potential emergencies that could occur.

If your business is set up as a sole proprietorship, one of the payment options is to have checks made out to you personally, so that you can cash them while you're on the road and pay the band in cash as you tour. If you decide to take this option, make sure that all of your contracts specify that the check is to be issued in your name (rather than in the band's name) before you sign them. You can't cash a business check (a check made out in the name of your band) while you're on the road. Banks insist that you deposit business checks in your business account. If one of your clients has specified that the check will be made out to the band's name, then contact the client and ask him or her about amending the contract. If the contact agrees to the change, he or she can either send you new contracts or you can change the contracts yourself and initial the change.

If your business is set up as a partnership, corporation, or a nonprofit, checks will need to be written in the name of your business, using its Tax Identification number. If you've agreed to pay your band in cash while you're on the road, you'll have to keep a reserve in your business account so that you can take cash for their salaries with you on the road. An alternative to this approach is to take enough cash so that your band members can pay their road expenses while you're on tour, and then you can pay the balance of their salaries by business check at the end of the tour, after you've deposited your checks.

Educational, nonprofit, and cultural institutions almost always pay by check. If you have salary commitments that you have to make while you're on the road, try to arrange it so that you receive the check in the afternoon of the date of the engagement. This way you can get to the local bank to cash the check before the gig. Or, if the gig is on a weekday and your travel schedule allows it, you can cash the check on the next day—on your way to the next gig. If you are paid on a Saturday and no banks are open, other gigs on the tour may pay enough in cash for you to meet your salary commitments, or give you checks that you have time to cash on the road. To avoid the risks that are involved with carrying large amounts of cash with you while you're on the road, it's safer for you to reserve some of these checks as your personal income from the tour, depositing them in your account when you return home.

Most musicians, with good reason, are wary of accepting checks for payment of services. I've never had an educational, arts presenter, or cultural venue's check bounce. You should, however, avoid accepting checks from jazz clubs—unless, of course, the client goes to the bank with you to cash it.

Handling Cash

Keeping cash secure while you're on the road is a major concern for most bandleaders. For example, you might put your cash in an old envelope on the desk in your hotel room when you come back from a gig at 1:00 A.M. And then, checking out at 5:00 A.M., with only four hours of sleep, you might overlook that envelope and inadvertently leave the cash in your room. To minimize the risks involved with carrying cash on the road, there are a handful of cautionary measures that you should follow.

Most hotels have safes in which guests can securely deposit cash and valuables. Before bringing cash to the front desk for deposit, put it in a sealed envelope and write your name and room number across the seal. This protects the envelope from being opened by anyone. Make a note of how much you have in the envelope—not on the envelope itself, but on a piece of paper that you keep. This is a precautionary measure, just in case you forget how much money you put in the envelope. And then, on your itinerary (next to the day you plan to check out of that hotel), make a note to yourself to pick up the envelope.

Under no circumstances should you ever leave cash in your hotel room while you're at a gig. Hotels don't accept responsibility for cash and valuables left in the rooms of their guests. If you're not comfortable checking your money into a hotel safe, carry the money with you to the gig and keep it on your person at all times. Don't put it into kit bags, equipment bags, or suitcases, or leave it in your dressing room.

Paying Your Band

One way to minimize the risk of losing cash while you're on the road is by keeping your band members' salaries up-to-date and paying them in cash as you go along. Of course, if you do this, you'll want to make sure that you keep enough cash on hand to manage any emergencies that might arise. After paying your band members through to the current gig, if you still have excessive amounts of cash on hand (and if your band members are financially mature), you might consider paying them as far in advance as the surplus allows. Both of these solutions relieve you of the responsibility of keeping the cash safe. Remember that, if the money is lost either by theft or by accident while it's in *your* possession, *you'll* be personally responsible for the money you agreed to pay your band members. However, once you have paid out the salaries, each of the band members is responsible for the safety of his or her cash.

Salary agreements vary, but most musicians prefer to be paid in cash rather than by check. If you have a cooperative group, the tour income after expenses will be divided evenly among you. If your band has this kind of agreement, the loss of income from a canceled gig or lost or stolen cash is shared equally. Under certain salary agreements, band members are guaranteed a total salary for a tour—irrespective of the number of days that they have worked. In this case, if money is lost or stolen while it is in your care, you'll be personally responsible.

Disagreements about who paid what to whom have created problems for many a band. To avoid possible conflicts, develop accurate and dependable payment practices and follow them strictly. Buy a carbonless petty-cash receipt book from a business-supply store and get signed receipts for all salary payments and reimbursements. Keep the "carbon" copy of each payment for your records and give each member the original. In addition to settling any questions that may arise with your band members, these receipts will come in handy every January when your accountant has to send your band members their W-2 forms.

While traveling abroad, you can avoid any of the speculative aspects that can be involved with salary payments by paying your band members in U.S. currency. You could win or lose when you exchange foreign currency to U.S. currency, but so could your musicians. If your band members need foreign currency for road expenses, pay them in U.S. currency and tell them to exchange the money into foreign currency themselves. That way they take the responsibility for any exchange-rate wins or losses.

Sending Income Home

When touring the United States, another way to reduce the risk of losing your cash (or checks for that matter) is by depositing it into your account by mail. You can also convert your cash to bank checks or postal money orders to avoid the risk of depositing cash by mail. Carry a few mail-in deposit forms with you for this purpose. This method can come in handy—particularly if no one is at home to pay important bills that may come due while you're traveling. You don't want your health, automobile, or house insurance to lapse while you're on the road. If you need to pay your bills while touring, carry your bills and your checkbook with you, or pay your bills using postal money orders. If you decide to pay your bills by postal money order, check your itinerary to determine when you'll have time to get to a post office.

While you're on the road, make sure that you take a moment—from time to time—to go over your budget spreadsheet and assess your income status. This simple precautionary measure can help you minimize the possibility that you will find yourself short of cash for expenses and emergencies. Check your itinerary and look for upcoming cash transactions. Keep enough cash on hand for expenses such as gas, tolls, tips, meals, and unexpected purchases of clothing or incidentals.

While touring Spain one year, the airline mistakenly sent our luggage to Addis Ababa. Everyone had to purchase clothing and incidentals, just to survive, until our luggage was returned to us. Most airlines will reimburse you for these expenses up to a certain limit, but not without accurate receipts. If this happens to you, ask about the airline's limit *before* you make any purchases. Our travel schedule was pretty tight the day we discovered that our luggage had been sent to Addis Ababa. When we arrived at our destination, just a few hours before the gig, it was siesta time and the stores were closed until 7:00 P.M. So we couldn't buy gig clothes. We played that evening's concert in our traveling clothes.

Sending income home from foreign countries is only slightly more complicated than sending it home when you're traveling in the United States. Many musicians elect to send excess cash home by going to a foreign bank and wiring money to their home bank accounts. Although this is—for the most part—a secure way of transferring funds, you have to pay transaction fees to both banks. Since these fees can add up, you will have to balance the expense of the transaction against your concerns for safety and determine whether or not this is the best method for you.

As an alternative to wiring money home, consider converting your cash into American Express checks as you travel from city to city. The fees for these checks are markedly lower than banks' wire-transfer fees, and you're protected against loss or theft. Although this method takes longer than bank transfers, you can then mail the checks to your home account with a "for deposit only to the account of" notation on each of the checks. However, there is always a risk that these checks will get lost in the mail. And if you are away from home for a long period of time, you may not know until after you have returned home whether the checks arrived at your bank safely. You *can* check in with your local bank from time to time, but that entails the extra cost of intercontinental phone charges.

On one European tour, I mailed my American Express checks to my bank and they never arrived. Luckily, as advised by American Express, I had saved all of the check receipts. If I hadn't, I would have lost all of that money. However, since I had the receipts, American Express reissued another set of checks for me. After that experience, I have been somewhat apprehensive of losing checks in the mail again, so I have adopted another technique: I convert my cash to American Express checks, tear them up, and flush them down the toilet, but keep the receipts. When I get home, I go to an American Express office with my receipts and tell the financial representative that the checks were lost in the mail. The American Express representative always reissues the checks for me right away.

Exporting and Importing Cash

Many foreign countries have restrictions about how much money you can take when you're leaving the country. While it may be unlikely that you will face this problem, some well-known musicians have had their money confiscated when they were leaving a foreign country because the amount of cash that they were carrying exceeded a country's currency-export laws. You can find out about any country's currency-export restrictions by calling the embassies of the countries to which you will be traveling. If you anticipate that you will make more cash than you can legally take out of the country, use the cash to pay off as much of your credit-card debt as you can while on the road. This is easy if the American Express card is your primary card, because you can simply go to an American Express office and pay your bill—up to $1,000 per day. (See pages 216–217 for more about this.) Alternatively, you can split the money among the members of your band until you have passed through customs.

Keep in mind that, according to U.S. Customs regulations, you're importing currency when you bring money into the United States from foreign tours. At the time of this writing, U.S. Customs has a currency import limit of $10,000. If you are lucky enough to have made that amount of income from a tour, you risk it being taxed, or even confiscated, when you enter the United States.

Exchanging Foreign Currencies

The following discussion about exchanging foreign currency was adapted from road warrior extraordinaire David Liebman's excellent book *Guide to the Road for the Touring Musician* (Jamey Aebersold Jazz, 1994).

Most musicians find themselves overseas at one time or another—especially in Europe. When you're abroad, depending upon your itinerary and how many countries you're traveling through, you may have to exchange money daily. After a week of traveling, many musicians end up with pockets full of various currencies and a lot of confusion about what to do with it.

When traveling, remember one important thing: If you take one country's currency to another country—for example, French francs to Germany—and want to get dollars, you will be losing money because the German bankers will first convert the francs to marks, and then to dollars. Every transaction involves some loss of your money. So you want to avoid scenarios like the one described above, where one transaction for you (francs to dollars) involves two transactions for the banker (francs to marks to dollars). This will be further explained later in this section.

The bank is the best place to change your money. However, if your schedule doesn't jibe with banking hours, which vary widely in different countries, then change your money at the airport. Although it may be convenient to change your money at your hotel, this isn't recommended because the rate for your exchange is usually less favorable at the hotel than it is at either the bank or the airport. The exchange agencies in locations in large cities are often not favorable either.

When you're traveling from country to country, it is a good idea to get a small amount of the new country's currency prior to entering the country, in case the exchange booths and banks are closed for a holiday, or have limited hours of operation, strikes, or sheer incompetence when you arrive. As you will discover as you travel, these kinds of glitches happen more in some countries than in others. When you're exchanging money, you should try to estimate how much currency you will need in that country. Use your judgment to estimate how much your food expenditures (which are expensive overseas) as well as extras—such as snacks and magazines—will cost. For these items, I usually allocate a minimum of sixty dollars per day. If I know that I will have time to shop in that country, I might exchange more. Most stores will take American dollars and give you the rate posted in the bank or paper for that day. But as you will discover in the explanation further on in this section, this sounds easier than it actually is.

Try to find time to exchange any leftover currency before you leave the country. This is easier to accomplish if you're flying or taking trains rather than driving, because airports and train stations both frequently have conversion booths. If you have more currency than you will need, exchange the currency to dollars in the country of departure before you leave to avoid the scenario that I mentioned earlier concerning double exchanges. Most of all, be careful not to wind up with foreign currency when you arrive home. If you do end up with foreign currency once you get home, you can forget about getting it changed into dollars at your local bank. Even a name bank will charge an exorbitant fee for this service and it will not happen on the spot. In New York City, I know of two agencies that do this type of exchange, but you have to take the time to get to them and their rates are not as favorable as those that you would receive if you exchanged the money in the foreign country before departure. Exchanging money can be a real pain at the last moment of a tour, so think ahead. And take into consideration that most airports will not have thousands of dollars to give you.

It is a good idea to carry small denominations of U.S. currency with you when you're traveling. This cash will come in handy if you need to exchange small amounts of currency if you are passing quickly through a country, or if you only plan to be in a country for a short while and anticipate that most of your expenses will be paid by the tour's promoter. However, since carrying cash is risky, I recommend that you carry your cash in some sort of ankle, shoulder, or waist bag on you at all times—even when you're sleeping! I cannot overstate this warning enough times. I can't think of anything more upsetting than coming home empty-handed after an extensive tour.

You should never accept a foreign check unless it has been certified for the foreign equivalent and can be cashed the morning after the gig personally by the payee. Hopefully the promoter will have worked this out before you leave for your tour. To avoid unfortunate situations, make sure, before you sign a contract, that you clearly understand the manner by which you will be paid.

If you are in the United States and can't readily get to a bank to deposit a check, you can secure this check by writing your account number on the back of the check as well as "for deposit only" along with your endorsement. If this check is lost or stolen, this notation will complicate matters if someone attempts to cash it. And by then you would have had the time to call the venue to stop payment and issue another check.

Now, I am going to attempt to explain how the monetary exchange system works and why words like "buy," "sell," and "official" are so confusing.

The official rates are products of international relationships, money supply, markets, etc. These rates are listed daily in the *International Herald Tribune* (the paper you will read for news when you're abroad), as well as in large national foreign-language daily newspapers. These official rates establish the basis for the subsequent buy and sell rates, which will directly affect you. A local bank or exchange service is always trying to make a reasonable profit from its services. Utilizing some hypothetical but realistic numbers, the following examples demonstrate how the exchange rate works.

Let's assume that the official rate is five French francs for one U.S. dollar. If I go to a French bank and wish to exchange French francs for dollars, I will get those dollars at the sell rate, which plainly means that the French bank is selling dollars. The sell rate is always higher than the buy rate. (To remember this, think of the old stockbroker advice: buy low, sell high; that is basically what the banks are doing.) Looking at the opposite transaction clarifies things. If I go to the same bank and wish to exchange dollars for francs, then the bank will "buy" my dollars from me, and in turn will give me francs. The buy and sell rates are usually equidistant—below and above—the official rate.

An example of a typical buy rate might be a ratio of one dollar to 4.7 francs. If one hundred American dollars are exchanged for French francs at this rate, then the customer receives 470 francs. An example of a sell rate procedure might be one hundred francs exchanged for American dollars at a ratio of 100 francs to 5.3 American dollars. In this scenario, the customer would receive $18.87.

What does this all mean? If I am paid the equivalent of $1,000 in French francs, it is to my advantage to specify in the contract that the venue must pay the franc-equivalent of the dollar amount at the *sell rate* of that day (as posted in the local bank). In other words, 1,000 American dollars would be converted to 5,300 French francs.

All banks will be the same, more or less. If your client refuses to give you your fee according to the sell rate, then insist that you at least get the official rate. The client may object because it will cost more francs if he or she uses the higher sell rate or the official rate, rather than the lower buy rate (5.3 or 5, rather than 4.7). However, if the client uses the bank rate, then when you exchange the francs back to dollars, you will not get the full 1,000 American dollars agreed upon. Why should you be paid less because of the exchange system? To summarize, consider the following two scenarios, unfavorable or favorable:

THE UNFAVORABLE SCENARIO You are owed 1,000 American dollars for your fee, air tickets, etc. If you are paid the equivalent French francs at the buy rate of 4.7, you will receive 4,700 francs (i.e., 1,000 multiplied by 4.7). Then, when you leave France and exchange the francs for dollars, you will have no choice but to exchange the money at the higher sell rate of 5.3 francs per American dollars. As a result, the total American dollars you will receive will be $887 (i.e., 4,700 divided by 5.3).

THE FAVORABLE SCENARIO Again, you are owed 1,000 American dollars for your fee, air tickets, etc. If you are paid the equivalent francs at the sell rate of 5.3, you will receive 5,300 francs (i.e., 1,000 multiplied by 5.3). Then, when you leave France and exchange the francs at the sell rate of 5.3, you will receive your full 1,000 American dollars (i.e., 5,300 divided by 5.3).

OTHER SCENARIOS There are other possible scenarios that can happen. For instance, you can be paid in one of the stronger currencies that do not fluctuate, like German marks or Swiss francs. With this scenario there is a possibility that you can make some money, but it is a gamble. The success of your gamble depends upon the value of the dollar going down between the time you received the German marks or Swiss francs and the time that you exchange them for American dollars.

For example, if the sell rate for German marks is 5.3 and you requested to be paid the equivalent of 1,000 American dollars in marks, then you will receive 5,300 German marks for the $1,000 fee. Let's say that by the time you get home the American dollar's rate of exchange has dipped to 4.5 as the official rate. If the official rate is 4.5, then the sell rate would be, let's say, 4.8. You can then exchange the 5,300 marks that you received as payment for dollars at the new and lower sell rate of 4.8. Because the dollar had dipped in value against the mark, at the exchange ratio of 5,300 divided by 4.8 you would net $1,104. But, if you requested to be paid in German marks and then by the time you return home the value of the American dollar went up, you will lose. My advice is to be safe and conservative, and to get those greenbacks.

With the oncoming advent of the Eurodollar, some of the confusion that is created by exchange rates will invariably be eliminated—simply because there will be fewer exchange rates in effect. However, not all European countries have agreed to the new monetary system—so currency discrepancies will still exist. At the time of this writing, the Eurodollar is being used solely among banks as a financial trading instrument. The paper Eurodollar is not expected to be circulated as a general currency until the year 2002.

When you exchange foreign currency to dollars, and vice versa, how much you decide to exchange will be determined by the dates of your tour, the timing of the events, and by the currency in which you were paid. If you are paid in dollars, use this cash as much as possible for paying your salaries and credit-card bills while you're on the road.

Every time you exchange a currency you lose money. Therefore, only exchange amounts that you'll need for your expenses. If you're going to be in a country only for a few days, it won't cost you *that* much to change your money to the local currency at a hotel—even though their exchange rates are the most expensive. It only amounts to a matter of pennies. However, if you plan to be in a country for a longer period, exchange your money at an airport, train station, or bank.

If you have local currency left over when you're getting ready to leave a country, use what you have to pay your hotel bill and pay the balance with your credit card. If you need to keep a little of the currency on hand for any reason (taxis, airport meals, etc.), you should try to estimate what your expenses will be. Then if you find that you have some money left over, you can exchange it later into the currency of your next country upon arrival. If you have large amounts of a currency and are going to another country, don't convert it to dollars *unless* you know you're going to be paid in the next country with foreign funds. For example, if you are paid in German marks and then are going to Italy, don't change the marks to dollars in Germany—only to have to convert the dollars to lire once you get to Italy. Every transaction has a fee attached to it. It makes more sense for you to convert your marks directly to lire once you get to Italy. That way, you're only making one transaction, and only being charged for one conversion.

About ten years ago when I was traveling with my trio we were paid for two nights' worth of work in Berlin in marks, and we were to be in Germany for six more days. I used as many of the marks as possible to pay my personal and band tour expenses, but I still had a lot of marks on hand when it came time to go to Italy. Since we were planning to spend ten days in Italy and I knew that we weren't going to be paid for any of the initial gigs in local currency, I changed my marks to lire upon arrival.

Another inexpensive way to exchange foreign currencies is to use it to pay off your credit-card bills while you're on the road. Credit-card companies give you the best exchange rates. You can also pay your bill in a currency from one country while you're in another country and avoid the double exchange. For example, in one instance I had been paid for a gig in Danish krona, but I didn't have time to convert it before leaving Denmark for Germany because our plane left the airport at 7:00 A.M. (before the banks were open). So the next day I went to the American Express office in Berlin and paid my bill using $1,000 worth of krona, which avoided the double exchange.

Organizing Your Tour Documents

While you're on the road make sure that you keep accurate records of all of your transportation, hotel, and salary expenses. I always travel with a digital diary that has a spreadsheet program containing a duplicate of my tour budget. This way I can enter any unanticipated expenses into the tour budget as the tour progresses as well as change the prices of transportation or accommodations, if necessary.

Make sure to save all of the necessary receipts. As you go, use your calculator to translate foreign receipts into U.S. currency and note the conversions on the back. Exchange rates fluctuate constantly and, if you ever get audited by the IRS, you'll need accurate figures to justify your deductions.

Keeping Receipts

Ensure that you save and protect all van rental, hotel, taxi, and miscellaneous business-expense receipts by keeping them in a manila envelope while you're on the road. Eventually you'll end up with a lot of these envelopes. Identify the tour by writing the date and the name of the tour on each envelope. This way you won't have to open each envelope to look inside when you need to find a particular receipt for a particular tour.

Although your transportation expenses will be listed on your credit-card bill, have your band members give you their airfare or train receipts as they are used. The more documentation you have for the tax man, the better. At the end of the tour, put all of these receipts in the manila envelope described above.

Keeping receipts for dining on the road is optional. The IRS has two standard daily deductions for meals while working on the road—one for U.S. travel and one for foreign travel. Oftentimes the government's standard deductions are slightly less than what your actual deductions would be. However, you'll have to balance the necessity of taking the time to get a receipt for every food purchase against the ease of taking the standard deduction.

If you decide to keep all of your actual receipts while you're on the road, there are a few tricks that can make the process easier. Using credit cards helps to facilitate the accounting process. If you use a credit card, you don't have to worry so much about losing a receipt—because if you do, you will have a second record of the expense when you receive your monthly statement. However, you must remember that not every restaurant takes credit cards. And, if you're in the habit of relying on credit-card receipts to document your purchases and then you stray from the routine, you might lose the deduction. For instance, if you're in an airport and you don't have enough time to use your credit card before your flight and you forget to take the receipt, then you'll lose the deduction.

You may decide that it simply isn't worth the effort to keep all of your meal receipts—especially since meal receipts for foreign travel will be in local currency, and at tax time you'll either have to go over each receipt to convert the amount to dollars, or pay your accountant to do it. If you decide to take the standard deduction, you'll simply need to count the number of days spent on the road each year and multiply that by the daily allowance.

As previously mentioned, one of the advantages of using a credit card for foreign-travel expenses is that you often get the best currency-exchange rates. To get these rates, the expense has to be entered on the card in the local currency, not in dollars. You'll want to make sure that your expenses are always processed in local currency. For example, during one tour, in an attempt to make a little extra on the deal, a hotel in Zagreb, Yugoslavia, put our hotel expenses on my card in U.S. funds. They figured the exchange rate at the hotel's lower rate and the hotel cost me more than it would have if I had been charged in the local currency.

ORGANIZING YOUR DOCUMENTS AFTER THE TOUR

If you are conscientious about keeping receipts for all of your expenses while you're on the road, then organizing your documents after your tour will be a painless process. The only things that you'll need to add to your manila folder after the fact are copies of the expenses that are processed on your credit card for that tour. As mentioned earlier, it is advisable to keep your personal credit cards separate from your business credit cards. If you mix the two expenses, you will need to spend time (or pay your accountant) to unravel your personal and business expenses at tax time. However, even if you keep your business expenses separate from your personal expenses, it still may be complicated to separate expenses from one tour to the next—especially when foreign tours are involved. This is because it sometimes takes several months for foreign charges to be processed. So you may find that a random charge from an Italian tour that you did in March will show up on a June statement—in the midst of charges for another tour.

The major thing that you will need to do after your tour is prepare your personal and band taxes.

Preparing Your Personal and Band Taxes

Avoid problems with the IRS, and your band members, by consulting with your accountant regarding the proper setup of your band and personal finances. You'll have to submit copies of the 1099 form to the IRS, as well as to your band members at the end of the tax year. Salary receipts will document how much each musician was paid. (This is discussed in detail on page 221.)

My first tour with my trio was audited by the IRS because I hadn't consulted my accountant and had neglected to submit 1099 forms to the IRS at the end of the year. Avoid the extra time, expense, and stress of a tax audit by checking with your accountant about the necessary paperwork that is required for your business type. This should be done well before you leave for your tour. However, if you have overlooked this part of the process, contact your accountant as soon as your tour is completed.

Keep your tour budget up-to-date. Any changes should be entered into your digital diary budget spreadsheet—as they occur. Once you return from the tour, go through the spreadsheet one last time—just to make sure that you didn't overlook something when you were on the road. Even though you may have paid for most of your touring expenses with a credit card, your tour budget will provide additional documentation. This will come in handy should you have any tax-deduction disputes with the IRS at a future point.

You will need to decide for yourself whether or not to declare all of the cash income you bring home from your foreign tours. Generally, the U.S. government won't know about this money. It's prudent to declare it though. Otherwise, if you are audited, your income and expenses will not match and you will be faced with having to pay back taxes.

Before you prepare your taxes at the end of the year, ask your accountant if there are any local or state taxes that may apply to your sole proprietorship or corporation. A well-known New York City guitarist, who had been touring with his own band for many years, got hit with $40,000 of city business taxes he had no idea existed. It nearly bankrupted him.

Chapter 13

Conducting Your Promotional Activities

Promoting your band and your music can be as labor-intensive as booking your band. Without help from friends or your spouse, you'll have to fit your promotional activities in between your booking tasks. The concept behind promotion is to have your name, and your band's name, appear in the public's—and the music industry's—consciousness, as many times and in as many places as possible. The goal of promotion is to get the attention of everyone in the world of jazz, and create a positive image for yourself and for the other members of your band.

UNDERSTANDING THE THREE TYPES OF ADVERTISING

Promotion is another word for advertising. And the opportunities for promotion are omnipresent. Take a look at industry magazines, such as *Down Beat* and *JazzTimes*, and notice how often there are appropriate spots where your name could appear. For instance, mentions of your name (or your band's name) in a "What's Going On" column or in a letter to the editor can help to increase your profile. Once you start to notice *where* promotion for you or your band could appear, you can start to visualize *how* to get it there.

You can exert control of the appearance of your name in numerous situations. An important factor in your favor is that the media has a ravenous appetite for information. But don't leave it up to the media to come to you. Your promotion in this industry, in a large part, will depend on your own efforts.

Any contact with the public and the music industry should be considered promotion. You don't have to be on the front page of the newspaper or be featured in a story on CNN to get in the public's eye. Sometimes gaining prominence in your field is just a matter of repeat impressions. Promotional opportunities appear everywhere and constantly. Cultivate an awareness to take advantage of them when they appear.

There are three categories of advertising. Listed from the most to the least effective, they are advertising that pays you, free advertising, and advertising for which you pay. Each of these three types of promotion should have its own place in your overall promotional plans.

Advertising That Pays You

This is the most effective form of promotion. It means that someone has invested money in you. A record label, for example, will actively work on your behalf to promote you. This is because the label wants to realize profit—monetary or otherwise—from its investment. The forms of advertising that pay you fall into the following five major categories. Each of these categories has free promotional spin-offs as well.

Record Dates and CDs: Unless it is a vanity recording, when you record a CD, you are paid for the recording itself, and you receive artist and mechanical royalties from record sales, airplay, and your compositions. If you write the liner notes and create the artwork, you'll get paid for that as well, and your name will be credited on the cover. On-site record sales is a form of promotion that pays very well. Promotional spin-offs that result from record dates and CDs include airplay, media advertising, reviews, catalog listings, word of mouth, and an increased fan base.

Concerts: Every time you appear in public for a fee, you have been paid to advertise yourself. This is your best form of promotion. Promotional spin-offs that result from concert appearances include advertisements for the concert and listings in local and national media, listings in venues' Web sites, increased word of mouth, on-site record sales, mailing-list cards, contacts for other gigs, return engagement requests, and an increased fan base.

Teaching: Instructing privately or as part of a school's faculty or doing a clinic or jazz camp is paid advertising. There is an expression in the music industry: The younger the convert, the longer they will be a fan. Teaching gives you access to a wide range of young musicians. Promotional spin-offs that result from teaching include having your name in school catalogs and advertisements as well as word of mouth.

Articles in Industry Magazines: Although the income received from writing and publishing educational articles is not very substantial, the exposure you get from publishing can be significant. Educational articles enhance and expand your public image and increase your ability to acquire educational venues for you and your band. Promotional spin-offs that result from written articles include having your name and/or image on the cover of the magazine.

Composing: If you develop a reputation as a composer, then when other musicians record your songs, that recording is a form of paid promotion. Promotional spin-offs that result from composing are airplay and concert announcements.

Free Advertising

Most music-industry magazines have "What's Going On" columns. These sections mention newsworthy musical events. Subscribe to as many industry publications as you can afford. (For a listing of such publications, see pages 94–95.) Many venues have these publications just lying around. Make a list of these publications and develop a preformatted news release on your computer. When you are about to go on tour, mail out individualized news releases to promote all of your musical events—both in the industry publications as well as specifically in the areas where you'll be touring. Some of these announcements will get published and some won't.

Regional Union and Jazz Society Newsletters: Ask each of your clients if he or she has contact information for the jazz societies in the region. Send these outlets press releases about upcoming record releases and concerts in their area.

Local Newspaper Free Listings: While on the road, keep your eyes open for local newspapers that offer entertainment listings. The local venue will probably cover this, but a little redundancy can't hurt. Add these local newspapers to your mailing list for the next time that you do a tour in the area.

Jazz Newsletters: Collect every jazz newsletter you encounter while you're on the road. They can usually be found at the venue. These publications are always looking for filler and they often publish listings of local events.

Radio Interviews: In addition to having your concerts advertised in local (and national, if you can manage it) publications, you should also think about radio interviews. These are an excellent source of free advertising. Most of the areas where you will perform will have radio stations that can help advertise your appearance. Don't wait for the venue to arrange this. Get the station's contact info from your client and call the station yourself. Many radio stations are equipped to do phone interviews in advance of the gig—no matter where you are located at the time of the interview.

Letters to the Editor: If you see something in a jazz publication that you think deserves comment, write a letter. However, you should avoid rehashing "sour grapes." The subject of your letter to the editor could be misinformation that was included in an article that was published, a controversy (either ongoing or one that you want to start yourself), or just an interesting viewpoint you might have to offer. Having your own words appear in print gives you instant credibility in the jazz community.

Interviews and Articles: Because of space limitations and the power that the major labels have in promoting their artists, it can be rather difficult to get a publication—especially a major jazz publication—to conduct an interview with you or publish an article about you. Competition is heavy for this kind of media space because it is an excellent way to promote yourself. Whether you're contacted by a major or a minor jazz publication, never refuse the opportunity to be interviewed. Also, you shouldn't feel shy about contacting various print publications to ask them if they might be interested in doing an article or interview on you. Magazines and newsletters often have issues with special themes, and you just might fit into one of them. It's good to establish relationships with the editors and publishers of these publications. Although these editors may not run an interview or article about you now, they may remember you next time. Since you're in this for the long run, you want to increase your chances that—sooner or later—these publications will write about you.

Advertising for Which You Pay

In his book *My Life in Advertising*, Claude C. Hopkins places paid advertising as fourteenth on his list of effective forms of advertising. Hopkins's theory is: The more you pay for advertising, the less effective it is. The following list cites the many different kinds of self-promotion—from the cheapest to the most expensive modes.

The Internet: This is one of the least expensive ways to promote yourself globally. The basic fees involved with having and maintaining a Web site will be the cost for your server to store your Web site (from $15 to $25 per month), the cost for your local regional calling plan to call the server and make changes (about $10 per month), and what it costs you to create and update your own Web site (from zero to $1,000). You may want to consider creating your own Web site. If you surf the Web, you'll see that many musicians are now doing this. To get an idea of how you'd like your site to look and function, visit the sites of other musicians. You can find these sites by accessing the Yahoo! site at http://www.yahoo.com and then searching under "jazz musicians."

Creating a Web site can be time consuming, but with today's simple Web authoring tools, learning curves are rapidly shrinking. You also have the option of paying someone to create your site, but at an average rate of $25 to $30 an hour for this service (or from $300 to $1,000 or more for a completed site) you may find this route prohibitive. A midway solution between designing the entire site yourself and hiring someone to design the site for you is designing the site graphics yourself then paying for a professional to code and upload the site. Although this approach is more costly than designing the site yourself, it bypasses the need to learn HTML coding.

In addition to creating the site, you must be able to promote it—otherwise no one will know it exists. If you decide to create a Web site, I strongly suggest that you read *Web Pages That Suck* by Vincent Flanders (Sybex, 1998). Although it has a rather unusual title, many people consider this to be the best book for learning how to create and promote Web sites.

The number of artists' Web sites grows daily. In fact, at this writing, there are nearly 17,000 jazz Web sites worldwide. And, the number of people connected to the Net also grows daily. So, the importance of utilizing this new medium cannot be underestimated. Your Web site can serve a multitude of functions. It will save you time and money—because instead of sending out press kits or CDs, you can have people visit your site, read your info, and listen to sound clips. Sound clips will significantly cut down on the expensive process of mailing promotional CDs to venues. Although not yet cost effective, a secure server connection that allows credit cards to be used for on-line buying, can be added to your site to increase your record sales. You can find many Internet credit-card companies that facilitate secure on-line sales for a small fee.

Internet Newsletters: Surf the Web for newsletter sites located in areas where you're going to be touring. Many are run by fans or jazz societies and will publish interviews as well as listings. Also ask if the venue has a Web site. If so, have your contact put a link on it to your Web site. Bookmark these sites for future use.

In addition to using the Internet to access newsletters, you should also do a search for your own name on a search engine such as Metacrawler at http://www.metacrawler. com. This is a great way to find out what is being said about you on the Web and in news groups. Quite often you can enter a dialogue with someone or start something going yourself by participating in one of the BBSes (bulletin board systems) that serve as a meeting place for the jazz community on the Web. One of the most popular BBSes is the Usenet newsgroup at http://www.bluenote.com.

Batch E-mailing: Collect a list of every E-mail contact you have and do a batch mailing before each tour, or to announce a new CD release or magazine article. Although they tend toward becoming junk mail, batch E-mails, if done tastefully, aren't too much of a burden on the receiver. As a courtesy, you can also put an unsubscribe note at the bottom of your E-mail message for those people who wish to be taken off your mailing list.

Batch E-mailing is an inexpensive way to distribute newsletters. Most E-mail software allows batch mailings by using a blind-carbon-copy (BCC) format. This format avoids that long list of recipients that you often see at the top of E-mails and creates the impression that each recipient was contacted individually. It is essential that you use this feature, especially if you have a long E-mail list.

E-mailing: This technology is good for establishing primary contact with a potential contact. One of the advantages of E-mail is that messages can be sent at any time of the day or night. This is especially helpful when you're contacting areas where time-zone differences make telephone communications problematic. Similar to telephone calls, E-mails can serve a promotional function. If you use E-mail to communicate, you're also likely to save about 30 percent on your phone bills. That's more than enough of a savings to finance your Web site.

Telephone Calls: Every phone call you make to anyone in the music business should be considered promotion. Every time you call another client, whether you get the gig or not, you put your name in front of him or her. The client may forget about you after you hang up, but your name still lingers in his or her mind. If the client sees your name somewhere else, in another context, he or she will be reminded of your contact. Since telephoning is going to be one of your most frequent activities, make these calls count for the long run. Think about it. If you make one thousand calls in a year, over several years the effect of that adds up to a heightened perception in the industry.

PREPARING PROMOTIONAL STRATEGIES

Doing your own promotion is as much a full-time job as booking your band. You need to make your strongest possible impression no matter what area of the music business you're dealing with at the moment. It's a matter of doing all you can to slant the odds for success in your favor. As with all of the other aspects of this business, you will improve your odds by paying attention to the details.

Developing a Strong Press Kit

Press kits, brochures, and CDs are probably the most expensive forms of advertising that you'll utilize as a bandleader. The press kit itself says something about you. Sometimes an effective press kit can get you a gig on its own merits. So everything about the kit itself must be totally professional. However, you don't want to go overboard because the cost of printing press kits, buying stationery, photos, mailers, postage, and the cost of promotional CDs adds up quickly. A complete press kit—including photos, CDs, and postage—can cost as much as $10 (if it is sent within the United States) and $20 (if it is sent to a foreign country).

Cold mailings, those that you make without first having contacted the client, must be handled with restraint, as this is not a cost-effective way of promoting yourself and your band. If you must do a cold mailing, consider making an inexpensive band brochure for this purpose. It can be mailed in a business-size envelope and the postage fees will be lower than for an entire press kit. Depending on your computer expertise, you may be able to create the brochure yourself. Or, if you don't feel that you have the necessary expertise, you can have a professional do it for you for about $300 to $500. If you expect your personnel to vary from tour to tour, it would not be cost effective to pay for a professionally designed brochure.

A good press kit should not be too large or too small. Remember that potential clients are bombarded with press kits on a daily basis and may not have time to browse through excessive pages of information. Put the odds in your favor. An attractive and concise press kit is more likely to be read than an unimaginative one. Present your accomplishments in a factual manner and avoid obviously self-aggrandizing statements.

Press kits come in a variety of formats, but certain things are universal for every one. To get an idea of what format will express your personality, research the press kits that other musicians use. They can be in black and white or in color. If you decide to use color, you might use a variety of colored papers for each section of the kit. Some venues don't like kits with colored paper, as they are difficult to xerox for promotional purposes. Print on both sides of the paper. This keeps your postage fees down and makes a smaller package. A kit can be in an appealing folder or just a mailing envelope. Here are the standard components of a press kit:

The Envelope: Your press kit must stand out in the crowd. Except for promotional CD mailings to clients that you have already contacted, avoid using plain manila envelopes for your first presentation. An attractive envelope will catch a client's attention. When making promotional mailings to newspapers and media contacts, keep the envelopes small. Use a brochure and a press-release format that will fit into a business-size envelope. Pick a color that is eye-catching and a material that is durable. The envelope will need to be able to hold CDs in it without it becoming trashed in the mail. Mailing labels can be printed on your computer, and attractive rolls of return address labels can be purchased anywhere. Expensive-to-make, custom-designed mailers and labels with logos create the impression that the material is coming from someone who is well established in the business. Potential clients will assume that you must be doing okay if you can afford custom items. However, with a little clever planning, and attention to detail, inexpensive and attractive press kits can be created using desktop-publishing skills and stock materials.

The Cover Letter: The first thing a client sees when he or she opens your kit is your cover letter. This letter should sum up your initial conversation, as well as any details you didn't discuss during the initial contact. It's easy to create a good-looking custom format for your band stationery on your computer. This approach is especially successful if you use interesting paper. Use a paper clip (a colored one is more eye-catching than a plain, metal one) to attach your business card to the letter for inclusion in the client's Rolodex. While in general I'm a proponent of DIY promotion, when it comes to business cards I think that the small expense of creating custom-made business cards (approximately $100 for 1,000 cards) is well worth the investment. Consider including your band brochure in the press kit as well. This gives an overworked client the option of learning about you and your band without going through your complete press kit. Quite often, the client will start with the brochure and, if interested, he or she will then read the complete kit.

Biographies: As the bandleader, you should have a bio that is as thorough as possible. Include your musical education, your credits with other bands, any notable events in which you've participated, as well as any awards or degrees that you've received. Include a short description of the style of music that you play and your band's musical goals. Put the band's bio on a separate page. Changing your press kit every time you have a personnel change can be expensive; you'll want to minimize this potential expense by keeping your own bio separate from the band's bio. Think of every musical event that might add to your credibility and use it—especially if it involves recognized names. The experienced client will be aware that you are doing this, but don't let this hold you back. No one is going to promote you as well as you.

Reviews: Keep a file folder of your recording reviews, performance reviews, and interviews. Use quotes from your reviews in your brochure, but include some complete reviews in your press kit. A photocopy of a good interview is an effective form of promotion. You can save the expense of updating your reviews by not including the dates of each review. However, if you do this, be sure to include the reviewer's name and the name of the publication. Use separate pages for your recording reviews and your performance reviews.

Discographies: List your recordings—starting with those that you've recorded under your own name, and following with those that you've recorded with others.

Awards: Have a page that lists any recording, performance, or educational awards you may have earned.

Educational Material: If you are developing an educational component for your band, request letters of recommendation from clients at the educational venues where you have appeared and include quotes from these clients in your press kit. Include educational reviews as well. Because you will only use these educational materials when you are applying to schools, store them separately from your press kit. Xerox and include any articles you may have written as well as a synopsis of your band members' educational strengths.

Photos: If your band has stable personnel, have photographs taken by a professional photographer. If your personnel is going to change often, just use a picture of yourself. Costs vary, but most photographers charge about $200 for a sitting. Don't have the photographer print your copies. You can save money by having your photos printed by a professional bulk printer. A year's supply of photos costs approximately $100. Check around with any actor-friends you might have. They usually know the most economical places to get promotional pictures developed and printed. Black-and-white glossy photos are best, although you may want to have some color copies available for venues that prepare their own brochures. Keep a well-scanned copy of both the black-and-white and the color photos in your computer. These will come in handy for attaching to E-mail messages. Avoid performance photos. They are usually taken from too far away to show up well in a newspaper. When sending photos in your press kit, use cardboard inserts for protection. They are very inexpensive, can be purchased from your printer, and ensure that your photos arrive at their destinations in good condition.

Artist Newsletters: Including an artist newsletter in your press kit will update your potential client about your latest news. Even if you don't have a mailing list, including a newsletter suggests that you do. Many venues value bands that have their own mailing lists. That in and of itself can be a strong selling point and may be the point that clinches the gig. Having a mailing list indicates that the group realizes the importance of self-promotion and building an audience. Clients appreciate that. Don't waste valuable time waiting until you have to mail a press kit to put together your artist newsletter. Put aside an evening and collate the press kits, leaving the addition of the cover letter, photos, brochures (if necessary), educational material (if necessary), and newsletter until mailing time.

Creating Artist Newsletters

One of the most effective self-promotion techniques is the ongoing development of your own mailing list. This list can be used to advertise career events, including tour itineraries, new recordings, reviews, etc. The only limiting factors to having an artist newsletter will be the time it takes to manage it and the costs required to distribute it. There are many books available on mailing-list management. A little research on this subject can go a long way toward improving artist-audience communication as well as keeping your expenses to a minimum.

To begin the mailing list itself, create a postcard-size mailing-list card that can be distributed at every performance. Your card should include a check box where the addressee can approve receiving unsolicited CD mailings from you. This is an effective method for mail distribution of your recordings. However, an unsolicited CD mailing can offend a recipient—as the receiver may feel that he or she is being pressured by a moral obligation to buy something.

If you run out of CDs for on-site sales, you can take orders and ask people to prepay for their CDs and then you can fill the orders once you return from the tour. Alternatively, if people don't want to prepay, you can fill the orders and then bill them. Either way, make a note on the back of the mailing card to remind yourself of what you discussed at the gig. If you run out of mailing cards, ask interested parties for their business cards and make your notations on the back of their business cards. These strategies will increase your CD sales.

If you decide to do mailing cards, ask your audience to fill the cards out (using printed, not cursive, type), so you can keep in touch with them. In an educational situation, ask that home addresses, not dormitory addresses, be used. Students' addresses change often. Leave a space on the card for E-mail addresses as well.

The frequency of your mailings will depend on your budget and how much time you have available to devote to the production and distribution of your newsletter. Infrequent mailings often unearth out-of-date addresses, which, because they add additional (and unnecessary expense), are the bane of most mailing-list companies' existence. Anything mailed for the cost of a standard first-class postage stamp or higher, will be returned to you if the address is defunct. You won't receive return mail for post-card mailings. So, if you use postcards, you could be wasting postage on addresses that are no longer current, and there is no way for you to find out. Newsletter mailings that are sent out between four and six times a year are the most practical. Foreign mailings can be arranged through friends in other countries. If you send your friend a package of preaddressed newsletters and a check (or cash) for postage and have him or her mail the newsletters within the country, you will save yourself a lot of postage. Of course, one of the drawbacks of taking this approach is that, if the addresses aren't current, the newsletters will not be returned to you. Another approach is to investigate the regulations for foreign bulk mailings.

There are many different ways that you can mail your newsletter. The post office has a free booklet that contains all the information you'll need to decide upon which method you use—including the pros, cons, and costs of each method. If you are set up as a nonprofit business, you can piggyback on another nonprofit organization's mailing permit. Nonprofit postal fees are the least expensive of any of those offered by the U.S.

post office. Although frowned upon by the postal service, piggybacking is also hard to catch. Many local nonprofit arts organizations won't mind helping out a local artist.

Depending on how large you want your mailing list to be, you might consider including all past venues, record companies, media publications, and radio stations on your list. If you can afford the extra cost, commercial mailing-list services offer expert mailing-list management for extensive mailing lists. They can charge from $.15 to $.20 per name for logging and updating the addresses on your list as well as additional fees for postage.

Artists' newsletters come in varied formats and can be sent using various distribution methods. Decide on a format that will be inexpensive to print as well as mail. Choosing a format that can be mailed without an envelope will save you a lot of money, and will also save on the labor involved with preparing the newsletter to be mailed. A double-page format that is printed on all sides and folded twice can hold a lot of information.

Take a careful look at other musicians' newsletters. Use lightweight, colored paper and monochrome printing. Multicolored printing can be quite expensive. You can create an attractive and inexpensive newsletter if you have desktop-publishing expertise as well as access to a color printer and a scanner. If you don't have access to these items and have to print the newsletter professionally, using photos in your newsletter will increase its production costs exponentially. So, you may want to avoid using photos if you're not producing the newsletter yourself.

Folding, addressing, and adding postage to your newsletter is labor intensive. You might consider hiring a student or a friend to do that for you. Your local printer can also fold the newsletters for a nominal fee. Time is money and hiring someone to do this kind of work for you is well worth the small extra expense—as it allows you to focus more fully on the more complicated aspects of keeping your business together.

Hiring Promotional Services

There are many individuals and companies that provide promotional services for artists—for a fee. The people who offer these services have good long-term relationships and connections within the media. Hiring one of these people is likely to increase the frequency of the appearance of your name in the media, which will enhance your media presence in general and create more attention in the public's mind. However, the fees for promotional services are very high and can start at $10,000 for a six-month contract.

Most musicians, especially emerging musicians, cannot afford to hire professional promotional services. And even if an emerging musician *could* afford them, the cost-benefit ratio is often doubtful. Professional promotion is probably most effective for those musicians who already have a fair degree of marquee value. Timing and research are the keys to the successful use of promotional services. If you have received a major award, like a Grammy, it may be worthwhile to hire a publicist to create a synergistic effect in the media. This will help to build upon your accomplishment.

If you're considering hiring a publicist, ask for the contact info of some of his or her clients. Call these people and ask them for an evaluation of the quality of the publicist's work. One of the problems of hiring someone to do your promotion is that you cannot check his or her work, and you, therefore, may not know how much labor is actually being expended on your behalf. So, it is important to hire someone who has a solid track record and with whom you feel comfortable working.

Securing Record Label Tour Support

Record labels are sometimes in a position to offer tour support to promote your engagements. However, the kind of support that is available often depends on the size and the stature of the record label with which you're dealing. Small, independent labels work on very tight budgets and usually cannot afford the extra expense that promotion usually entails. Medium-size labels might be able to offer minimal support. So, it is definitely worth your while to approach the personnel in the publicity department and—within reason—ask them to help promote you. Major labels can afford very powerful tour support, as they have large staffs that are specifically geared toward this aspect of the music industry.

When organizing promotion with a record label, remember that tour support can come in many forms. Small-scale and focused local advertising may help to draw crowds just as much as extensive media campaigns. So, when organizing promotion for your tour, don't get caught in the mind-set that bigger is better. That simply isn't always the case.

MAJOR-LABEL SUPPORT Promotional support from a major record label often includes print ads in local newspapers, which are published in coordination with the venue and local retailers. This is a very expensive form of promotion and generally corresponds with a specific event. Major record labels may pay for advertising or share the expense with the venue to increase the size of an ad. Record stores, which assume that an artist's appearance at a local venue will stimulate their own CD sales, will often share advertising costs with major labels in exchange for product. The label's expense is the cost of producing the CDs, and the record store will pay for its share of the advertising out of the profits it makes from acquiring the CDs at a less-than-wholesale price. The average wholesale price of a CD is $7.50, yet the common retail price is $15. Thirty CDs will sell for a total of $450, which will then be added to the record store's advertising budget to create a larger ad that includes the artist and venue information. This is usually the case when you see a record store advertising an artist's appearance at a local venue.

Major labels also have a telephone staff that contacts area radio stations in order to lobby them to increase airplay for their artists. These labels also can arrange radio interviews and often share expenses with a venue for radio advertising. Major labels also contact recording and performance reviewers at local newspapers in the hopes that these reviewers will cooperate to support an artist's appearance.

INDEPENDENT-LABEL SUPPORT Independent-label support often makes the difference between getting certain gigs or not—especially in larger cities. Independent labels often work with artists to enhance tour opportunities and promotion, but such support generally has to be requested by the artist. The label may add this expense to an artist's account as an advance against royalties.

If you are in the position of asking for independent-label support, your intent should be to maximize the *frequency* of tour support, not the *size* of it. Keep your requests minimal in size, and only use the label's support in highly competitive areas. Ask the label to absorb the costs for printing and posting your mailings, using a venue's mailing list.

Coordinate with the label's promotion department to have your CD sent to radio stations. The promotion personnel will know if they have previously sent one to a particular station. So, by working directly with the promotion personnel at the label, you can avoid redundancy. Labels keep lists of these stations and how many hours a day or week they present jazz music. They tend to concentrate on those stations that have the most airtime. As a result, smaller stations in your touring area may not be on the label's list. Call the local jazz disc jockeys to see if they have your CD, and if they don't, forward the information to the label's promotion department so they can send one.

Clever and judicious use of independent-label support is advised. Independent labels do not have large staffs. You should focus your efforts on compensating for the department's lack of staffing, and not overwork the staff. When working with an independent label, it is important to remember that you are not the only artist that the label is promoting.

Orchestrating Pretour Promotion

The amount of pretour promotion you can do will depend on how much time you have available and your budget. Emerging artists may want to consider the extra time and expense of promoting a tour as an investment in audience and image building. Pretour promotion for artists with minimal to moderate marquee value is integral to the success of the tour. This is especially true in larger cities, where venues are in direct competition with other venues. If a competing venue has booked an artist with a higher marquee value than you have, your venue may be concerned about drawing an audience for your performance. Of course, since venues are booked so far in advance, your contact will have no way of anticipating this and you may only find out about a competing gig a few weeks or months before your gig. Call your venues a month in advance of your tour to see if anything may be working against you.

Some clients are promotionally savvy and work hard to make your appearance successful, others are not. Many venues have their own promotion techniques that you can enhance, such as sending out mailings, organizing radio interviews, and placing media advertising. Always ask what promotional techniques a venue will be using to promote your gig, and tailor your offers of support to fit that plan. Begin pretour promotion six weeks in advance of the tour. If you have publicity too far in advance of the gig, your audience may forget about it by the time it actually happens. However, if you have publicity too late, your audience may not have time to plan to attend your show. With the exception of national magazines (which require more advance notice), most media outlets prefer the six-week advance window.

Many venues have their own monthly or quarterly newsletters. Some gigs may confirm after the newsletter mailing date. If this happens for your gig, offer to share the extra expense of a separate mailing for your engagement, and if the venue accepts, send your client your own preprinted postcards for the venue to mail. These postcards can be inexpensively printed, four to a page. The printer can then cut the pages into separate postcards for mailing. Be sure to include the venue's address and contact number, as well as the set times and the price of the performance. If you have a new CD to promote, mention it.

Another idea is to create an inexpensive generic, hard-paper poster and send fifty (or more, as required) of them to each venue in advance of your tour. Before you go to the trouble of making these posters, however, it is a good idea to contact the venue and ask your contact if he or she is interested in this kind of promotional material. If your contact is interested, the venue can organize to have these posters hung around the city or town.

With information gained from your client, research the radio stations that are in broadcast range of the venue. Contact the jazz disc jockeys and send them each a CD along with a personal letter. Many venues are on personal terms with their local disc jockeys and will send them CDs for you. You'll be pleasantly surprised to discover how much you have in common with disc jockeys. Personal contact with a local disc jockey is well worth the effort and expense. It is advisable, however, to not directly ask for free promotion for your engagement. Radio promotion time is expensive and is one of the ways radio stations support themselves financially. Leave it up to the disc jockey whether or not he or she will mention your gig when playing your CD.

Your venue client should also have local media contacts. Ask your contact what media promotion, if any, is being planned for your gig. If the venue isn't specifically sending material to local media, then ask your contact for the venue's media list and tell him or her that you plan to telephone these people and send them CDs for review. Then, when talking to each of the media contacts, offer to put his or her name on the guest list for your appearance.

Promotion can be a very creative process. For an eye-opening look at how creative self-promotion can be, read *Guerilla Marketing*, which is listed in the business reading list that begins on page 243.

Afterword

When I was coming up in Boston in the early 1960s, I knew in my bones that eventually I would have to leave town and go to New York City. Tales of the dues that the city could put on you abounded. To prepare myself for this momentous move, I buttonholed all of the New York musicians who came through town and asked them to recount what had happened to them. No two stories were alike. It was obvious that whatever happened to you in New York City, happened just to *you*.

Does this sound scary? Unpredictable? For sure. Going to the Big Apple was like closing your eyes and, with fingers crossed, jumping off a cliff and hoping that everything would turn out okay. There were no guidelines to survival. It was overwhelming. Then I realized the other side of the coin: That this was an opportunity to be creative with my life. Going to New York could be an exciting adventure. It was a chance to reinvent myself.

Since you've gotten to this point in the book, I suspect that you have a really good idea of what booking and touring your band might be like. Does the prospect of booking and touring your own band seem like a daunting prospect? Does it feel like a tremendous amount of work? You could look at it that way. But the other side of this coin is that every moment is a chance to be creative, to reinvent yourself. The difference between what happened to me when I went to the Big Apple and what can happen to you when taking your career into your own hands is that you have this book to guide you.

It says on the cover that this book is about survival. The ideas in *The Touring Musician* were my techniques for survival. No two people will interpret them the same way. They will not guarantee that you'll become a star. However, adopting some of these techniques will put the odds of success in your favor. Good technique is integral to survival. Good luck is integral to success. And good luck is not an accident. It is made.

You will find your own individual way to use the guidelines in this book—and that way will, undoubtedly, continuously change as you absorb these ideas. By embarking on the road to self-empowerment, you will discover the creative joy of making something out of nothing. After all, that's what creativity is about, isn't it?

Having your own band is a full-time job that requires dedication, intelligence, and talent. The rewards are commensurate with how well you apply these abilities. The years I've spent booking and touring with my own groups have been the most rewarding of all my years of being a professional musician. Playing the music I want to play for people all over the world while offering my band mates the same opportunity at a decent wage is an accomplishment that sustains me through thick and thin. I hope that this book helps you to reach your goals and realize rewards both rare and exceptional. Good Luck!

—Hal Galper
January 2000

Business Reading List

Americans for the Arts Publications Catalog. New York: Americans for the Arts, 1999. To order copies, call (1-212) 223-2787 or view it on-line at http://www.artsusa.org.

Anschell, Bill. *Who Can I Turn To? A Guide to Jazz Funding and Support Services.* Atlanta, Georgia: Southern Arts Federation, 1993. To order copies, call (1-404) 874-7244 or check the Web site at http://www.southarts.org.

Avalon, Moses. *Confessions of a Record Producer: How to Survive the Scams and Shams of the Music Business.* San Francisco: Miller Freeman Books, 1998.

Baker, Bob. *101 Ways to Make Money Right Now in the Music Business: The A–Z Guide to Cashing in on Your Talents.* Gary Hustwit, ed. San Diego, California: Rockpress Publishers, 1993.

Brabec, Jeffrey, and Todd Brabec. *Music, Money, and Success: The Insider's Guide to the Music Industry.* Indianapolis, Indiana: Macmillan Publishing Company, 1994.

Cypert, Samuel A. *Believe and Achieve: W. Clement Stone's 17 Principles of Success.* New York: Avon Books, 1991.

Dannen, Fredric. *Hit Men: Power Brokers and Fast Money Inside the Music Business.* New York: Random House, 1991.

Dearing, James. *Making Money Making Music.* Amherst, New York: Writer's Digest, 1982.

Garrett, Marty R. *How You Can Break into the Music Business: Without Breaking Your Heart, Your Dream, or Your Bank Account.* Broken Arrow, Oklahoma: Marty Garrett Entertainment, 1997. To order copies, check the Web site at http://www.telepath.com/bizbook.

Gibson, James. *Getting Noticed: A Musician's Guide to Publicity and Self-Promotion.* Amherst, New York: Writer's Digest, 1987.

Halloran, Mark, editor and compiler. *The Musician's Business and Legal Guide.* Upper Saddle River, New Jersey: Prentice Hall, 1996.

Hustwit, Gary. *Getting Radio Airplay.* San Diego, California: Rockpress Publishers, 1993.

Jenkins, Willard V. *A Musician's Guide to Increasing Performance Opportunities (Insights on Jazz Series).* Minneapolis, Minnesota: Arts Midwest, no date. To order copies, call (1-612) 341-0755.

Kashif, Gary Greenberg. *Everything You'd Better Know about the Record Industry.* Venice, California: Brooklyn Boy Books, 1996.

Kohn, Al, and Bob Kohn. *The Art of Music Licensing.* New York: Aspen Law, 1992.

Krasilovsky, M. William and Sidney Shemel. *This Business of Music: A Practical Guide to the Music Industry for Publishers, Writers, Record Companies, Producers, Artists, Agents.* New York: Watson-Guptill Publications, 1995.

Levinson, Jay Conrad. *Guerrilla Marketing Weapons: 100 Affordable Marketing Methods for Maximizing Profits from Your Small Business*. New York: NAL, 1990.

Lewis, Herschell Gordon. *Mail Order Advertising*. Upper Saddle River, New Jersey: Prentice Hall, 1983.

Lewis, Herschell Gordon. *More Than You Ever Wanted to Know About Mail Order Advertising*. Upper Saddle River, New Jersey: Prentice Hall, 1983.

Passman, Donald S. *All You Need to Know about the Music Business*. New York: Simon & Schuster, 1997.

Rapaport, Diane S. *How to Make and Sell Your Own Recording: A Guide to the Nineties*. Jerome, Arizona: Jerome Headlands Press Books, 1998.

Ringer, Robert J. *Million Dollar Habits*. New York: Fawcett, 1991.

Support Services Alliance, Inc. *Your Guide to Free Self-Promotion*. Schoharie, New York: Support Services Alliance, Inc., 1993. To order copies, call 1-800-322-3920.

Uscher, Nancy. *Your Own Way in Music: A Career and Resource Guide*. New York: St. Martin's Press, 1993.

Whitmyer, Claude, and Salli Rasberry. *Running a One-Person Business*. Berkeley, California: Ten Speed Press, 1994.

On the Internet: Visit Maureen Jack's *Music Books Plus* on-line catalog for additional reading material on music and the music business at http://www.musicbooksplus.com.

For links to many valuable tour information Web sites, visit the Bookmarks page on my Web site at http://www.upbeat.com/galper.

Index